COME YE APART

Come Ye Apart

Daily Bible Readings in the Life of Christ

By

J. R. Miller, D.D.

THOMAS NELSON PUBLISHERS
NASHVILLE

PUBLISHED BY THOMAS NELSON INC.,
PUBLISHERS, Nashville, Tennessee. Manufac-
tured in the United States of America.
1980 printing

PREFACE

THIS volume of a year's readings has been prepared in the hope that it may prove daily food to some earnest children of God in their life of care, struggle, and duty. It is made to cover the earthly life of our Lord, from its beginning to its close. The texts are selected from the several gospels, following the order of Robinson's "Harmony." The book thus provides a year's daily readings on the story and the words of Jesus.

The readings themselves are only fragments of thought suggested by the texts. They are neither exegetical nor expository, but are rather practical and devotional hints. The author's aim has been to put a life-thought on each page—a word that may give a little glimpse of some phase of the beauty of Christ, or unveil in some of our Lord's sayings a suggestion of duty or of encouragement or of comfort. The book has but a single aim—to honour and glorify Christ in the eyes of those who follow its pages.

There is a tendency to leave the Bible out of the closet. We hear a great deal of earnest counsel concerning secret prayer. We are urged both to open and close the day at God's feet. We are taught that prayer is the Christian's vital breath. And not a word too much can be said on this subject. If we would live strong, noble, beautiful, radiant, and useful Christian lives, we must get seasons of secret prayer into all our busy days. But we must take our Bibles with us into the closet. While we talk to God, we must also let God talk to us. God feeds us through His Word. It is *into all truth* that the Holy Spirit leads Christ's disciples. Seasons of prayer without meditation on some word of God cannot yield the full blessing that we need.

For devotional pondering it is well always, however much of the Scripture we may read besides, to fix our thought on some one verse or clause, taking it as a word for the day. It is in this way that it is hoped this book may prove a help in the closet. Its daily text, with the few words of practical suggestion that accompany it, may help the reader to make the day's life more beautiful, more victorious, more radiant, more beneficent.

Life is hard for most of us; at least, it is hard to live nobly, grandly, purely, Christianly. We can do so only by getting a great deal of help from Christ. We need, therefore, daily to heed His invitation, "Come ye apart." In communion with Him we shall receive strength and blessing to enable us to fulfil our mission of obedience and ministry in His name. We shall rob ourselves, therefore, of Divine anointing and Divine help if we do not make room in our busiest days for quiet retreats from noise and strife —apart with Christ, where we may sit at His feet to hear His words, or lie on His bosom to absorb His spirit, for the refreshing and transforming of our own lives. A sweet-voiced poet thus writes of "The Valley of Silence:"—

> "In the hush of the valley of silence
>   I dream all the songs that I sing;
> And the music floats down the dim valley,
>   Till each finds a word for a wing,
> That to hearts, like the dove of the deluge,
>   A message of peace they may bring.

> "But far on the deep there are billows
>   That never shall break on the beach;
> And I have heard songs in the silence
>   That never shall float into speech;

And I have had dreams in the valley
Too lofty for language to reach.

" And I have seen thoughts in the valley,—
Ah me, how my spirit was stirred !
And they wear holy veils on their faces,
Their footsteps can scarcely be heard ;
They pass through the valley like virgins,
Too pure for the touch of a word.

" Do you ask me the place of the valley,
Ye hearts that are harrowed by care ?
It lieth afar between mountains,
And God and His angels are there :
One is the dark mountain of sorrow,
And one the bright mountain of prayer."

It is only in the valley of silence with Christ that we can dream the dreams and see the visions which we desire to translate into actual life and character among men. There alone can we get the heavenly inspirations and impulses for holy earthly living. Only in the mount can we be shown the patterns of the sacred things which our hands should fashion in this world.

This book is sent out with the earnest prayer that the Holy Spirit may use it to bless some of the Father's children by helping them to get better acquainted with Christ, and to get grace, peace, and joy from Him.

J. R. M

PHILADELPHIA.

COME YE APART

The Lord's Prayer

Our Father which art in heaven,
Hallowed be thy name.
Thy kingdom come.
Thy will be done
in earth as it is in heaven.
Give us this day our daily bread.
And forgive us our debts,
As we forgive our debtors.

And lead us not into temptation,
but deliver us from evil:
For thine is the kingdom, and the power,
  and the glory, for ever. Amen.

DAILY READINGS
IN THE LIFE OF CHRIST

In the Beginning

*"In the beginning was the Word, and the Word was with
God, and the Word was God."*—JOHN i. 1

LIFE is full of beginnings. We are now at the beginning of a year. But here is a beginning that carries
our thought back beyond all years, all dates of history, all
imaginable periods of time, beyond the beginnings of creation. Then Christ was. What a sublime stretch of being
these words give to Him who is our Saviour ! We cannot
grasp the thought, but we can find security and comfort in
it when we think of Christ, and when we rest in Him as
our hope and salvation. We trust in human friends, and
the comfort is very sweet ; yet we can never forget that
they are but creatures of a day, and that we cannot be sure
of having them even for to-morrow. But we trust in
Christ, and know that from eternity to eternity He is the
same, and therefore our confidence is for ever sure and
strong.

Our trust is still more stable and firm when we read
on and find who this Person is in whom we are confiding.
" The Word was God." There is nothing doubtful in this
language. No kind of exegesis can blot from this brief
clause the truth of Christ's divinity. The Saviour, into

whose hands you have committed your life, is the eternal God. Earthly trusts are never secure, for everything human is mortal; but those who commit themselves to the keeping of Christ are safe for ever. It is very sweet to think of Christ's humanity. It brings Him near to us. He is like one of ourselves. He is our own brother, with tender sympathies and warm affections. We study the gospel and learn the graciousness of His character as seen in His compassion, His tears, His love. Then when we know that behind these qualities are the Divine attributes, that He is very God, what glorious confidence it gives us! Let us set this glorious truth at the gate of the New Year; it is a shining point from which to start.

> " Come and hear the grand old story
>   Story of the ages past;
> All earth's annals far surpassing,
>   Story that shall ever last.
>
> " Christ, the Father's Son eternal,
>   Once was born, a Son of man;
> He who never knew beginning
>   Here on earth a life began......
>
> " Hear we then the grand old story,
>   True as God's all-faithful word,
> Best of tidings to the guilty
>   Of a dead and risen Lord.
>
> " Hear we then the grand old story,
>   And in listening learn the love
> Flowing through it to the guilty
>   From our pardoning God above."
>
> DR. BONAR.

A Plan for each Life

" There was a man sent from God."—JOHN i. 6

HE had his commission from God. He came as God's messenger on God's business. But each one of us was likewise "sent from God" into this world. If we are sent from God, it is on some definite errand. God has a plan, a purpose, for each life. No immortal soul ever came by accident into this world, and none ever came without a mission. We ought to think of this. People sometimes suppose that such men as Moses and John Baptist and Paul were exceptions. They had their own specific mission ; God sent them on very definite errands. But surely we common people are not sent from God in the same sense. We never saw God in a burning bush, or received our commission directly from his lips. No angel came before our birth to announce what we were to be and to do in this world. We had no revelation of bright glory smiting us down in blindness.

Yet nevertheless are we "sent from God," every one of us, and have as definite a work allotted to us as had Moses or John or Paul. Are we living out God's thought for us, what He had in view when He made us and sent us hither ? Are we doing in this world what He wants us to do ? These are important questions ; and we should not stop short of honest answers to them, for we shall have to account to God at the end for the way we have fulfilled our mission. Any life is a failure which does not accomplish that which God sent it into the world to do. We find our work and our mission by simple obedience to God and submission to Him. He first prepares us for the place He is preparing for us, and then at the right time leads us into it. We can, indeed, miss our mission in this world, but only by taking our own way rather than God's.

Bearing Witness of Christ

" He was not that Light, but was sent to bear witness of that Light."—JOHN i. 8

THE mission of every Christian is likewise to bear witness of the Light. The Bible says that the spirit of man is the candle of the Lord ; but in our natural, unregenerate state the candle is unlighted. It is capable of being lighted ; but until the Divine Spirit touches it with heavenly fire and sets it ablaze, it is dead and dark. When the candle is lighted, however, it shines within us and makes us light. Thus it is that we bear witness of the Light : it is Christ in us that shines ; our light is but a little of His light breaking through our dull souls. Every one that sees us sees in us a few gleams of the true Light.

There is another way also in which we may bear witness of the Light. We cannot alone light any one to heaven ; we cannot save any perishing one, or give life to any dead soul. But we can point lost and dying ones to Christ, who is the great and true Light ; we can tell others, in their experiences of need and sorrow, of the fullness there is in Christ. We should bear this witness to Christ in many ways. We can do it by our words, telling what He has done for us. There certainly is great honour for Christ, and also great blessing for others, in simple testimony for Christ. If a physician heals us, we speak his praise among all our friends. Why should we not thus bear witness of Christ ? We can bear witness, too, by our lives, showing in ourselves what Christ can do for others who will come to Him. We should all be good witnesses, true representatives, never giving any wrong impression of our Master either by word or by act. It would be sad indeed if any one looking at us should get a wrong thought about Christ. We need to be most careful that we never in any way misrepresent Him.

Rejecting Christ

" He came unto His own, and His own received Him not."
JOHN i. 11

THE picture represents Christ coming with infinite grace to those He loved, and to His own people, only to be rejected by them and turned away from their doors. This was one of the saddest things about the Saviour's mission to this world. He was the God of glory and of life ; He came to bring heaven to earth : but when He stood at men's doors and knocked, the doors were kept closed upon Him, and He had to turn and go away again, bearing back in His hands the precious gifts and blessings He had brought and wished to leave. We say the Jews, " His own," were very ungrateful to treat their Messiah in this way ; and also that their rejection was a terrible wrong to themselves, for they thrust away in Christ the most glorious things of heaven and eternity. But how is it with ourselves ? Christ comes to us ; He is continually coming. His hands are full of blessings ; He has eternal life to bestow. Do we receive Him ? Is it not true of us that He comes unto His own, and His own receive Him not ? Do we really take from the hand of Christ all that He offers to us ? Do we not daily grieve Him and rob ourselves of blessings by declining what He brings ? Especially do we reject Christ often when He comes to us in the garb of pain or sorrow. Many times the blessings He brings to us then are the very richest and the most precious in all His store. But how many of us receive Christ as gladly, and take the gifts from His hand as cheerfully and gratefully, when He comes in grief or suffering, as when He comes in the garb of joy or worldly prosperity ? Why should we not do so ? Can we not trust His love and wisdom ? He never sends pain unless pain is best. He never chastens unless there is a blessing in chastening.

Accepting Christ

" *As many as received Him, to them gave He power to become the sons of God.*"—JOHN i. 12

THE people who shut their doors on Christ always shut out great blessings ; those who open to Him let all heaven's love and joy into their lives. Some say it does not matter whether they receive Christ or not ; they believe in God's mercy and love, and do not see why they need accept Christ. Here it is made very plain that the only way to receive God's love and mercy is by receiving Christ. They, and they only, who accept Him become God's children. Christ is the only way to God, the only door into the Father's house. To refuse Christ is to refuse adoption into the family of God. Then we learn also from this morning's text another thing. Some people are puzzled to know how to become Christians. Here the way is surely made as plain as a pathway of light. Christ comes to us as the one Mediator, the Son of God, the Divine Saviour ; and we have only to receive Him, to accept Him with our hearts, and commit ourselves to Him. " But there is that mystery of the new birth ; I can't understand that," says some one. You have nothing whatever to do with that ; for does not this verse say that if we receive Christ we become the children of God ? The same sentence goes on to say that those who thus receive Christ are born again ; but it says expressly that this change is not their own act, not the act of any man, but is divinely wrought, —they are born of God. All that belongs to us is simply to receive Christ. We have nothing whatever to do with the mystery of the new birth. That is God's work, and He is able to effect it. Our part is the acceptance of Christ ; God will change our hearts. If we accept God's Son as our Saviour, the new life will at once flow into our heart, and we shall become children of God, not by any fiction of name, but by the communication of Divine life.

The Incarnation.

" The Word was made flesh, and dwelt among us."
JOHN i. 14

WE must notice that it is the same person who was in the beginning, who was God, and who made all things, who is here said to have become flesh. The Jesus of the gospel story is the God of eternity, the Jehovah of the Old Testament. The reason for the incarnation was the salvation of man. The Good Shepherd came to seek and to save His sheep which were lost. He came in human form that He might get nearer to the sinner. A Moravian missionary went to preach the gospel to the slaves in the West Indies. Failing as a free man to reach them, he became a slave himself, and went with them to their toils in the field and into all their hardships and sufferings, thus getting close to them. Then they listened to him. This illustrates Christ's condescension to save the world. We could not understand God in His invisible glory; and Immanuel came, and in human form lived out the Divine life, showing us God's thoughts, character, and feelings, especially God's grace and His love for sinners. This was one object of the incarnation,—it revealed in a way which men could understand the invisible things of God.

Then Christ became man also that He might learn life by actual experience, and thus be fitted to be our Saviour, and to sympathize with us in all our experiences of temptation, struggle, sorrow. We are sure now, when we come to Christ in any need, that He understands our condition and knows how to help us. We have a high priest in heaven who can be touched with the feeling of our infirmities, because He was tried in all points as we are. Christ became man also that He might taste death for every man, thus abolishing death for His people. He remembers what He suffered being tempted; and when He sees His people in their struggles, He remembers when He endured the same, and is ready to sympathize with and help them.

God Revealed in Christ

*" No man hath seen God at any time ; the only begotten
Son......He hath declared Him."*—JOHN i. 18

SO we never can know God save through His Son ;
there is no other possible revelation of Him. There
is no ladder by which to ascend to God's blessedness but
the ladder of Christ's incarnation. Christ came in lowly
form, and appeared to His friends as a man ; but when
they learned to know Him, they found that He was God
Himself. This is one of the most precious truths about
the incarnation ; and we understand its meaning only
when we see in every act and word of Christ a manifestation of the Divine heart and life. When we find Him at
a wedding-feast, we see God putting His sanction anew
upon the sacred ordinance of marriage, and upon innocent
human gladness and festivities. When we behold Him
taking little children in His arms, laying His hands upon
their heads and blessing them, we learn how God feels
toward children, and that He wants parents now to bring
their infants to Him. When we see Him moved with compassion in the presence of pain or of sin, we have a glimpse
of the Divine pity toward the suffering and the sinning.
When we look at Him receiving the outcast and the fallen,
treating them with kindness, forgiving them, and transforming their lives into beauty, we see how God feels
toward sinners, and what He is ready to do for the worst
and guiltiest. When we behold Him going at last to the
cross in voluntary sacrifice, giving His life for the lost, we
see how God loves sinners. Thus the whole of the incarnation is a manifesting of the invisible God in acts and
expressions which we can understand. Thus it is literally
true, as Jesus said, " He that hath seen Me hath seen the
Father." If we would ever see God, and know Him, and
enter His family, we must receive Christ. To reject Him
is to shut ourselves for ever away from the vision of
God.

A True and Holy Life

" *In the days of Herod, the King of Judea, a certain priest.....
and his wife.*"—LUKE i. 5

IT makes a great deal of difference in what times and amid what circumstances and influences a man lives. In godly days, when piety pervades all life, it is not remarkable that one should live righteously ; but when the times are ungodly, and the prevailing spirit is unrighteous, the life that is holy and devout shines with rare splendour, like a lamp in the darkness. Such were the times and the spirit of " the days of Herod ; " and such were the lives of the blameless old people who are here mentioned. Amidst the almost universal corruption of the priesthood and hypocrisy of the Pharisees, they lived in piety and godly simplicity. The lesson is that it is not necessary for us to be like other people, if other people are not what they ought to be. The prevalent standard of living ought not to satisfy us, if the prevalent standard is low. No matter how corrupt the times, we should strive to live righteous and godly lives. Nor is this impossible. God is able and willing to give us all the grace we need to enable us to live a true and holy life in the most unfavouring circumstances ; and He will do so if He has really placed us in these circumstances. God makes no mistakes in planting people in this world. He does not put any of us in a spiritual climate in which we cannot grow into beauty and strength ; and wherever He plants us, He sends the streams of grace to refresh us. So, whatever our circumstances may be, it is possible for us to live a godly life. The darker the night of sin about us, the clearer and steadier should be the light that streams from our life and conduct. Any one should be able to live well in the midst of friendly influences and favouring circumstances ; but it is doubly important that we be loyal and true to Christ when surrounded by those who care not for Him.

The Test of Life

" And they were both righteous before God."
LUKE i. 6

THIS is a beautiful thing to have said of them. Yet, after all, that is the test which every life must endure. It is not enough to have human commendation ; how do we stand before God ? how does our life appear to Him ? No matter how men praise and commend, if as God sees us we are wrong. The Pharisees were righteous before men ; but if you would see how they stood in God's eye, read the twenty-third chapter of Matthew. We are in reality just what we are before God,—nothing less, nothing more. The question always to be asked is, " What will God think of this ? " If we would meet His approval, we must first have our hearts right, and then we must be true in every part of our life.

One of the old artists was chiselling with great pains on the back part of his marble. " Why do you carve so carefully the tresses on the head of your statue ? " asked one ; " it will stand high in its niche against the wall, and no one will ever see its back." " The gods will see it," was the reply. We should learn a lesson from the old heathen artist. We should do our work just as honestly where it will be covered up and never seen by human eyes, as where it is to be open to the scrutiny of the world ; for God will see it. We should live just as purely and beautifully in secret as in the glare of the world's noon. There really is no such thing as secrecy in this world. We fancy that no eye is looking when we are not in the presence of men ; but really we always have spectators—we are living all our life in the presence of angels, and of God Himself. We should train ourselves, therefore, to work for the Divine eye in all that we do, that our work may stand the Divine inspection, and that we may have the approval and commendation of God.

God Looketh on the Heart

" Walking in all the commandments and ordinances of the Lord blameless."—LUKE i. 6

OF course, this does not mean that they were absolutely faultless, but that their lives were so beautiful, so sincere and faithful, that God saw nothing in them to blame or rebuke. This truth is very beautifully illustrated in one of Mrs. Herrick Johnson's tender little poems. A mother is sitting at her work, her mind perplexed as she thinks of her poor faulty life. She had longed to serve the Master, and had tried to do so; but it seemed to her that she had utterly failed. Just then she turned the garment she was mending, and her eye " caught an odd little bungle of mending and patchwork " done by some other hand. Her heart grew tender as the truth flashed over her. Her little daughter had wanted to help her. To be sure, she had made a botch of it; but the mother knew it was the best she could do, and she felt a strange yearning for her child. Then a voice whispered, " Art thou tenderer for the little child than I am tender for thee? " She understood it all in a flash, and her perplexed faith brightened into peace.

> " For I thought, when the Master-Builder
>   Comes down His temple to view,—
> To see what rents must be mended,
>   And what must be builded anew,—
>
> " Perhaps, as He looks o'er the building,
>   He will bring my poor work to the light,
> And seeing the marring and bungling,
>   And how far it all is from right,
>
> " He will feel as I felt for my darling,
>   And say as I said for her:
> ' Dear child! she wanted to help me,
>   And love for me was the spur:
>
> " ' And for the true love that is in it,
>   The work shall seem perfect as mine;
> And because it was willing service,
>   I will crown it with plaudit divine.' "

Messengers from God

*" And when Zacharias saw him, he was troubled, and fear
fell upon him."*—LUKE i. 12

YET the angel had come on an errand of love,—had
come to announce to Zacharias tidings which would
fill his heart with great joy. It is often so. All through
the Bible we find that people were afraid of God's angels.
Their very glory startled and terrified those to whom they
appeared. It is ofttimes the same with us. When God's
messengers come to us on errands of grace and peace, we
are terrified, as if they were the messengers of wrath.
Angels do not appear to us in these days in their heavenly
garb. They come no less really and no less frequently
than in the Bible days; but they wear other and various
forms. Sometimes they appear in robes of gladness and
light, but ofttimes they come in dark garments. Yet our
faith in our Father's love should make us confident that
every messenger that He sends to us, whatever the garb,
brings something good to us.

> " All God's angels come to us disguised,—
> Sorrow and sickness, poverty and death,
> One after other lift their frowning masks,
> And we behold the seraph's face beneath,
> All radiant with the glory and the calm
> Of having looked upon the face of God."

The things which we call trials and adversities are really
God's angels, though they seem terrible to us; and if
we will only quiet our hearts and wait, we shall find that
they are messengers from heaven, and that they have
brought blessings to us from God. They have come to
tell us of some new joy that is to be granted,—some
spiritual joy, perhaps, to be born of earthly sorrow, some
strange and sweet surprise of love that is waiting for us.
We want to learn to trust God so perfectly that no messenger He ever sends shall alarm us.

Magnificat

" And Mary said, My soul doth magnify the Lord."
LUKE i. 46

NO wonder that Mary sang that day. At the shut gate of the garden of Eden there was a promise given of a Saviour,—a Saviour who should be " the seed of the woman." Ever after that, all along the line of the covenant, each woman hoped that she might be the mother of this Saviour. Centuries passed, and generations of disappointed hearts saw their hopes fade. At length one day a heavenly messenger came to this lowly Nazarite maiden, and announced to her that she should be the mother of this long-expected Messiah. What a glorious honour ! No wonder she rejoiced. One strain of her song was, " My soul doth magnify the Lord." We cannot make God any greater ; He needs nothing from us. Can the candle add to the glory of the sun's noonday splendour ? Yet we can so tell others of God that He will seem greater to them. It was said in praise of a distinguished preacher that in his sermons he made God appear very great. We can declare God's goodness and grace. Then we can so live ourselves as to honour Him, and thus magnify His name.

Retzsch, a German sculptor, made a wonderful statue of the Redeemer. For eight years it was his dream by night, his thought by day. He first made a clay model, and set it before a child five or six years old. There were none of the usual emblematical marks about the figure,—no cross, no crown, nothing by which to identify it. Yet when the child saw it he said, " The Redeemer ! the Redeemer ! " This was a wonderful triumph of art. We should exhibit in our life and character such a reproduction of the nobleness and beauty of Christ that every one who looks upon us may instinctively recognize the features, and say, " Behold the image of our Redeemer ! " There is no other way of magnifying the Lord that so impresses the world.

The Christian's Joy

" *My spirit hath rejoiced in God.*"—LUKE i. 47

THIS is another strain of Mary's song, and it has for us the secret of all deep Christian joy. We have no real and lasting joy till we are in God's family, and in God as the refuge of our souls. One of the old prophets says, " Let the inhabitants of the rocks sing ! " None can sing with lasting gladness but the inhabitants of the Rock —those who are in the shelter of the Rock of Ages. The world's songs soon change to cries of terror. During the battle of Gettysburg there was a little bird on a tree that would sing a few notes every time there was a lull in the awful roar of battle ; but when the crash began again, its song would cease. That is the way with this world's joy. It sings a few strains now and then in the pauses of life's struggle and discontent. When the waves of sorrow break, its voice is drowned ; it cannot sing in loss, in bereavement, in the hour of dying. But one who rejoices in God has a joy that sings on through all the roar of battle, through all the darkness of night. Troubles come to the Christian, but they do not rob him of his joy. He may be in deep sorrow, but all the while there is a fountain of joy welling up in his heart. Sometimes there is a fresh-water spring by the sea-shore. Twice every day the salt tides roll over it, but the spring never ceases to flow ; and when the brackish waves have rolled back, the waters of the spring are still sweet as ever. That is the way with the Christian's joy. It is a living well in his heart. Even in his sorrow he has a deep peace in his soul. Then when the sorrow is past, the joy springs fresh as ever. The permanence of all joy depends upon the source from which it comes. If it be in God that we rejoice, then earth has no power to take from us the gladness.

Christ is Mine

" *My Saviour.*"—LUKE i. 47

IT is a great thing when any one can say, " My Saviour ! " Many people can talk about Christ very beautifully and eloquently. They can linger upon the story of His life, and speak with tender accents of His sufferings and death. They can paint the beauties of His character, and tell of the salvation which He has provided. Yet they cannot say, " He is my Saviour.". And what good does all this knowledge of Christ do them if they are not saved by Him ? I saw a picture of two little beggar children standing on the pavement before a beautiful house, looking in at the windows, where they beheld a happy family gathered around the table at their evening meal. There were evidences of luxury and great comfort within the house. It was winter, and the night without was bleak, and the snow was falling. The poor children outside saw all the brightness and beauty that were within ; they could describe it, but they could not call it their own. And while they looked in upon the happy scene, the storm swept about them, and they shivered in their thin rags, and felt the gnawings of unsatisfied hunger. So it is with those who know of Christ and His salvation by the hearing of the ear, but who cannot say, " He is my Saviour." They see the deep joy of others in time of trouble, but around them the storm still breaks. They look at others feeding upon Christ, and witness their satisfaction, but they themselves stand shivering in the winter of sorrow, and their hungry hearts find no bread to eat. All our study about Christ will do us no good if we do not take Him as our own personal Saviour, and learn to call Him " My Jesus." But when we can say of Him, " He is my Saviour," all life is bright and full of joy for us. He is ready to be ours, to give Himself to us with all His blessed life, and all the privileges of heirship in the Father's family, the moment we will accept Him.

Lowly Service

" For He hath regarded the low estate of His handmaiden."
LUKE i. 48

WHAT a beautiful name by which to call one's self !
A handmaid is one who devotes herself to the
service of another. A young girl is the handmaid of the
Lord when she gives herself to Him, and then lives all her
life just to please Him and serve Him. This does not always mean that she must give up her home and the comforts of life in her own country, and go away to a heathen
land. Sometimes it may mean that. It did for Harriet
Newell, and it has meant that for hundreds of other young
Christian women along the years. But for most young
girls it means to serve Christ and live for Him just in the
ordinary life of every day. There are a great many ways
of serving Him. One is by always doing right. We are
serving Him whenever we are listening for His voice and
promptly following Him. He says, " If ye love Me, keep
My commandments." Another way is by doing everything
we can to make friends for Him, by getting other people to
love and serve Him. A little girl is a handmaid of Christ
when she is trying to get other little girls to come to the
Sabbath school. Another way is by doing every kindness
we can to others in His name. When Jesus was on the
earth as a man, some women left their homes and went
with Him, ministering to Him. It is probable that they
made garments for Him, prepared food for His meals, and
did every little personal kindness they could. That was a
very sweet privilege. No doubt if He were here now many
noble young girls and women would do the same. He is
not here in human form ; but He has told us that if we
do these same kindnesses even to the least and lowliest
of His friends who are in need, it is the same as if we
did them to Himself. So it is not hard to be a handmaid
of Christ.

"Ḃe Careth for You."

" He that is mighty hath done to me great things."
LUKE i. 49

IS it not wonderful that the mighty God, so great, so holy, should ever think of a poor, lowly sinner on this earth ? But does He really ? It scarcely seems possible. Only consider how many million people there are in this world. Can it be that the glorious God ever gives a separate, special thought to any one person among so many ? He may give personal thought to a few great people,—to kings and rulers, and to certain very good men and women ; but surely He does not think of any one so small and obscure as I am. Ah yes! He does. You remember that a child was once dying of thirst in a desert, and God heard its cries amid all the noise of the world, and sent an angel to point out a spring of water and thus save its life. You remember, too, that story of the baby that the mother could not herself longer shelter, and which she put into a little ark and laid among the sedge beside the river ; and you remember how God cared for that helpless infant and provided for it in a wonderful way. Then you remember that Jesus said our heavenly Father cares even for a sparrow and feeds it, and that He even clothes each little flower in the field. If there is not a bird or a flower that He does not think of and care for, surely He gives thought and care to us. We are better than a sparrow, better than a flower. We have immortal souls ; we are God's own children ; and was there ever a true father who did not think of, and love and care for, his children ? He calls each one of us by name. He hears our prayers. He knows when anything is going wrong with us, or when we are in any trouble. He watches over us, and sends blessings to us every day. What a wonderful thought, that God thinks of each one of us, and does *great things* for us !

Spiritual Hunger

" He hath filled the hungry with good things ; and the rich
He hath sent empty away."—LUKE i. 53

A GREAT many people attend church and Sabbath school, where the blessings of grace abound, and yet are " sent empty away." They are not fed. They do not carry anything with them from all the fullness before them. They are no better, no stronger, no happier for the privileges they have enjoyed. Is it the minister's fault or the teacher's fault ? No ; the fault must be their own. They were not really hungry, or they would have been filled. A lady was ill with consumption. She was advised to go to Florida to spend the winter. She wrote home glowing letters about the salubrious climate, the wonderful foliage, the luscious fruits. While it was midwinter at her old home in the North, it was summer where she was. She spoke of the table,—how it was covered with all manner of tempting fruits. But in every letter she wrote there was one sad lament : "I have no appetite. If I only had an appetite, I am sure I should soon grow well amid such luxuries." Then in a little while word came that she was dead,—dead in the midst of abounding plenty, not for want of food, but for want of appetite. So it is with many souls. They live amidst abundance of spiritual provision. God spreads full tables before them continually. They sit down beside them, and then are sent away empty ; not because there is nothing there for them, but because they have no hunger for such things. Others sit close by them, at the same tables, with the same provisions before them, and are richly fed, and go away rejoicing in strength and hope, and refreshed in all their nature ; but these came with spiritual appetite. Our constant prayer should be that God would make us hungry for Himself. The beatitude is, " Blessed are they *which do hunger and thirst* after righteousness : for they shall be filled."

The Divine Visitor

" He hath visited and redeemed His people."—LUKE i. 68

WHAT a beautiful thought it is that God pays visits to His people in this world! We remember a number of visits He made in the olden times,—to Adam and Eve, to Abraham, to Jacob, to Moses, to Joshua, and to others. But the most wonderful visit He ever made was when Christ came and stayed so long, and did so much to bless the world. After a while He went away; yet we must not think that He went away to stay, and that He never pays visits to this world any more. Every time any of His children are in trouble He comes to help them. They do not always know it; for He comes unseen, and often so softly and silently that people do not know they have such a glorious visitor within their doors. He visits those who are not saved, to try to persuade them to accept salvation. When we are in great danger, He visits us to deliver us. When we are sick or suffering, He visits us to give us grace to bear our suffering. Then ofttimes He comes and knocks at our doors, and wants to visit us and give us some rich blessing, and we will not open the door. There was an old Scotch woman who could not pay her rent, and the landlord said he would seize her goods. A good friend heard of it, and went to her house to give her money to save her property. He knocked, but could not get in. Next day he met her and told her of his visit. " Was that you ? " she said with amazement; " I thought it was the officer coming to take my goods, and I had all the doors and windows barred, and would not let him in." So Christ comes and knocks. He knows of our need, and wants to bless or help us; and we bar our doors and keep Him out, not knowing who He is nor why He comes. We must remember that when Christ comes it is always to do us good, and that we shall rob ourselves if we ever keep Him out or refuse His visit.

The Door of Mercy

" *The tender mercy of our God.*"—LUKE i. 78

WHAT would we ever have done if God had not been merciful ? There could never have been a soul saved in this world. There is a story of a man who dreams that he is out in an open field in a fierce driving storm. He is wildly seeking a refuge. He sees one gate, over which " Holiness " is written. There seems to be shelter inside, and he knocks. The door is opened by one in white garments ; but none save the holy can be admitted, and he is not holy. So he hurries on to seek shelter elsewhere. He sees another gate, and tries that ; but " Truth " is inscribed above it, and he is not fit to enter. He hastens to a third, which is the palace of Justice ; but armed sentinels keep the door, and only the righteous can be received. At last, when he is almost in despair, he sees a light shining some distance away, and hastens toward it. The door stands wide open, and beautiful angels meet him with welcomes of joy. It is the house of Mercy, and he is taken in and finds refuge from the storm, and is hospitably entertained.

Not one of us can ever find a refuge at any door save the door of Mercy. But here the vilest sinner can find eternal shelter ; and not mere cold shelter only, for God's mercy is " tender." We flee for refuge, and find it. Strong walls shut out all pursuing enemies, and cover us from all storms. Then, as we begin to rejoice in our security, we learn that we are inside a sweet home, and not merely a secure shelter. Our refuge is in the very heart of God ; and no mother's bosom was ever so warm a nest for her own child as is the Divine mercy for all who find refuge in it.

" He that dwelleth in the secret place of the most High
Shall abide under the shadow of the Almighty......
He shall cover thee with His pinions,
And under His wings shalt thou take refuge."

Ps. xci. 1, 4.

The Light of the World

"To give light to them that sit in darkness and in the shadow of death."—LUKE i. 79

SUPPOSE the sun were never to rise again, and the light of every star were put out, what a gloomy world this would be! This is the picture of the world, in a moral and spiritual sense, without Christ, as it is painted in these words, "darkness and the shadow of death!"—no light to guide, to cheer, to produce joy and beauty. A world without Christ would be utter blackness, unillumined by a single ray of sun, or even by a single burning far-away star. Christ is light. Only think what light does for us! It makes our days very bright; it shows us all the beautiful things that are around us. But it does far more. It produces all the life of the earth, and then nourishes it. There would not be a bud or a root or a leaf were it not for the sun. Nor would there be any beauty, for every lovely thing in nature the sun paints. Think of Christ, then, as light. His love brooding over us causes us to live, and nourishes in us every spiritual grace. Every beam of hope is a ray of light. What the coming of light is to a prisoner in a darkened dungeon, that is the bursting of mercy over the guilty soul. Light gives cheer; and what cheer the gospel gives to the mourner, to the poor, to the troubled! Is it not strange that any will refuse to receive this light? If any one would persist in living in a dark cave, far away from the light of the sun, with only dim candles of his own making to pour a few feeble, flickering beams upon the gloom, we should consider him insane. What shall we say of those who persist in living in the darkness of sin, with no light but the candles of earth's false hopes to shine upon their souls? There are many such, too. They turn to every "will-o'-the-wisp" that flashes a little beam—anywhere rather than to Christ. It is like preferring a tallow candle to the sun.

Jan. 21

Paths of Peace

"*To guide our feet into the way of peace.*"—LUKE i. 79

FIRST Jesus made the way of peace for us. Sin had destroyed the road to heaven, leaving only a rough and thorny way for human feet to go upon. There never would have been a path of peace had not Jesus Himself made it. All ways in life save that one which He has opened for us are full of pain and trouble, and lead only to sorrow, despair, and death. But Christ prepared a highway that is beautiful and blessed, and that leads to eternal joy and glory. It was not easy work building this road. In the construction of some of this world's great thoroughfares thousands of human lives were sacrificed. We forget sometimes, as we move on in the highway of redemption, amid peaceful scenes, with soft music in our ears, and rich comforts in our hearts, and heavenly hopes to woo us forward, what it cost our blessed Lord, what toil and tears and blood, to prepare the way for us, to bridge over the chasms and level down the mountains. But now the way is open, and from beginning to end it is a way of peace.

A great many people think that the Christian life is hard and unpleasant, that it is a rough and steep road; but truly it is a way of pleasantness and peace. The only really happy people in this world are those who are following Christ along the way of redemption. They have their share of troubles, disappointments, sorrows; but all the time in the midst of these they have a secret peace of which the world knows nothing. There are paths in the low valleys, among the great mountains, which are sweet pictures of the Christian's way of peace. High up among the peaks and crags the storms sweep in wild fury, but on these valley-paths no breath of tempest ever blows. Flowers bloom and springs of water gurgle along the wayside, and trees cast their grateful shadow, and bird-songs fill the air. Such is Christ's "way of peace" in this world.

Blessed Night-Watch.

*" There were......shepherds abiding in the field, keeping
watch over their flock by night. And, lo, the angel of
the Lord came."*—LUKE ii. 8, 9

WE should notice that it was while these shepherds
were at their common, humble work that they
had this wonderful vision. The best place to have the
angels come to us is always at our post of duty, no matter
how lowly it is. They never show themselves to one who
is ashamed of his calling, or too indolent to be faithful at
his proper work. It did not seem a very pleasant way
to live—to be poor, and to have to stay out all night
in the field, and keep awake and watch the sheep. No
doubt the people who lived in the great houses thought
the poor shepherds had a hard time of it, and perhaps
they even despised them for their lowly work and their
poverty. It may be that the shepherds themselves sometimes envied the people who had fine houses and lived in
luxury, and never needed to work hard or to stay up
nights. At least, a good many people, in these modern
days, who have to work hard are disposed to be envious
of the rich. But it is quite certain that these shepherds
were never sorry after that night that they were poor
shepherds, and that they were at their post at that time.
If they had thought themselves too good or too fine to do
such work, and had given up their position for something
more elegant or more respectable, they would have missed
the angelic visit that night, and would have lost the
honour of being the first to hear the announcement of the
Saviour's birth.

We never know what we lose by being out of our place of
duty. Celestial visions do not come to those who despise
God's allotments in life. The angel honoured poverty
and faithfulness when he came to the shepherds rather than
to the door of some lordly palace, to proclaim his glorious
tidings. The best place to be in is always the place of duty.

Good News

" Behold, I bring you good tidings of great joy."
LUKE ii. 10

EVERY word of the gospel is a joy-bell. In Eastern poetry they tell of a wondrous tree on which grew golden apples and silver bells. Every time the breeze went by and tossed the fragrant branches, a shower of the golden apples fell, and the bells chimed and tinkled forth their sweet and airy music. Like this tree of fable is the gospel-tree, ever dropping rich and mellow fruits, and ringing joy-bells whose music thrills our hearts with its celestial sweetness. The gospel is always good news. Who was ever made sad by it ? It brings good news to the guilty sinner when it comes to tell him of forgiveness. It brings good news to the struggling soul in the strife of temptation, when it comes to offer him help to overcome. It brings good news to the man or the woman who has failed, and is in despair over a ruined life and hopes dashed to the dust, when it says, " You may rise yet to a glorious life." It brings good news to the mourner when it breathes comfort, the assurance of Divine sympathy and love, and a promise that good shall come out of sorrow. So wherever the gospel goes it tells good news, never bad. Think what joys it has started in this world, what sadness it has chased away, what ruin it has restored to beauty. Think of the hymns of joy that have been sung along these Christian centuries, and are yet echoing in countless human hearts. Think of the heavenly songs in which millions will unite eternally. Then remember that all this song and gladness will be but the prolonged echo of that joy which the angel proclaimed. We must be sure that we let this good news into our hearts, else we can never share this great gladness. Then we should in turn become joy-bearers, by ourselves repeating the good news, and likewise by letting all about us see in us what deep victorious joy the gospel of Christ can give.

The Christ-Child

" *Unto you is born this day in the city of David a Saviour, which is Christ the Lord.*"—LUKE ii. 11

HOW wonderful this was ! We must remember who it was that was thus born. The birth of another child in this world was nothing strange, for thousands of children are born every day. But this was the Lord of glory. This was not the beginning of His life. He had lived from all eternity in heaven. His hands made the universe. All glory was His. All the crowns of power flashed upon His brow. All mighty angels called Him Lord. We must remember this if we would understand how great was His condescension. Every schoolboy has read that Peter the Great left his throne, and in lowly disguise apprenticed himself at Zaandam and Amsterdam as a shipwright. Among the common labourers he wrought, dressed in their working-garb, living in a hut, preparing his own food, making his own bed. Yet in doing so he never for a moment ceased to be the autocrat of Russia. His royal splendour was laid aside for a time; his regal power and majesty were temporarily veiled beneath the disguise he wore; but there was never an hour when he was not an emperor.

So Christ's glory was folded away under robes of human flesh. He never ceased to be the Son of God ; and yet He assumed all the conditions of humanity. He veiled His power, and became a helpless infant, unable to walk, to speak, to think, lying feeble and dependent in His mother's bosom. He veiled His knowledge, and learned as other children do. He laid aside His sovereignty, His majesty. What condescension ! And it was all for our sake, that He might lift us up to glory. It was as a Saviour that He came into this world. He became Son of man that He might make us sons of God. He came down to earth and lived among men, entering into their experiences of humiliation, that He might lift them up to glory to share His exaltation.

Jan. 25

Strange Insignia

" This shall be a sign unto you ; Ye shall find the babe wrapped in swaddling clothes, lying in a manger."—
Luke ii. 12

WHAT a strange sign this by which to recognize the King of glory ! The shepherds would not find Him robed in purple garments, like the child of a prince, but wrapped in swaddling clothes. They would not find Him in a palace, but in a stable, with a manger for His cradle. Is it not strange that the very marks and authentications of Messiah's character and mission, by which these shepherds recognized Him when they found Him, were these tokens of poverty and humiliation ? This tells us what empty things are the world's marks of greatness. No one would expect ever to recognize earthly royalty by any such insignia as these. When Christ came, He despised all the badges of rank by which men indicate greatness, and wore the insignia of earthly poverty and meanness. Yet was He less great because He bore not the world's stamp of honour ?

True greatness is in the character, never in the circumstances. No matter about wearing a crown ; make sure that you have a head worthy of wearing a crown. No matter about the purple ; make sure that you have a heart worthy of the purple. No matter about a throne to sit on ; make sure that your life is regal in its own intrinsic character—that men will recognize the king in you though you toil in the field or mine, or serve in the lowliest place.

These strange tokens tell us also of Christ's sympathy with the lowliest phases of life, with the plainest and poorest of the people. None can say that Christ never came to them. If He had been born in a palace amid splendours, the common people would never have felt that He was their Saviour as they feel now that He is. Christ went down and touched life at its lowest point, that there might be none to whom His mission of love and grace should not reach.

God is Love

"*Good will toward men.*"—LUKE ii. 14

YES! that is the meaning of it all. It tells of the good will of God toward all men. There is a strange mediæval legend which illustrates this truth. An infidel knight, in the wildness of his mad, Heaven-defying infidelity, determined to test, by the method to which as a knight he was accustomed, the reality and power of the God whose existence he denied. So, going out into the field, armed as if for combat, he cast his glove down upon the ground, after the manner of the ancient challengers, and cried out to the heavens : "God !—if there be a God—I defy Thee here and now to mortal combat ! If Thou indeed art, put forth Thy might, of which Thy pretended priests make such boasts." As he spoke his eye was caught by a piece of parchment fluttering in the air just above his head. It fell at his feet. He stooped and picked it up, and found inscribed upon it these words, "God is love !" Overcome by this unexpected response, he broke his sword in token of his surrender, and kneeling upon the fragments, consecrated his life henceforth to the service of that God whom he had just before defied. Thus to all men's defiance, to the rebellion of a world, to the godlessness of nations, to the blasphemy of individuals, the answer that heaven has always let fall has been, "God is love !" This was the message that came wafted down that night on the silent air in this sweet note of the angels' song. This was the meaning of the coming of Christ. Cold was the world ; shut were men's hearts against God ; defiant was the attitude of nations. Yet to this coldness, this defiance, this revolt, the answer was not swift judgment, but the gift of the Son of God as the Saviour—"On earth peace, good will toward men." Wherever the gospel goes to-day, it breathes the same loving message. God does not hate us ; He loves us with a love tender and everlasting.

Daily Duty

"*The shepherds returned.*"—LUKE ii. 20

THEY might have been so enraptured with the sight of the Christ-child that they would not have cared to go away again to their own dull work in the fields. Some people in their ecstasies feel disinclined to devote themselves longer to the prosaic things of this common work-day life. Peter wanted to stay on the Transfiguration Mount; earthly life, with its toils and struggles, would be too tame, he thought, after such ecstatic visions. And surely no human eyes ever gazed on a more glorious vision than that these shepherds beheld that night. Yet they went back to their lowly toil, and no doubt they were just as faithful shepherds after that as they had been before.

We need to learn a lesson here. All our spiritual enjoyments ought to make us only the more diligent and faithful in the duties of our ordinary callings. It is not a true devotional experience which draws us away from our daily duty. The nearer we get to Christ the better should we do all our work. Our love for communion with God and with His people should never make us negligent in the doing of the tasks that the common days bring to us. After our most heavenly experiences on the Sabbath or in the closet of prayer, we should return to our work ever with fresh earnestness and zest. God gives us our spiritual raptures, our glimpses of His face and His glory, our foretastes of celestial joy, our fragments of heavenly vision, for the very purpose of making us stronger and braver for duty. It will be sad indeed, then, if they make us less fit for life here with its burdens and cares. We should seek to bring the heavenly visions down and give them reality in our lives, that others may see the beauty too, and be cheered by it. Our hours of communion with Christ should leave some gleams of brightness on our faces as we come to walk again in life's dusty ways.

Upright Devotion

" *The same man was just and devout.*"—LUKE ii. 25

HE was *just* in all his dealings with men, and *devout* in his feelings toward God. It takes both these elements to make true religion. Some people are *just*, and not devout. They are scrupulously honest in all their dealings, yet they never think of God or of their duties to Him. They do not bow to Him in prayer ; they never lift their hearts to Him in praise. They do not love Him. They confess no obligations to Him. Their whole religion simply is honesty toward their fellow-men, while they utterly ignore God, their Creator and Redeemer, in whom they live, from whose grace every hope in their lives flows, and upon whom they are dependent every moment for breath, for protection, and for all the blessings of life. It is readily seen that such religion is no religion at all. While we are just and honest in our transactions with men, it is to God that we owe the first and highest duties. We are His creatures ; we are saved, if at all, by His grace ; we owe to Him obedience, faith, love, honour, service. So we must be devout as well as just. On the other hand, there are some people who profess to be *devout* who are not just. They attend upon ordinances, they sing and pray ; and then they go out into the week-day world, and are hard, unjust, greedy, oppressive. It is very evident that this kind of religion does not please God. He wants our praise and honour, but He wants us to honour Him by our lives and actions as well as by our lips.

There are two tables of commandments ; and the second table commandments are as binding as the first. We are to love God with all our heart, but we are also to love our neighbour as ourselves. While we are devout toward God, we are to be honest, true, unselfish, toward men. The two things must go together, and must never be torn asunder.

Are we Ready?

" He should not see death, before he had seen the Lord's Christ."—LUKE ii. 26

IT is a fearful thing for any one to see death before seeing Christ. Death is terrible. It is a vale of shadows. It ushers us into the presence of God to be judged. What if we have never seen Christ ? No matter how many great men we have seen during our life ; no matter what we may have done in the way of good or great deeds. We may have seen the wonders of every land ; we may have achieved honour and fame. But if we have not seen Christ we are not ready to die. Even wicked men want to see Him before death, although all through their life they have rejected Him. They can live without Him, but without Him they dare not die.

There is a story of an infidel whose wife was a lovely Christian. Their beautiful young daughter was dying. Her father had always ridiculed Christ in her presence. When she was near death she asked him whether he wanted her to die in his or in her mother's belief—as an infidel or as a Christian. With great emotion he said, " Mary, I would rather you would die in your mother's faith—die as a Christian." He was not content for his child to meet death as an unbeliever ; all his scepticism vanished in the presence of the dread mystery.

Death tests all creeds. A belief that is not good to die in, which a man wants to give up and throw away as he enters the portals of eternity, surely cannot be worthy of acceptance by an immortal being. No one, as he entered the valley of shadows, was ever heard regretting that he had trusted his soul in Christ's hands. When we have truly seen Christ, we are ready for death any moment. We have already passed from death unto life, and have nothing to dread in the experience of dying. Departure will only be translation from darkness into light.

"Asleep in Jesus"

"Now lettest Thou Thy servant depart in peace."—LUKE ii. 29

NO one is ready to die in peace until he has seen Christ; but when he has seen Him, he needs no further preparation for dying. He may never have looked upon any of the wonders of this world; but it is not necessary that he should have done so, if he has beheld the Lamb of God. He may not have carried out one of his own ambitious plans in life, nor have achieved anything great or beautiful; but no matter—the one essential achievement in life is to see Jesus. When we have truly seen Him, dying has no more terrors, for He has robbed death of its sting and the grave of its victory.

The Christian has a soft pillow of peace to rest upon when he comes to die. Christ has lifted the curse from his soul, and made death but the way to glory. He Himself tasted death for His people; but now there is no death for any of them. He said to Martha, by her brother's grave, "I am the resurrection and the life. Whosoever liveth and believeth in Me shall never die." That means that those who are saved by Christ find no terror, no darkness, nothing to harm them, in dying, but pass through the experience as through a beautiful gate into life everlasting.

The word "lettest" here means "set free,"—"Set thy servant free to depart;" implying that what we call life is like the imprisoning of the eagle; and what we call death, after one has seen Christ, is blessed and glorious emancipation. What a beautiful thought of dying! On the gravestone of a little child are the words: "Out of the darkness into the marvellous light!" All we need, then, is truly to see Christ before we die: When He has lifted away the curse of sin, and put His own holy life into our souls, we are already in the portal of heaven while in this world; dying will be but entering in, to behold Christ face to face for ever.

Jan. 31

Looking unto Jesus

" *Mine eyes have seen thy salvation.*"—LUKE ii. 30

TRAVELLERS come home from abroad, and tell of the wonderful sights they have seen. They have stood among the mighty Alps, and been awed by their grandeur. They have walked on the streets of famous cities. They have visited the old cathedrals. They have stood enraptured before the pictures of the old masters. And they speak with pride of what they have seen. Yet it is a far greater thing to be able to say, "I have seen Jesus." The sight of earth's beautiful and wonderful things may have a refining and inspiring influence upon one's mind, may add to one's intelligence and broaden one's experience. But seeing Jesus changes one's whole life and destiny. It makes one an heir of heaven and glory; it transforms one into the likeness of Christ Himself. He that sees Jesus is saved.

Some writer says: " Never lose an opportunity to look on a beautiful thing, for it will leave a touch of new beauty in your own soul." We may say: " Lose not the opportunity to look upon Jesus, for it will print glory in your soul." St. Paul tells us that by beholding the glory of Christ as it lies in the mirror of the Scriptures, we are changed into the same image. The old monks had a superstitious notion that if they would gaze continuously and intensely on the figure of the Christ on His cross which hung upon their cell wall, the marks of the wounds would appear in them,—the print of the nails in their hands and feet, and the scar of the spear-gash in their side. This is but a gross representation of the spiritual truth which lies under it,—that beholding Christ produces the real " marks of the Lord Jesus " in our souls. Looking upon Him with steady, loving gaze, the glorious vision that our eyes behold prints itself deep in our hearts, and the " beauty of the Lord " shines out in our dull faces.

Homage

" *When Jesus was born in Bethlehem of Judæa......there came wise men from the east to Jerusalem.*"—MATT. ii. 1

THAT was the most wonderful birth that ever occurred in this world. It is not strange there were so many remarkable events accompanying it—that angels came down to announce it and to sing their song of rejoicing, and that wise men came from afar to pay their homage. It was the Son of God incarnate that slept His first sleep in the manger of Bethlehem.

This is so great a mystery that we cannot understand it ; yet we know that the same One who then became flesh had been from all eternity with God, that He was God, that He made all things, that in Him was the fountain of all life and blessedness. That a child should be born was not a strange thing ; a child is born in this world with every heart-beat. That a child should be born in a stable was not a remarkable occurrence in that country. But when we remember who it was that was made flesh that night, we find ourselves in the presence of the most stupendous wonder of all ages.

We should certainly come with the shepherds and the Magi to pay our homage at the cradle of this same glorious child-King. The Magi came hundreds of miles to find Christ. The journey was difficult, and perilous, and very costly. We ought to count no toil or sacrifice too great to find Christ. We ought to be ready to go thousands of miles, if need be, to find Him. He is the pearl of great price, and we shall be well repaid for our quest, though it cost us the loss and sacrifice of all things, and though we even have to lay down our lives to gain Him.

We notice also that it is not always those who are nearest to Christ who first see His glory. He was born right among the Jews, but nobody went out from Jerusalem to worship Him. Shall it be so with us ? Shall we miss the blessing of seeing the Saviour who is so near ?

The King of Kings

" *Where is He that is born King of the Jews? for we have
seen His star in the east, and are come to worship Him.*"
MATT. ii. 2

SURELY it was strange that the Jews did not know of
the birth of their own King. Usually when future
kings are born the whole realm rings with joy. But when
the Messiah was born there was no rejoicing on earth. A
few humble shepherds came to look with wonder on the
new-born Babe which lay in the young mother's arms; but
that was all. The Jews had been looking for their Messiah,
but did not recognize Him when He came.

For one thing, we learn how quiet His advent was.
There was no blare of trumpets. Noise and show are not
necessary accompaniments of power. The mightiest energies in this world are ofttimes the quietest. The grace of
God always comes quietly. Angels minister noiselessly and
often unseen. The most useful Christians are not those
who make the most ado in their work, but those who in
humility, unconscious of any splendour shining in their
faces, go daily about their work for Christ.

Another thought here is, that we do not always know
when Christ comes to us. " He was in the world, and the
world was made by Him, and the world knew Him not.
He came unto His own, and His own received Him not."
Yet why should we complain so of the Jews? Are we any
better? Our King is in our midst: do we recognize Him?
do we worship and honour Him? These wise men had only
a dim star to guide them; yet they followed it with loving
trust and unfaltering step, and it led them to the feet of the
King of glory. Even the faintest glimmerings of light should
be welcomed and their guidance accepted. We should not
wait to know all about Christ, and to see Him in all His
glory, before we set out to seek Him. We should follow the
first faint gleams, and as we go on the light will brighten,
until we see Him in all His blessed beauty, face to face.

Offering Gifts

*" They saw the young child with Mary His mother, and fell
down, and worshipped Him : and when they had opened
their treasures, they presented unto Him gifts ; gold,
and frankincense, and myrrh."*—MATT. ii. 11

THOSE who follow the light will surely be led at last
to the Christ. There is always joy, too, in the
heart when one has found the Saviour. The first act is to
adore and worship Him. These men saw only the little
Babe lying in the young mother's arms. There was no
crown on His head. No glory gleamed from His face. His
surroundings were most unkingly, without pomp or page-
ant. The Child did nothing in their presence to show His
royalty—spoke no word, wrought no kingly act of power.
Yet the Magi believed and worshipped Him.

Think how much more we know about the Christ than
they did. We see Him in all the glory of His life and
death and resurrection and ascension ; we see Him sitting
at the right hand of God, King of kings, wearing many
crowns. It is not hard for us to see the regal marks in
Him. Shall we be behind the Magi in our adoration ?
They were not content merely to worship the King, showing Him homage in word and posture ; but they also laid
their gifts at His feet. It is not enough for us to sing our
songs of praise to Christ, to look up adoringly into His
face, to bow before Him in reverent worship, and to speak
our heart's homage in words. We should bring our gifts,
too, to lay at His feet. There is a great deal of mere senti-
ment in the consecration of many people : when there is
call for gifts of sacrifice, or for real service, it instantly
vanishes. People sing missionary hymns heartily, and
when the collection-box comes to them they have no gifts
to offer. These men not only brought presents, but they
brought those that were costly. We should bring our best,
our gold and frankincense and myrrh, the alabaster box of
our heart's deepest love, and the best of our life and service.

Guardian Angels

" *When they were departed, behold, the angel of the Lord appeareth.*"—MATT. ii. 13

WE have a glimpse here of the closeness of Heaven's watch over this imperilled Babe. A wicked king was plotting for the life of the Child, and His earthly friends could not protect Him. But in the hour of human weakness Heaven came quickly to shelter and save Him. The destinies of the human race were in that Child's life, and all God's power would have been used to deliver Him. It is a precious truth, too, that over every child Heaven keeps a like close and sure watch. A poet says : " Heaven lies about us in our infancy ; " and it is very true of every child. Jesus Himself said, speaking of the children, " Their angels do always behold the face of My Father which is in heaven." This means that Heaven's strongest, holiest, and most favoured angels are set to guard children in this world.

Fathers and mothers should never forget that their children are very dear to God, and are under His unsleeping protection. This should give them great comfort and confidence, as their little ones go out into the midst of the world's dangers. No human eye can be always upon them. No human hand can ward off the evils that lurk in every shadow. But there are unseen guardians that never leave them for a moment. Heaven is interested in the keeping of every tender child-life in this world. Christian parents may commit their little ones to God with implicit confidence. If they are only faithful as parents, God will not disappoint their hopes.

Children also should know that they are being cared for by celestial guardians whom they cannot see. Angels may not appear to men in these days, but they are continually around us, encamping about our homes, and watching over us by day and by night. Though their bright faces are not seen by our dull eyes, their loving ministry never ceases.

Heavenly Guidance

" Be thou there until I bring thee word."—MATT. ii. 13

ALL our movements should be under the direction of God. In very olden times God guided His people by a pillar of fire and cloud, which lifted and moved when they were to move, showing them the way, and which rested and settled down when they were to halt. In these days of so much fuller revelation there is no need for any such visible token of guidance, yet the guidance is no less real and no less unmistakable.

It was an angel that brought to Joseph the bidding to flee into Egypt. Angels do not now appear to our eyes ; but who will say that they do not whisper in our ears many a suggestion which we suppose to come from our own hearts ? At least we know that in some way God will always tell us what to do ; and if only we have ears to hear we shall never fail of guidance. We should always wait for God's bidding before taking any step. Especially in times of danger, when we are moving under His guidance, should we wait and not move until He brings us word.

It ought to give us great comfort and a wonderful sense of safety to know that God is caring for us so faithfully. Some people laugh at the simple faith of child-like believers in God, and say that it is all fancy—that there is no one in heaven taking care of us. But we need not be worried by such sceptical ones. There *is* a God in heaven, and He is our Father. He never sleeps. He has charge of all the affairs of this universe, and is always " at the helm." This should give us all confidence. Our whole duty is to be ready always to obey. Whenever the voice comes bidding us arise and depart, there is some reason for it, and we should not hesitate to obey. Wherever we are sent we should quietly stay till again God sends to call us away. The place of duty is always the place of safety, and we should never move until God brings us word.

The Nazareth Home

" He came and dwelt in a city called Nazareth."

MATT. ii. 23

IN that little village, until ready for His public ministry, Jesus made His home. It is a sweet thought that the Son of God dwelt for so many years in a home on earth. His pure and sinless life opened out there as a bud opens into a lovely rose, pouring fragrance over all the lowly place.

The study of the childhood and the youth of Jesus, even from the few fragmentary glimpses of those years given us in the gospel, ought to prove an inspiration to every child and young person. No doubt, we wish that we could know more of that sweet and blessed home-life ; but the little we are told about it is enough, or God's Spirit would have given us more of the story. We know there was no sin in Jesus, and we can think of His gentleness, His obedience, His love, His unselfishness, and of all His other graces and beauties of character. He was a natural child, glad, joyous, interested in beautiful things, studious, earnest without being precocious or morbidly religious. He was such a boy as God loves, and as He would have every other boy strive to be. We have one glimpse of Him at twelve, when He began to think of His relation to the heavenly Father ; yet we must note the fact that He went back to Nazareth and resumed his place of filial duty, staying there for eighteen years longer. The Father's business on which He entered at twelve was not preaching and working miracles and going about doing good in a public manner, but for the time remaining at home, a dutiful child, a glad, helpful youth, and an industrious, growing man.

Some young men chafe under the providence that keeps them so many years in a quiet, obscure home, where they can do only plain, common duty. But if Jesus found His Nazareth home a wide enough sphere for His blessed life, surely we should not think any home too narrow for our little lives to grow in.

The Mother of Christ

" *And the child grew, and waxed strong in spirit, filled with wisdom.*"—LUKE ii. 40

ONE of the chief influences in moulding Christ's life was His mother. When God wants to prepare a man for a great mission, He first prepares a noble mother, and puts the child into her bosom to be trained. The Jews had a saying, " God could not be everywhere, and therefore He made mothers." Nearly all the truly great men of the world have received the inspiration and stamp of their lives from their mothers. When Moses was to be trained for his work, the Lord put the little babe back in the hands of its mother as his first teacher. There is no doubt that in preparing Mary to be the mother of the Saviour, the rarest and loveliest graces of womanhood were wrought by God into her nature. She was not sinless, but surely we may believe that no more perfect woman ever lived.

" Woman ! above all women glorified ;
Our tainted nature's solitary boast ;
Purer than foam on central ocean tossed ;
Brighter than eastern skies at daybreak strown
With fancied roses."

" In whom did blend
All that was mixed and reconciled in thee
Of mother's love with maiden purity."

Such a mother would exert a wonderful influence over the child Jesus. She was His first teacher. Her love wrapped Him around in its warm folds in His earliest infancy and through all His youth and young manhood. Her sweet life was the atmosphere that hung over His tenderest years. Her prayers kept heaven lying ever close about Him. Her hands guided His feet and shaped His character. What a blessed mission is that of a mother, any mother ! What woman in whose arms God has laid an immortal life will despise her glorious calling ? What woman so honoured will not die rather than prove unfaithful to her holy trust ?

The Rock of Salvation

" Jesus Christ, the Son of God."—MARK i. 1

MARK does not intend that there shall be room for mistake concerning the person of our Lord. Each of the names He here uses represents one particular phase of His character.

Jesus means Saviour. " Thou shalt call His name Jesus: for He shall save His people from their sins." None of His names can be sweeter than this. It is enshrined in every Christian heart. This is the name that brings hope into our souls. The first thing we all need is to be saved, and He is the only Saviour.

Christ means the Anointed One. He is the One whom the Father has anointed to be prophet, priest, and king. He is our prophet, our teacher; He is our priest interceding for us, having already made Himself an offering for our sins; He is our king, and we ought to obey Him.

Son of God tells of His Divine nature and His eternal sonship. This is the name that gives security to all our hopes and trusts. If He were only a man, He might be very tender, loving, and kind, but could He do for us everything we need? Could a man make atonement for our sins? Could a man put his own life into our dead souls? Could a man fight our battles for us, and rescue us out of the hands of Satan? Could a man be with us in all the ways of toil, sorrow, need, and struggle? Could a man save us in death and bear us through the dark mystery to glory? Could a man stand for us in the judgment? The divinity of Christ is the rock of our hope and our salvation. Our Saviour and anointed King is the Son of God. We can lean upon His breast and know that we are folded about with divinity, that our refuge is the eternal God, and that the arms which are clasped about us are everlasting. In all danger we may rest secure, for the power that would pluck us out of our resting-place must be mightier than God's.

Repentance

" Repent ye."—MATT. iii. 2

THIS was John's gospel. At first it seems very unlike the story of love which Jesus preached, and yet it is part of the same story. Repentance must always come before forgiveness and peace. Perhaps we need to be reminded of this in these days. We are in danger of making salvation too easy a matter and of being altogether too tolerant with ourselves. We forget, some of us, that sin is such a terrible thing, and we are too careless about getting rid of our sins. We misunderstand God's forgiveness if we think of it merely as an easy forgetting that we have done the wrong thing. Jesus did not come to save us merely from sin's penalties ; He came to save us from the sins themselves, by leading us to forsake them for ever. Unless we repent of our sins we never can have forgiveness.

We must make sure, too, that we do thorough work in our repenting. Repentance is not merely a little twinge of remorse over some wrong thing. It is not simply a gush of tears at the recollection of some wickedness. It is not a mere shame at being found out in some meanness or uncleanness or dishonesty. It is the revolution of the whole life. Sins wept over must be forsaken for ever. Repentance is a change of heart, a turning of the face just the other way. It is well for us to make diligent quest to be sure that we always abandon the wrong-doing which we deplore, that we quit the evil course which we regret, that we turn away from the sin which we confess.

A good many people get only half the gospel. They talk a great deal about believing, but very little about repenting. It needs to be remembered that a faith which does not lead to genuine repentance is not a faith that saves. He who bewails a sin and confesses it, secretly intending to return to it again, has no good ground to hope that he is forgiven.

The Coming of the Lord

" Prepare ye the way of the Lord."—MATT. iii. 3

THE Lord is always coming to us, or is always ready to come to us, if the way is open for Him. Yet no doubt we are continually losing heavenly visitations because the road is blocked up. If we would receive the visitations we must keep the way always open. Sins clung to, unconfessed, unrepented of, unforsaken, block up the path, and Christ cannot come to us until we get them out of the way. Then there is another sense in which we need to prepare the way of the Lord. He may come any moment in death to call us away from all our busy work. Is there no preparation needed now in our hearts for this coming of the Lord ? Are we ready for Him any moment ? Are our lamps trimmed and burning ? Are our loins girded, and have we our shoes on our feet and our staves in our hands ? If He came this hour, how would He find us ? Peter gives us good counsel when, speaking of Christ's coming again, he says, " Be diligent, that ye may be found of Him in peace, without spot, and blameless." Would He find us thus if He came to-day ? Are we in peace—in peace with God, in peace with ourselves, in peace with all the world ? Would He find us without spot ? Have we kept our hands clean and our hearts pure, and ourselves unspotted from the world ? Would He find us living blameless lives, so sincere, so true, so without blemish that the world can find no cause of reproach in us, and that He Himself will approve us ?

It will be well for us to think of these things, and if the way for His coming is not prepared, to hasten to have it ready, for He may come any moment. The Jews were taught to prepare a way for the coming of the Lord by repenting of their sins and turning their hearts to God. That is just what every one must do who desires Christ to come to him with blessing—every sin must be swept out.

The Wrath to Come

" *Who hath warned you to flee from the wrath to come ?* "
LUKE iii. 7

THERE are a good many people who want to flee from
wrath, but are not willing to give up that which
draws down the wrath upon them. When a godless man
becomes sick, and it seems as though he may die, straightway he begins to look about for some way of flight from
the wrath that he feels hangs over him. He sends for a
minister or for some good man. He has his long-neglected
Bible brought from his parlour-table and laid beside his
bed. He will find refuge from his peril, if he can. He
wants to have the Bible read to him: perhaps there is
virtue in that which will shield him. He wants the minister to pray for him: he has heard that a good man's prayers
will save a soul. He wants to be baptized and to receive
the Lord's Supper: he hopes that these holy ordinances
may somehow shelter him from the wrath. All the while
he has not really thought of trying to unload the burden
which is crushing him. He is carrying his sins unconfessed
and unforgiven. He has no true sense of sinfulness, no
realization of God's holiness or of his own debt to Him;
He is simply terrified, and is trying to flee from the im-
pending wrath. If he gets well again, he will very likely
return to his old life and live on in sin as before, proving
the insincerity and worthlessness of his repentance. If
he were asked, " Who warned you to flee ? " his answer
could not be " Love for Christ," or " A sense of my guilt,"
but " Fear—the terrors of death and eternity."

It was a very proper question, therefore, which John
asked the multitudes who came to him desiring to be baptized. The only flight that saves is away from sin, to
Christ. No man is saved who carries his sins with him in
his flight. The door of the refuge is wide enough to admit
the worst penitent sinner, but not wide enough to admit
any cherished sin.

Evidence of Repentance

" *Bring forth therefore fruits meet for repentance.*"
MATT. iii. 8

THERE is only one way to prove that we have truly repented. It will not be enough to tell people that we have; they will wait to see the evidence in our lives. Suppose a wicked man joins the Church and then goes back on Monday morning to his old wicked ways, will anybody credit his Sunday's profession ? He must go on Monday morning to a new life if his repentance is to pass for anything. Everybody knows what is right in such a case. None are quicker to cry out against the insincerity and unreality of the man's profession than wicked men themselves, when they see him continue in his old evil ways. Even bad men know what it is to be good ; thus they pay high compliment to Christianity. Repentance amounts to nothing whatever if it produces only a few tears, a spasm of regret, a little fright as a flash from eternity reveals to a man his guilt and danger, and then a return to-morrow to the same old wicked ways. What are the works that are worthy of repentance ?

A grocer went home from the meeting one night where he had heard a sermon about false weights and measures and burned the " bushel " he had been using to cheat his customers. A father who had been living carelessly in his home, when awakened to the truth took down the old family Bible and confessed to his household his neglect, and re-established the family altar. These are illustrations of work worthy of repentance. In short, we must leave the sins we repent of, and must do them no more, and we must walk in the new, clean ways of holiness. The heart is the important matter in all spiritual life, but the heart makes the life ; and if the life be yet evil the heart can be no better, whatever external profession of betterment it may have made. The way to prove to men that we have really repented, is really to repent, and the fact will soon speak for itself.

The Divine Patience

" The axe is laid unto the root of the trees."—MATT. iii. 10

THE picture is very suggestive. The axe lying at the tree's root, or raised in the woodman's hand to strike, shows that judgment impends, hangs ready to fall. Any moment the tree may be cut down. The axe lying at the tree's root unused tells of patience in the husbandman; he is waiting to see if the fruitless tree will yet bear fruit. The axe leaning quietly against the tree is very suggestive. The meaning is very plain.

God waits long for impenitent sinners to return to Him; He is slow to punish or to cut off the day of opportunity; He desires all to repent and be saved. Yet we must not trifle with the Divine patience and forbearance. We must remember that while the axe is not lifted to strike, still there is not a moment when it is not lying close, ready to be used; when the summons may not come, " Hasten to judgment." The axe of death really lies all the while at the root of every life. There is not a moment when it is not true that there is but a step between us and death.

The lying of the axe at the root suggests that its use is not pruning but cutting down. God has two axes. One He uses in pruning his trees, removing the fruitless branches, and cleansing the fruitful branches that they may bring forth more fruit. The work of this axe is not judgment or destruction, but mercy and blessing. It is the good, the fruitful tree that feels its keen edge. Then God has another axe which He uses only in judgment, in cutting down those trees which after all His culture of them bring forth no fruit. Life is all very critical. There is not a moment in any day on which may not turn all the destinies of eternity. It certainly is an infinitely perilous thing for an immortal soul to rest an hour with the axe of judgment waiting to strike the blow that will end for ever the day of mercy. Only supremest folly can be blind to duty in such a case.

Our Every=Day Life

" *He answereth and saith unto them.*"—LUKE iii. 11

IN John's several answers to the different inquiries made of him we see that religion is not something entirely apart from our every-day life. He did not tell these men to fast for a week, or to leave their business and retire to a monastery, or to enter upon a long course of devotions. Nothing of the kind. They were to begin at once to live according to God's commandments in their own particular calling—to do their every-day work religiously. The " people " were to begin to practise the law of love, thus giving up their greed and selfishness. The " publicans " were to cease to practise extortion, and begin to deal honestly and justly with all men. The " soldiers " were to refrain from all acts of violence. He did not tell them to give up their calling, but to do their duty as good and true men in their calling—to carry the principles of true religion into all their actions.

It is well for us to catch this lesson. A good many people think that being a Christian is to pray a few moments morning and evening, to read a daily chapter or two in the Bible, and to attend church on the Sabbath. These duties are important as means of grace, but they are not religion. Religion is living out the principles of Christianity in one's ordinary week-day life. It is getting the Bible and the prayers and the services into thought and act and character. We must not cut our lives in two and call one part secular, governing it by one set of principles, and regarding the other part as sacred, to be controlled by another set of rules. All life is to be made religious in the sense that everything is to be done in such a way as to please God, under the direction of His counsel. We have just as much religion as we get into our week-day life, and not a whit more. Whatever we do, even to eating and drinking, we should do in the name of the Lord Jesus.

Self=Renunciation

" John answered......one mightier than I cometh."
LUKE iii. 16

THERE is something very fine in John's behaviour on this occasion. The people were expecting Christ, and when John rose up in such brightness they were ready to accept him as the Messiah. So intense was the excitement, so wild was the enthusiasm, that almost the whole nation flocked to the Jordan to see and hear John. One word from him claiming to be the Messiah would have kindled a feeling among the people which would have crowned him as king. But the picture which we see is this great man pushing away the honours which lay within his grasp, and saying, " Nay, they are not mine to wear ; put them on the head of Him who is coming after me."

Many of us are ready to accept honours for ourselves when we are doing Christ's work. We like to have people praise us and commend us. Sometimes we are in danger of striving to get honour for ourselves, rather than to put honour upon Christ. How much more beautiful was John's self-renunciation ! It is pleasant when we have helped people to have them come to us with their grateful tributes, to have them show their love to us and put honour upon us. Let us beware, however, lest we take that which belongs to Christ, and also lest our friends see only us and see not Christ. Let us keep ourselves out of the way, that they may behold Him. Let us remember always that there is One coming after us, yea, standing unseen beside us, while we do our work, that is far mightier than we, and that we should strive only and always to put the honour upon Him, utterly forgetting ourselves. He will look after us and honour us, if we will only seek always His honour and never our own. But if we rob Him here of the praise that is His, to wreathe chaplets for our own brow, we shall find ourselves stripped of honour and crown in the day of Christ's manifesting.

Baptism

" *I indeed baptize you with water......He shall baptize you with the Holy Ghost.*"—LUKE iii. 16

BAPTISM with water is right. It is one of God's appointments, and He would require nothing that is useless. Some people think that there is no necessity for being baptized ; but they make themselves wiser than Christ in saying this of that which He commanded to be done. Baptism has a meaning, and must never be despised. It teaches by picture, showing us, first, that we are unclean and need washing, and then depicting the deep work of grace by which the heart is cleansed.

We should not lightly esteem a rite which has such solemn Divine sanction. But while baptism with water is proper and should not be omitted, it cannot wash away sin or save our souls. We must not think that because we have been baptized we are necessarily Christians. There must be change within us. We must be converted, born again. And no amount of washing with water will produce this change. Christ must baptize us with the Holy Ghost. There is danger that many are satisfied with the baptismal water, and do not look for the regenerating grace. It is the peril of all forms of service that people trust in them and do not realize their need of Christ. A few drops of water on the brow make no impression on the life, and it is only when the baptism symbolized by the water is received by faith that real blessing comes upon the one who is baptized. When Jesus was being baptized He prayed, and the heavens were opened, and the Holy Spirit descended and abode upon Him. Like blessing descends from heaven upon every one receiving the symbol who also by prayer seeks the heavenly baptism. The same is true of the Lord's Supper and other Divine ordinances. When the ordinance is received in faith and with prayer, God gives the grace of which the emblem is but the image.

Wheat or Chaff?

" He will throughly purge His floor, and gather His wheat
into the garner ; but He will burn up the chaff."—
MATT. iii. 12

THE illustration which the preacher of the desert here
uses is very striking. The wheat-sheaves were
gathered on the threshing-floor and trodden over by oxen
to free the grains from the chaff. Then came the process
of winnowing, when the chaff was blown away and the
wheat left on the floor ready for use. After that the wheat
was carried to the garner, and the chaff was swept up and
burned. God's penitent, believing ones are wheat, and the
finally impenitent and unbelieving are chaff. Christ's
gospel has a stern side. The same breath that cleanses the
wheat drives away the chaff. Which are we—wheat or
chaff ? Very evidently our eternal destiny will depend on
which we are, and we ought to be very sure of it ourselves.

There is a great difference between wheat and chaff.
Wheat has life in it ; wheat-grains dropped into the earth
grow and yield a harvest. Wheat is food ; it makes bread
and satisfies hunger. Wheat is precious ; it is highly
prized in the market. Chaff has no life in it ; it does not
grow, and only rots in the ground. It is not food ; it
satisfies no hunger. It is not of any value ; and it is good
only to throw away or to burn. Which of these descrip-
tions best fits our lives ?

What sadder thing is there in this world than a human
life, made to be golden wheat, to feed men's hunger, yet
proving only worthless chaff ? Apart from the doom of
impenitence, who, with an immortal soul and almost infinite possibilities of usefulness and blessedness, should be
content to be worthless chaff ? Made to be children of
God and heirs of glory, and to live in blessedness in heaven
for ever, shall we tear ourselves away from our high destiny,
and, by our own unbelief and folly, doom ourselves to be
swept by the Divine wrath into unquenchable fire ?

External Rites

" *Then cometh Jesus from Galilee to Jordan unto John, to be baptized of him.*"—MATT. iii. 13

WE may look at the baptism of Jesus in several ways. For one thing, it tells us that He honoured the external rites of religion. Some people cannot see why it is necessary to make a public confession and to observe the ordinances of the Church. These are only forms, they argue, and do no good. What benefit is it, they ask, to a man or woman or to an infant to have a few drops of water sprinkled on the forehead, or even to be plunged into water ? What blessing can come to one's soul from eating a little piece of bread and drinking a sip of wine as a religious ceremony ? Or what good does it do to one to " join the Church " ? There are many reasons that might be given why we should observe the ordinances which God has appointed, but none ought to have more weight than Christ's own example. He thought external rites to be of sufficient importance to be observed by Him. He came all the way from Galilee to the Jordan to be baptized, and then insisted on receiving the ordinance. He was *publicly* baptized, thus showing all men where He stood, enrolling Himself under the banner of righteousness.

Shall we say, then, that there is no necessity for public confession of Christ, for declaring ourselves on His side, for uniting with His Church ? The disciple is not above His Lord. Surely Christ would not have ordained baptism if baptism is a mere empty and valueless form. He would not have commanded us to observe the Lord's Supper if the Lord's Supper is nothing more than a common meal. So of all means of grace. The fact that the wise and holy Christ ordained them ought to make them sacred to every loyal Christian heart. And the fact that Christ Himself thought these necessary for Him ought to silence men's shallow talk that they do not need to observe these " forms."

The Baptism of Jesus

" Jesus came from Nazareth of Galilee, and was baptized of John."—MARK i. 9

ONE meaning of Christ's baptism was that it was His consecration to His public ministry. For thirty years He had dwelt in the quiet home at Nazareth, doing no miracle, wearing no halo, manifesting no Divine glory. But He had been sent into this world on a definite mission, and now the time had come for Him to enter upon the work of that mission. So, obeying the heavenly bidding, he left His home and came to the Jordan to be baptized, and thus consecrated to the ministry of redemption. He knew what was involved in His work. From the edge of the Jordan He saw through to the end. The shadow of the cross fell on the green banks and on the flowing river, fell also across the gentle and holy soul of Jesus as He stood there. He knew what that baptism meant, to what it introduced Him, what its end would be. Yet, knowing all, He voluntarily came to be baptized, thus accepting the mission of redemption.

It was a solemn hour to Jesus when He stood before John waiting for the ordinance that would set Him apart to His work. It was a literal laying of Himself on the altar, not for service only, but for death. It is always a solemn hour when any one stands before God and men to make a public confession of Christ and to enter His service. The act is nothing less than the consecration of a human soul to a service for life or for death. On the seal of an old missionary society an ox stands between the altar and a plough, and below is the motto, " Ready for either "—ready for service or for sacrifice. This should be the heart-legend in every public confession ; it should be a solemn devotement to Christ—an entire surrender to Him for obedience, duty, sacrifice ; a consecration of the whole life to Christ and His service. Such consecration all have made who have publicly given themselves to Christ.

The Shadow of the Cross

" Suffer it to be so now : for thus it becometh us to fulfil all righteousness."—MATT. iii. 15

ONE meaning of Christ's words here is that, as man in the place of sinful men, He must take upon Him all the conditions of humanity. He had no sins of His own to confess, and yet He came to John as other men came. He did this because He was in the place of sinners. A little later John pointed to Him and said, " Behold the Lamb of God, which taketh away the sin of the world." So we see Jesus coming to be baptized, because " all we like sheep have gone astray, and the Lord hath laid on Him the iniquity of us all." This baptism with water, however, was but the merest shadow of what the bearing of our sins cost Him.

In Holman Hunt's picture, " The Shadow of the Cross," Jesus is represented at thirteen, standing in the carpenter's shop at the close of the day. He stretches out His arms, and the setting sun casts His shadow in the form of a cross on the opposite wall. The artist's thought is that across the soul of the gentle youth thus early fell indeed the shadow of the cross. No doubt the thought is true. Especially here, however, as Jesus entered His public ministry, did this shadow fall upon Him. This baptism was but the emblem of the other baptism. This was only with water, and was but symbolical. He had another baptism to be baptized with—the baptism of sorrow, of death, and of curse, when He " redeemed us from the curse of the law by being made a curse for us." Here we see Him entering the edge of His sore baptism from which He finally comes on the morning of His resurrection. We ought never to forget, as we enjoy the blessings of redemption, what it cost our Lord to procure them for us. He endured His nameless baptism of sorrow, pain, and death, that we might receive the blessings of peace and joy. He tasted death for us that we might have deathless life.

The Spirit Like a Dove

" He saw......the Spirit like a dove descending upon Him."
MARK i. 10

EVEN Christ with all His Divine power needed the anointing of the Holy Spirit to set Him apart for His life-work, and to make Him ready for it. How much more do we, His disciples, need the same anointing before we are truly set apart for work and qualified for it.

There is rich suggestion also in the form in which the Spirit descended. A great many tender thoughts cluster around the dove. It was the dove that the very poor were permitted to bring to the altar as an offering, as a substitute for a more costly animal. The appearance of the dove was one of the harbingers or prophecies of coming spring. The dove was always remembered by the Jews in connection with the abatement of the waters of the deluge, when it returned to the ark bearing the olive-leaf; and it has become among all Christian nations, as well as the olive-branch, an emblem of peace. The dove was also referred to by Christ as a symbol of gentleness and harmlessness. All these associations made the dove a most fitting emblematic form for the Holy Ghost to assume when descending upon Jesus. For Jesus came to be a sacrifice for all, even the poorest. He came as the spring comes, bringing life to a dead world. He came bringing a message of peace from heaven to every one who will open to Him. And He is like the dove in gentleness and harmlessness.

It is this same holy dove that must descend upon us if the kingdom of heaven is truly to begin in our hearts. Until the Holy Spirit has been given to us and received by us there is no life in our souls and no power in us for work. But this Divine anointing is promised to all who truly consecrate themselves to Christ and believe on Him. No vision of cloven heavens and descending dove appears to human eyes, but above every scene of holy devotion to Christ this blessed reality hangs.

Enduring Temptation

*" Then was Jesus led up of the spirit into the wilderness to
be tempted of the devil."*—MATT. iv. 1

THE time is to be noted. It was just after the wonderful scenes of our Lord's baptism. The heavens were opened, and the Spirit descended and abode upon Him, and the Father's voice was heard from heaven in approval and witness; then immediately came the terrible experience here described. Spiritual privileges do not save us from fiery trials. Indeed there is no time when Satan is so sure to come with His subtle arts as just when we have passed through some season of special blessing. When we go from our prayer closet after a time of tender communion He meets us at the door with some evil suggestion. It is after we have been nearest to God that we are sure to find the devil most active. He is not half so anxious to tempt worldly Christians as those who are glowing with spiritual zeal.

An old writer says: "All the while our Saviour lay in His father's shop and meddled only with carpenter's chips, the devil troubled Him not; now that He is to enter more publicly upon His mediatorship the tempter pierceth His tender soul with many sorrows by solicitation to sin." It is the same with us. So long as we move on quietly in our ordinary life he does not trouble himself to harm us; but when we rouse up to new consecration and new activity in God's service he pounces upon us and tries to destroy us. It is therefore in our times of greatest spiritual exaltation that we need to be most watchful. We learn here also that we may expect to endure temptation in this world. New power came to Jesus through His conflicts. His life was developed and made perfect through sufferings. Then He was fitted for sympathy with us in our temptations by Himself being tempted in all points as we are. Temptations resisted always bring new strength. Victorious struggle prepares us for helping others in their temptations.

Our True Life

" *Man shall not live by bread alone, but by every word that proceedeth out of the mouth of God.*"—MATT. iv. 4

THERE are other needs of life besides those which bread supplies. Sometimes we hear it said as a pretext for doing wrong or debasing things, " Well, I must live," as if hunger excused stealing or fraud or other sinning in order to get bread. But it is not true that we *must* live, or that living is in itself the best thing for us. It certainly is not true that we must live if we cannot live without sinning. We have a higher life than our physical, and this, our true life, is nourished by communion with God.

It is never right for us to starve our spiritual nature to get bread for our bodies. It is our first duty to keep God's commandments, and in obedience is the highest good that we can attain in this world. Sometimes the best thing that we can do for our life is to lose it ; we had better any day starve to death than commit the smallest sin to get bread. Jesus said, " Seek ye first the kingdom of God, and His righteousness ; and all these things shall be added unto you." Getting bread should not be our first object in living, and is really not our business at all. Life's true object is to obey every word of God and seek His righteousness. So let us settle it once for all that we are never to do any wrong thing to get bread ; that we are to be true to God always and everywhere, and then leave to Him the caring for our bodies. He promises that He will do this if we seek first and only His kingdom and righteousness. If He wants us to suffer, it will be because in some way suffering will be best. At least we should leave that to Him. Then if we are to go hungry for a time, He will give us strength to endure the pangs until He sees fit to send relief. Even if we are to die for want of bread, our soul, our true being, shall live, and shall pass unstained into God's eternal blessedness.

Scripture with Scripture

" Jesus said unto him, It is written again."—MATT. iv. 7

CHRIST is our example in all things. Here we see how He met the tempter so as to conquer him. We see just what weapons He used in His victorious conflicts. He used His Bible as a quiver, and He drew from it the sharp arrows which He hurled so successfully against His opponent. We notice, too, that He did not have to get down His Bible and search through it to find texts to use in His battle. He drew them from memory. This shows that He had made the Scriptures a study in the quiet days at Nazareth, and had His heart filled with the precious words, so that when He needed them they were ready. The lesson for us lies on the surface. If we would be ready to meet the assaults of the tempter, we must have our quiver filled with the polished shafts of Scripture. We must have the words of the Holy Book laid away in reserve in our hearts, so that at the most sudden call we may use them.

There is another thought here. Said Jesus, " It is written *again*." We must compare scripture with scripture, so as to be sure of the will of God. A single text taken by itself may not give us the whole mind of the Spirit on any subject ; it may be necessary to take other passages, presenting other phases of the truth, in order to get the whole truth. Here the case is very plain and very instructive. The devil had quoted a sublime promise, but had distorted it, omitting the qualifying or limiting words in it. It is very true that God gives His angels charge over us, but it is true also that to get this heavenly care and protection we must walk in the ways of obedience and duty ; the moment we turn away unbidden into other paths and go where God has not sent us, we forfeit this protection. So we must remember always, when we are tempted to expect God's care or blessing in any sinful or wilful course of our own, that it is written again, " Thou shalt not tempt the Lord thy God."

The Lamb of God

" *And looking upon Jesus as He walked, he saith, Behold the Lamb of God!* "—JOHN i. 36

THIS was the first gospel sermon, and it is a model for all preachers and teachers. The preacher pointed his own followers away from himself to Christ. This same beautiful unselfishness appears in all John's course. He was only a voice, announcing the coming of a King. He was not that Light, but only one bearing witness of that Light. With throngs following him, the moment Jesus came John asked the throngs to leave him and go after Jesus. His whole ministry was simply a pointing of men to another.

This is what all Christian workers should do : they should preach and teach Christ, not themselves. They should not seek to win attention to themselves, but to get all to see Christ and to love Him. Like John, they should be willing to decrease that Christ might increase ; they should be satisfied to fade away like the morning star in the brightness of the sun's rising. Then this name by which John drew attention to Jesus is important. He called Him the Lamb of God. This meant that Christ had come into the world not alone to be a teacher, but chiefly to be a sacrifice for the sin of the world, to die in the place of sinners. He was called a lamb, no doubt, because of His gentleness and meekness ; but the principal reason was because He was to save us from our sins by bearing them Himself. Just the day before this, John said of Jesus, " Behold the Lamb of God, which taketh away the sin of the world." Not only did He take our sin upon Himself ; He bore it away into eternal forgetfulness, to be remembered no more for ever. Now all who come to Him are safe for ever from condemnation. Long ago their sins were laid on the atoning Lamb, and they will never have to be borne a second time. "There is therefore now no condemnation to them that are in Christ Jesus."

What Seek Ye?

" They followed Jesus. Then Jesus turned, and saw them following, and saith unto them, What seek ye ? "—JOHN i. 37, 38

HERE we see how easy Christ makes it for those who set out to find Him. When we start to seek Him, ever so timidly and tremblingly, He does not leave us to seek unencouraged, but quickly turns to meet us and to cheer and help us. Then He does not stand apart on some lofty mountain-top far away, or hide Himself out of sight, compelling us to seek alone and struggle through sore difficulties to get to His feet. He sees us when we take our first steps toward Him, and notes the very beginnings of our heart's longings for Him. In the parable, the father was watching and saw the prodigal as he came painfully and wearily homeward; and when he saw him he ran to meet him. It is just in this way that Christ does when He sees a penitent sinner turn his face toward Him.

Notice His question also, " What seek ye ? " This is Christ's question to all who begin to go after Him. He wants us to know ourselves just what it is that we are seeking for. Once, when two blind men cried after Him, He turned and asked, " What will ye that I shall do unto you ? " It is good for us to get our desires into definite form. Many people are unhappy, and know that they need something, but do not know what it is. They are unsatisfied with themselves; they are conscious of imperfection, of sin, of unrest; they bend their faces toward Christ and begin to pray to Him, but their prayers are vague and indefinite. Then Jesus turns and asks, " What seek ye ? " If we will settle definitely what we want, He will be ready to answer. The form of this question also veils a promise: " Tell Me what ye seek, and I will give it to you." The question is nothing less than a key to Christ's treasure-house. We need only to be sure that we seek truly, but we must remember that seeking is a very strong word.

Begin at Home

" He first findeth his own brother Simon..... and he brought him to Jesus."—JOHN i. 41, 42

NOBODY told Andrew to go after his brother; it was the impulse of his own heart that sent him so quickly away on his love-errand, after he had found Christ himself. The lesson lies on the surface. " Even a dog," says one, " that has had its leg mended will bring other limping dogs to the man that was kind to it." One who has been cured of some disease will bring all his afflicted friends to the physician who cured him.

You have had your soul saved. All about you are those whose souls are lost, as yours was a little while ago. How many have you brought to Jesus ? Do you think you can hold up clean hands, free from the blood of souls, unless you try very earnestly to bring some others to Christ ? Notice that it was his own brother that Andrew brought; and the words indicate that the other man—John—brought his brother too, only Andrew was the quicker. Home, then, is the place where we ought to begin. Yet, strange to say, it is the last place many of us speak about Christ. The old proverb has it, " The shoemaker's wife is always the worst shod." Often it is the preacher's or the teacher's own home that gets the least benefit and blessing from his messages of love, or from his Christian life and influence. Surely the dearest in the world to you are home's precious ones ; go first to them, therefore, if any of them are unsaved, and try to bring them to your Saviour, that they may find what you have found. Of course you will not stop with home ; let the circle widen until your influence reaches as widely as possible ; but do not overlook home and those nearest and dearest to you while you stretch out your hands towards the heathen in China or in Africa, or even reach over the fence to save a neighbour next door. That is a mistake some people make.

Finding Christ

" We have found the Messias."—JOHN i. 41

WE must notice the kind of argument Andrew used with his brother. He just went to him with a great joy in his heart—the joy of discovery and of satisfaction—and told him about it. An English preacher gives in a sermon this illustration, showing how much more convincing power there is in a little bit of real Christian life than there is in a large amount of apologetics. A minister delivered in his pulpit a very fine course of lectures in refutation of some form of infidelity. He delivered the course chiefly for the benefit of one man that attended his place of worship. The man was sceptical, and the preacher hoped to remove his doubts. Shortly after the close of the lectures this man came and declared himself a Christian. The minister was very glad, and said to him, " Which of my discourses was it that removed your doubts ? " The answer was, " Oh, it was not any of your sermons that influenced me. The thing that set me to thinking was a poor woman that came out of the chapel beside me one night and stumbled on the steps. I reached out my hand to help her, and she said, ' Thank you ; ' then she said, ' Do you love Jesus Christ, my blessed Saviour ? ' I did not, and I went home and thought about it ; and now I can say, I love Jesus." An ounce of heart is worth more than a ton of head in winning souls.

When we have really found Christ ourselves, the best way to bring others is just to tell them what Christ is to us. One word of genuine and hearty confession of Christ by a person whose soul is full of the new-found joy, is worth more than the most eloquent sermons to lead others to believe in Christ. Let us be sure that people know from us that we have really found Christ ; then they cannot but be impressed. It will surely be a sad pity if we should so live that they will not suspect that we are Christians.

The Wedding=Feast

" *There was a marriage in Cana......And both Jesus was called, and His disciples, to the marriage.*"—JOHN ii. 1, 2

JESUS approved, sanctified, and adorned marriage by attending this wedding-feast. The Bible from the beginning to the end puts high honour upon marriage. God Himself ordained it in Eden. It is not without peculiar significance that Christ made this His first public appearance, and wrought this His first miracle, at a marriage, thus showing His approval, and putting His sanction upon the relation. There is no subject on which young people in these days need to receive more careful instruction than concerning marriage. The many ill-advised and unhappy marriages, the alarming frequency of separation, and the ease with which, for the slightest reason, divorces are obtained, show that the ordinance is losing its sanctity in the public mind. Jesus should be invited to every wedding, as He was to this at Cana. No marriage relation should ever be entered into when His presence would not be welcome, and on which His blessing cannot be sought and obtained.

It should be noted further here that it was a wedding-*feast* which Jesus attended. His ministry opened amid scenes of human happiness. We need to learn that Christ is not merely a friend for our sorrow-hours, but also for our times of joy. We do not think enough of this. We regard religion too much " as a lamp burning dimly in a sepulchre," and not as a sun shining amid the brightness and the radiance of the fairest day. No doubt it is when trouble comes that Christ seems most precious to us ; but He is a Friend for our gladness as well. This lesson from the Cana wedding we should not lose. Our Lord does not frown upon pure, innocent pleasures. Mirth is a duty in its place as really as prayer. We need not be afraid to invite Christ to our social enjoyments ; indeed, if we cannot invite Him something must be wrong with the pleasures themselves.

Unfailing Joys

" *The wine failed.*"—JOHN ii. 3 (Revised Version)

THIS incident is a very fitting illustration of the failure of all this world's joys. The wine gave out at a wedding-feast. There was not enough of it to last through to the end of the feast. It is just so with all pleasure. It comes in cups, not in fountains, and the supply is limited and soon exhausted. It is so especially with sin's pleasures. The prodigal soon runs through with his abundance and begins to be in want. A poet compared the pleasures of sin to a snowflake on the river—" a moment white, then gone for ever." But it is true in a sense also of pure pleasures. Even the sweetness of human love is but a cupful which will not last for ever. The joy which so fills us to-day, to-morrow is changed to sorrow. Amid the gladness of the marriage altar there is the knell of the end in the words " till death us do part." One of every two friends must hold the other's hand in farewell at the edge of the valley—must stand by the other's grave and walk alone part of the way.

The best wine of life and of love will fail. If there were nothing better in this world, how sad it would be ! But it is here that we see the glory of Christ's gospel. Jesus comes when earth's wine fails, and gives heaven's wine to supply the lack. How beautiful and how true is the picture here—the failing wine, and then Jesus coming with power and supplying the want ! That is what He is doing continually. He takes lives which have drained their last drop of earthly gladness and He satisfies them with spiritual good and blessing, so that they want nothing more. When human joy fails, if we have Jesus with us, He gives new joy, better than the world's, and in unfailing abundance. How sad it is for those who have not taken Christ into their lives, and who have nothing but the empty cup when earth's wine gives out !

The Lord's Time

" *Mine hour is not yet come.*"—JOHN ii. 4

HE meant that His time for beginning to work miracles had not yet come. With all Divine power slumbering in His hands, He would do nothing at any bidding but His Father's. Even His human mother's request He could not in this matter regard.

One thought here is our Lord's perfect devotion to His Father's will. We find the same all through His life. He did nothing of Himself. He took His work moment by moment from His Father's hand. He waited always for His " hour." He had no plans of His own, but followed the Divine purpose in all His acts. All those early years at Nazareth, with omnipotence in His arm, He wrought no miracle. Even now, though appealed to by His mother whom He so deeply loved, He would not do anything even one minute before His hour came.

The practical lesson for us here is devotion to God's will. We should always wait for God. Too many of us run before we are sent. In our zeal for God's cause and kingdom we do not wait for Divine direction. We speak words out of season which, despite their earnestness and sincerity, do harm rather than good. We try to feed others with unripe fruits. We address men before they are prepared to hear, and ofttimes in words that drive them beyond our reach. We hurry out to preach when we ought ourselves to be sitting quietly at our Master's feet as learners. The most common fault among Christians is that they are too slow in doing Christ's work and in heeding His calls ; but it is a fault also to go too fast for God, to go before He sends us. With all warm love for Christ we must learn to wait for Him, to wait till our hour is come. He must prepare us for the work before we are ready to do it, and then He must prepare the work for our hand. In Christian work we need patience and self-restraint as well as zeal and earnestness.

March 3

Obedience

"*Whatsoever He saith unto you, do it.*"—JOHN ii. 5

THAT is the word for all Christ's servants. That is the motto of true consecration at all times and in all places. Every word in this sentence is emphatic and intense in its meaning. "Whatsoever *He* saith." There is no other one who has a right to command us. We belong to Christ because He has redeemed us. He is our only Lord and Master. "*Whatsoever* He saith." We may not choose some of His commands for obedience and some for neglect, inattention, or rejection. We are not to do the pleasant things He bids us to do, and leave undone the things that are not according to our own taste and feeling. We are to do even the things that cost pain and personal sacrifice. It was thus that Jesus did the will of His Father. That will took Him to His cross; but He did not shrink from accepting it when He saw the way growing dark, or when He felt the thorns under His feet and the burdens increasing into crushing weight upon His shoulders. If we would walk in His steps our obedience must be complete.

"Whatsoever He *saith*." But how can we know what He saith? We cannot hear His voice as the servants at the wedding heard it. He speaks now in His Word, and the reverent heart may always hear what He says, as the sacred pages are prayerfully pondered. He speaks in the conscience that is kept tender by loyal obeying; He speaks in the providence that brings duty to our hand. There never is any real uncertainty as to what He says, if we are truly intent on knowing His will. "Whatsoever He saith unto you, *do* it!" It is the doing that is important. We should never ask questions nor make suggestions when Jesus has spoken; the one thing for us is obedience. We should never ask what the consequences may be, what it may cost us; we are simply to obey. Christ knows why He wants us to do the thing, and that should be reason enough for us.

Co=Workers with Christ

" Fill the water-pots with water. And they filled them up
to the brim. And He saith unto them, Draw out now."
JOHN ii. 7, 8

THE servants' part in this miracle was important : they
had to carry the water and fill the vessels, and then
draw out and bear the wine to the guests. Thus they became co-workers with Christ in His miracle. So our Lord
calls His people always to be His helpers in blessing the
world. We cannot do much. The best we can bring is a
little of the common water of earth ; but if we bring that
to Him He can change it into the rich wine of heaven, which
will bless weary and fainting ones. If we take simply what
we have and use it as He commands, it will do good. Moses
had only a rod in his hand, but with this he wrought great
wonders. The disciples had only five barley-loaves, but
these, touched by Christ's hand, made a feast for thousands.
So the common water carried by these servants, under the
Master's benediction, became wine for the wedding.

Christ passes the gifts of His love and grace through
human hands to others. The redemption is Divine, wrought
by Christ alone, but the priesthood that mediates is human ;
human hands must distribute the blessings. Gifts of mercy
can get to the lost only through those who have been saved.
Then how striking is the other side of this truth : the
servants carried only common water from the spring, but
with Christ's blessing the water became good wine. So it
always is when we do what Christ bids us to do—our most
prosaic work leaves heavenly results. No labour is in vain
which is wrought in the Lord. Our commonest work amid
life's trivialities, in business, in the household, which seems
but like the carrying of water to be emptied out again, is
transformed into radiant service like angel ministry, and
leaves glorious results behind. The simplest things we do
at Christ's bidding may become immortal blessings to other
souls or to our own !

March 5

Silent Change

" The ruler of the feast......knew not whence it was."
JOHN ii. 9

CHRIST wrought this miracle without noise or ostentation. He said nothing to call attention to what
He was going to do. The people about Him did not know
of the wonderful work He had wrought. So He works
to-day. He is not in the storm, the earthquake, the whirl-
wind, but in the " still small voice." His kingdom comes
into men's hearts, not with observation and show, but
silently, without parade. The bad life is changed by His
word into moral purity, and yet no one saw the change
made or the hand that wrought it. Silently help comes in
the hours of need, silently prayer's answers glide down,
silently the angels come and go.

It is significant also that the " servants which drew the
water knew." Those who work with Christ are admitted
into the inner chamber where omnipotence is unveiled. The
lesson is very simple and beautiful. Christ takes into His
confidence those who serve Him ; calls them no more servants but friends. Those who do Christ's will know of His
doctrine, and see His ways of working. If we would see
Christ's power and glory, we must enter heartily into His
service. Ofttimes it is in the lowliest ways, and in the
paths of humble, self-denying service, that the most of His
glory appears. The ruler did not know whence the wine
came ; is it not often so with us ? People do not know
whence the blessings come which glide so softly into their
hearts. Many a troubled Christian kneels in prayer in great
fear, oppressed by a sense of need, and rises with new, rich
joy in his heart, yet knowing not whence the strange, sweet
blessing came. We drink the cups which God fills for us
with heavenly sweetness, we receive the gifts which are
brought down to us from the very throne, and yet ofttimes
we do not know whence these things come, nor recognize
the Divine presence that works so close beside us.

"More and More" of Blessing

*" Every man at the beginning doth set forth good wine ; and
when men have well drunk, then that which is worse :
but thou hast kept the good wine until now."*—JOHN ii. 10

THE world gives its best first, and the worst comes
afterwards. It is so in all sinful pleasures—first
exhilaration, and then bitter remorse. It is so in the chase
for wealth, power, fame—gratification first, and then painful disappointment. At first money brings gladness, a sort
of satisfaction ; but as time rolls on and wealth increases,
cares multiply, anxieties thicken, burdens grow heavier, and
at last the rich man finds that in all his riches he has less
comfort than he had in the days when he was a poor boy.
It is so in all mere worldly ambitions. The first cups of
fame are sweet, but soon they pall upon the taste. This
truth holds especially in the sinful life. We need not deny
that at the beginning sin is sweet, but bitterness is found
at the bottom of the cup. In grace, however, this is re-
versed ; the good wine is kept to the last. Christ Himself
had humiliation, darkness, and the shame of the cross, then
exaltation, power, glory.

In Christian life the same law holds. First there comes
bitterness, but out of the bitterness sweetness flows. There
is the deep sorrow of penitence, but this gives way to the
blessed joy of forgiveness. First there are self-denial and
cross-bearing, but out of these experiences comes a holy
peace that fills all the heart. Sorrows are to be endured,
but the good wine of comfort is poured into the emptied
cup. There is also a constant progression in the blessings
of the Divine life. We never get to the end of them ; indeed
we never get to the best. There is always something
better yet to come. Then Christ keeps the really best wine
to the very last, in heaven. Sweet as is earth's peace to
the Christian, he will never know the fullness of the love of
God until he gets home to the Father's house.

March 7

The First Miracle

*" This beginning of miracles did Jesus in Cana of Galilee,
and manifested forth His glory."*—JOHN ii. 11

THE glory was there before ; it had been slumbering
in His lowly, human life all along those quiet years
of toil and service at Nazareth ; but it was now manifested
for the first time. This was the first shining out before
men of the Divine splendour. We should notice also that
it was in a simple act of thoughtful kindness to a perplexed
household that this glory was first manifested. Christ did
not wait for some great occasion, but threw the earliest
gleams of His Divine manifestation upon this homely scene.
It should be further noticed that it was in the midst of
gladness and festivity that these first beams shone forth.
Thus we see that the glory of Christ was the radiance of
love. We follow on, and we find the same glory burning
out more and more brightly, until at last He goes to His
cross, manifesting forth in one great act the amazing splendour of the love of God for the world. No wonder His disciples believed on Him when they saw this miracle at Cana.
It was a gleam of divinity which flashed forth from His
lowly form and wrought the marvellous sign.

We should note, too, before leaving the story of this first
miracle, that this transformation of water into wine was a
fitting symbol of the whole work of Christ in this world.
We have but to look about us and back along the Christian
centuries to see the same glory blazing everywhere, the
same transformation perpetually going on. Wherever the
gospel goes wonderful change is wrought. The desert is
made to blossom like a garden. The worst lives are
touched and transfigured into spiritual beauty. Who
that looks upon the perpetual miracle of Christianity in
the world can refuse to believe on Christ ? No mere
empty creed could produce such results. There is a life
in Christianity which quickens and transforms whatever
it touches.

Secret Discipleship

" The same came to Jesus by night."—JOHN iii. 2

IT was better to come by night than not to come at all, though we usually think that it showed timidity on the part of Nicodemus. We must remember, however, that Jesus did not rebuke him, nor did He refuse to accept even his secret discipleship. He seems to have received him with loving welcome, and to have taught him in the quiet way Nicodemus chose to come. We must remember, too, that the times then were not as they are now. Christ had not yet died, nor had the Christian Church been established. Certainly, secret discipleship is not justifiable now, whatever excuse Nicodemus may have had for it in his time. We know too that it was not satisfactory even in his case. We know that the time came when he could no longer remain a secret friend. When Jesus was dead on His cross, and when His body, as that of a crucified malefactor, was about to be buried in dishonour among criminals, it is remarkable that the two men who came forward and rescued it from such ignominy and gave it honourable sepulture, had both until that day been secret disciples. The death of Christ so touched their hearts and aroused their timid, hesitating love, that they could not longer continue secret disciples. The true love of their hearts could not be repressed, and they came forward and risked and dared all for Him whom they had never before had courage openly to confess.

Secret discipleship is not satisfactory. It does not get the hearty approval of one's own conscience. It does not bring full, rich peace to the heart. It yields but a crippled and hampered Christian life at the best. If we love Christ we should come out boldly and confess Him at a time when our confession will honour Him and bring blessing to ourselves. We have a glorious promise that those who confess Him here, He will confess at the day of judgment before angels and men.

March 9

The Gospel

" *For God so loved the world, that He gave His only begotten Son, that whosoever believeth in Him should not perish, but have everlasting life.*"—JOHN iii. 16

THIS verse is a little Bible in itself, for it contains the whole gospel. It shows us the source of man's redemption—God's love. It shows us the measure of this Divine love—God gave His only begotten Son. It shows us how the redemption was accomplished—by the sacrifice of Christ. It tells us how to be saved—by believing on the Son of God. It tells us who will be saved—whosoever believeth on Christ. It shows us what the salvation is—deliverance from perishing, and the gift of eternal life.

Any one who truly believes that God loves him is saved ; the consciousness of this blessed truth is life in the soul. A story is told of a child in Luther's time who thought of God only with dread, as of a terrible Judge. In her stern home God had been held before her only in this way, to terrify her. She had never heard a word about God's gentleness or affection. But one day in her father's printing-office she picked up a scrap of paper and found on it just the first part of this verse, " God so loved the world that He gave—" The remaining words were torn off, but even this mere fragment was a revelation to her. God *loved*—loved the world—loved it well enough to *give* something. What He gave she did not know, but it was enough for her to know that God loved at all, and that He loved the world enough to give anything to it. The new thought changed all her conception of God. She learned from this time to think of Him as one who loved her, and this thought brought sweet comfort to her. We have the whole verse, and we know that God is love ; we know just what His love gave—the most costly and most valuable gift in all the universe ; and this revelation should fill us with unutterable joy.

Ibe Sat on tbe Well

" *Jesus therefore, being wearied with His journey, sat thus on the well.*"—John iv. 6

IN all the gospel story there are few more tenderly suggestive pictures of Jesus than that which we have in these words. He has been travelling all day in the hot sun, and coming to this resting-place He sits down on a well-curb. He is weary and wayworn with His long journey. He is both hungry and thirsty. This is the picture of Jesus for tired people. In other places we have pictures for the tempted, and for the bereft and sorrowing, for the penitent, and for mothers and children, and for the blind, the deaf, the lame, and the persecuted. Here, however, is the picture for the weary. As we look at it we see the human side of Christ's life. Here is one of His experiences which we can understand. As we see Him healing, teaching, raising the dead, transfigured, He is far above us, and we cannot enter into His feelings. But in His bodily weariness, after His long journey in the heat and dust, He is down amongst us, and we can tell just how He felt. The chief comfort comes to us from the fact that He is able now to sympathize with us when we are tired, because that day, so long since, He was tired.

Do we get all the blessing we might get from the truth of our Lord's actual human experiences ? When we have been working hard all day, and are weary and faint, let us remember this picture—Jesus, footsore and dust-covered, sinking down in sheer exhaustion on the stone curb. He has not forgotten even in His glory how He felt that day, and as He sees us in our weariness, His heart feels tenderly for us. He looks down upon us in compassion, and sends to us a benediction of strength and cheer. Let all the people whose work is hard, and who ofttimes are very tired, frame this picture in their memory and keep it always hanging up on the wall of their heart.

March 11

Give Me to Drink

" There cometh a woman of Samaria to draw water : Jesus saith unto her, Give Me to drink."—JOHN iv. 7

THIS illustrates to us how full the world's common walks are of Christ. This woman went out from her home on a very ordinary and commonplace errand, to draw a little water from the public well, and before she returned she had met the Messiah and He had revealed Himself to her soul as her Saviour. She was not seeking for Christ save as the unsatisfied yearning of her heart was a faint cry for Him whom she knew not. We never know when we are to meet Christ. He waits for us in all the paths of life. She was in the way of simple duty when He met her.

The way of duty is always the surest place to come upon Christ. No one ever yet found Him in the path of disobedience. This woman was unaware of the glory of the presence beside her. Jesus met her in the form of a weary and wayworn man, and won His way to her conscience and heart before He revealed to her the glory of His personality. Christ continually comes in unrecognized ways, getting near to us and drawing out our love and trust before we know that it is Christ we are loving and trusting ; then He drops the veil and shows us His blessed face.

There is another suggestion here : Jesus began His ministry of blessing to this woman by asking a simple favour of her. "Give me to drink," He said. Thus He continually stands before us in some disguise, asking some service. He Himself has told us that in the least of His little ones who appeal to us for bread in their hunger, or relief in their distress, He Himself comes, and that what we do for these we do for Him. So we never know when it is Christ that stands before us, in some suppliant or needy one, with timid request for help. We should be careful how we treat the lowliest, lest some day we deny a cup of water to the blessed glorious Christ.

Earthly Joys

" Whosoever drinketh of this water shall thirst again "
JOHN iv. 13

THAT is just as true of all earth's springs of joy as it was of Jacob's well. Men and women drink of them to-day and find a measure of satisfaction for a little time, but soon they are thirsty as ever again. The human soul cannot be satisfied with any of earth's good things. This is not the fault of the things of earth—they are good and beautiful in their way and in their place. But the soul is spiritual and immortal, and cannot be filled with any good that is not also spiritual and immortal. Money and fame and power can never be food for a soul made in the Divine image ; nothing less than God Himself can answer its cravings. We could not make the angels happy by giving them gold and diamonds, and building them fine marble palaces to live in, and putting crowns and fine clothes on them. No more can we satisfy our own souls with such things. Men try to do so, but their thirst is only momentarily quenched, and soon they must drink again. Gratification only intensifies desire.

There is said to be a strange plant in South America which finds a moist place, and sends its roots down and becomes green for a little while, until the place becomes dry, when it draws itself out and rolls itself up and is blown along by the wind until it comes to another moist place, where it repeats the same process. On and on the plant goes, stopping wherever it finds a little water until the spot is dry ; then in the end, after all its wanderings, it is nothing but a bundle of dry roots and leaves. It is the same with those who drink only of this world's springs. They drink and thirst again, and go on from spring to spring, blown by the winds of passion and desire, and at last their souls are nothing but bundles of unsatisfied desires and burning thirsts. We must find something better than this, or perish for ever.

A Living Spring

" *Whosoever drinketh of the water that I shall give him shall never thirst ; but the water that I shall give him shall be in him a well of water springing up into everlasting life.*"—JOHN iv. 14

THE soul was made for God, and when it returns to God it finds peace and satisfaction. It is not meant here, of course, that the Christian has no more desires ; for longing is the very condition of more blessedness. " Blessed are they that hunger and thirst after righteousness : for they shall be filled." If there is no thirst there really is no life. The dove that flew away from the ark went on weary wing everywhere, but found only a wide waste of desolate waters, with no place to alight. Then she flew back to the ark, and was gently drawn inside, where she found warmth, safety, and rest.

The story of the dove illustrates the history of the soul that wanders everywhere seeking rest, at last returning to God. How much better if men believed this truth of universal experience and went at once to God ! An immortal soul, from its very nature, cannot find what it needs anywhere save in God Himself. This word of Christ tells us also what true religion is. It begins in the heart. It is not something outside—a mere set of rules to be obeyed, an example to be copied. It is new spiritual life in the soul. It is Christ coming into the heart and dwelling there. It is a fountain of life—not a mere cistern, but a living spring open and ever flowing. It is fed from heaven, and no matter how dry this world may be, this living fountain in the heart shall never be exhausted, for its connection is with the river of life, which flows out from under God's throne. Wherever we go we have our religion with us, in us, if we are true Christians. We are not dependent upon circumstances. Trouble does not destroy a Christian, because the fountain of his joy is within. This new fountain of life when opened in the soul is the beginning of eternal life.

True Worship

" God is a Spirit : and they that worship Him must worship Him in spirit and in truth."—JOHN iv. 24

GOD loves to be worshipped—to have the praise, the adoration, and the homage of His children. In the olden days burning incense was the symbol of worship ; its odours rose up toward heaven, and God smelled a sweet savour. What the fragrance of flowers coming up from dew-anointed fields and gardens is to us, the breath of true worship as it ascends from earth's believing hearts is to God. God is well pleased with it. He is not satisfied with bare, cold obedience. What parent would be content with mere dutifulness, such as a slave might render to a master, without affection, confidence, regard ? God cannot be pleased with the most scrupulous external obedience if there be no heart in it. We must obey Him because we love Him.

This word tells us also how we may worship God if our worship is to be acceptable. It must be spiritual worship that we render Him. Stately forms please Him not in themselves. The music of splendid choirs and the repeating of creeds and prayers do not make worship. Worship is heart adoration, and the only true homage that rises from an assembly or from a private closet where one bows alone is just the love and praise and prayer and devotion of hearts ascending in the words of human lips. No mere forms of worship are acceptable ; the form must be breathed full of love and life. No offerings or gifts avail in worship unless they are the expression of holy affections. The teaching is not that we are not to use forms of worship ; we cannot well worship without forms. The baldest ritual and the tamest ceremonial will be pleasing to God if heart's love fill them ; but the most magnificent ritual will be empty of real worship, and will be an abomination to God, if there be no true worship of the spirit in it. All depends upon what we put into the forms.

March 15

Bread from Heaven

" *I have meat to eat that ye know not of.*"—JOHN iv. 32

THE disciples had left Jesus hungry when they went away to buy bread ; they came back to find His hunger departed, and in these words we have the reason He gave for it. He was intently engaged in His Father's work, doing His will, and in this He found perfect satisfaction. He had found spiritual refreshment, and His bodily weariness and hunger had vanished. His joy in saving a poor lost soul was so great that it made Him forget His hunger. But the joy was not the only food which Christ had ; while doing His Father's work special Divine grace was imparted to Him from heaven, which nourished and strengthened Him. He literally fed on bread from heaven—spiritual bread.

We have other examples of the same. When He had gone through His sore temptation and was an hungered, we are told that angels came and ministered unto Him. In Gethsemane also, after His bitter agony, we read that there appeared an angel from heaven strengthening Him. May we not suppose that always when He had any special service, costing Him an outlay of strength, spiritual refreshment was imparted to Him in some secret way by His Father ? Certainly we have the promise of this in our lives. When Paul asked that his trouble, his " thorn in the flesh," might be removed, the answer was, " No : My grace is sufficient for thee ; for My strength is made perfect in weakness." When we are united to Christ, our weakness to His strength, our emptiness to His fullness, for all our need there flows to us from Him a supply adequate to our want. We see constant illustrations of this in our homes, where frail ones called to nurse the sick are sustained in a wonderful way through long, wearisome days and sleepless nights of vigil, as if nourished with supernatural food. They have meat to eat that others know not of. There flows from Christ's fullness a strength for their need.

March 16

Doing the Father's Will

" My meat is to do the will of Him that sent Me."
JOHN iv. 34

THUS Jesus explained to His disciples how He had been nourished during their absence. He had been labouring in His Father's work, and this labour had revived Him. There is for all of Christ's people a wonderful secret of hidden blessedness in these words. There is a life higher than mere bodily existence. As our Lord elsewhere said, " Man shall not live by bread alone, but by every word that proceedeth out of the mouth of God." It is only the lower life that can be nourished by bread, and this may be well fed while the true life is famishing : the higher existence is sustained by communion with God, and this communion is maintained by doing God's will. It was this communion with the Father that sustained Christ in all His sufferings. At one time He said, " He that sent Me is with Me : the Father hath not left Me alone; for I do always those things that please Him." The simple joy of doing the Father's will was another element in the " meat " on which Christ here fed. There was also the joy of saving a lost soul. We do not begin to realize the joy that it gives Christ to see penitents coming home. It was this same " meat " that sustained Him in all the sorrows of the cross—" who for the joy set before Him endured the cross, despising the shame."

These are but a few of the many deep and rich suggestions of truth which lie in this one Divine sentence. We should learn the lesson for ourselves, for it is true for us as it was for Jesus that doing the will of God nourishes our souls. Complete and loving submission to the Divine will in time of suffering lifts the spirit above its pain. Entire devotion to God's work brings a Christian into such living communion with his Lord that he even rejoices in toil and sacrifice. To do God's will brings us into living communion with Him, and that is life.

March 17

Fruit unto Life Eternal

" He that reapeth receiveth wages, and gathereth fruit unto life eternal."—JOHN iv. 36

THOSE who work for this world often fail of reward; but those who do God's work are sure of good-wages and of glorious harvest. "The wages of sin is death," and the wages of much of earth's toil is disappointment; but the wages of doing good is life, and the joy is sure and eternal. It is often hard work which the Christian has to do. The sowing is ofttimes in tears, but the reaping is always in joy. Christ Himself found the sowing hard and sorrowful, but He has never been sorry in heaven for what it cost Him here. The old prophet having spoken of the sorrows and sufferings of Christ's life, said, "He shall see of the travail of His soul, and shall be satisfied." As He sits now on His throne and sees the millions of the redeemed coming home to glory, all saved through His sufferings, He never regrets that He gave such a price for their redemption, but rejoices and is satisfied with the wages which He receives. So it will be with all His followers who are permitted to suffer in any way in bringing lost ones home. The wages will a thousand times compensate for all the sacrifice and cost.

No true work for Christ has ever been in vain. On earth many a seed is dropped which dies in the soil; but no seed of heavenly truth which is sown in faith and watered with tears ever fails to spring up somewhere and some time into a plant of righteousness. It may not always grow as the sower hoped, nor always just where he hoped, nor when; yet no living word of God can ever die. We should notice the kind of wages God gives His reapers. He does not pay them in gold and silver, but in life—life eternal. Those who work in God's harvest-fields may not grow rich in men's eyes, but they themselves grow into richer, riper, holier spiritual blessedness.

Sowing and Reaping

" One soweth, and another reapeth."—JOHN iv. 37

THIS word of Christ is ofttimes illustrated in its literal sense. Many a man sows a field of wheat, and before the harvest lies in his grave. Many a man plants a tree, and does not live to taste its fruits ; others coming after him enjoy the benefit of his labour. Then still more frequently is this word illustrated in its spiritual sense. Ofttimes the sower does not reap any harvest in this world. Many people work hard and faithfully for Christ all their life and see no results. Then, by-and-by, others come, and with almost no toil gather from the same fields abundant harvests. One pastor preaches and prays for many years, and sees but few souls brought to Christ. He dies, or goes away, and a new man comes. Almost immediately a revival begins, and many souls are brought into the kingdom. One sowed, another reaps. But who will say that the sower's work was not just as important as the reaper's ? If the first pastor had not laboured so faithfully and so long, could the second have gathered such a harvest ? We are sure that in heaven they will both rejoice together. There is no danger that there will be any jealousy there as to whose is the just meed of honour.

Many a mother teaches her children the story of the love of Christ, and presses upon them the acceptance of the Saviour. With prayer and faith she awaits the result, hoping to see them confess Christ. But at length her eyes are closed upon earth, and her children are still unsaved. At last, however, there comes a gentle reaper, and they are gathered into the garner. So it is with many a faithful teacher or other Christian worker. We need not then concern ourselves about the reaping. Let us sow everywhere the good seed, and whether we reap the harvest, or some other hand gather it, it will make no difference ; sower and reaper shall rejoice together.

March 19

Trials Leading us to Christ

" *When he heard that Jesus was come......he went unto Him, and besought Him that He would come down, and heal his son.*"—JOHN iv. 47

THE trouble in his home sent this man to Christ. Perhaps he never would have gone at all had it not been for his son's sickness. Many of those who went to Christ in the olden days were driven by their distress of heart. They tried everything else first, and then at the last moment they hurried to Jesus. The same is true in these days. Many persons who have never prayed before have gotten down upon their knees by the bedside of their sick and dying children and cried to God on their behalf. Many persons have first been sent to God by their own troubles. It was not until the prodigal was in sore want, and every other resource had been exhausted, that he said he would arise and go to his father. Many sinners never think of Christ until they are in despair under the sense of guilt. Not until they see the storm of wrath gathering do they seek the shelter of the cross. But what a comfort it is that even going so late to the Saviour He does not reject or cast away those who come !

We ought to remember always that when any trouble comes to us, whatever other purposes it may have it is certainly intended to send us anew to Christ. Perhaps we have drifted away from Him, or grown careless, or lost our first love. The trouble that touches us is the merciful hand of God laid on us to lead us back to our place of safety and blessedness at His side. A man was travelling and was hungry, but did not know where to go to find food. There came up a sudden and violent storm, compelling him to seek shelter. Fleeing under a tree for refuge, he found not shelter only, but food, for the storm brought down fruits from the tree's branches for his hunger. Those whom trouble drives to Christ also find both shelter from the storm and food to meet their cravings.

Death the Gate of Life

" He was at the point of death."—JOHN iv. 47

HE was just on the edge of death, just at its door.
The point of death is a point to which all of us
some time must come. We pass through this world by
many different roads. Our ways run in diverse directions,
crossing each other at every possible angle. No two of
us go in precisely the same path. If we could see a map
of the world, with all human paths marked out on it, it
would be a strange network that we should behold. But
however diverse our courses, every one of us comes at last
to the " point of death ! " This is a point no one can ever
evade. There is no road in life which goes around it. It
is a strange point ! At it the life suddenly passes out of
sight, passes from earth, and enters on a new existence in
the eternal world.

What preparation have we made for this " point of
death " ? Are we ready for it, so that our sudden coming
to it at any moment shall not terrify us ? What preparation is necessary ? Only this—that we be saved in Christ,
and have our work for Him well and faithfully done up to
the last moment. Christ changed this " point of death "
to a " point of life." He tasted death for every man, and
absorbed all death's blackness and curse. Now if we are
true believers in Christ, dying is but leaving darkness and
sin and danger to pass into light and holiness and safety
A poet represents one coming up to a gate on a mountain-
side, over which were written the words, "The Gate of
Death ; " but when he touched the gate, it opened, and he
found himself amid great brightness and beauty ; then
turning about he saw above the gate he had entered the
words, " The Gate of Life." If we are in Christ, death is
abolished, and the point which earth calls the point of
death is really the point of life. We need then to make
sure of only one thing—that we are truly Christ's by living
faith and loving obedience.

March 21

The Return to Nazareth

" *He came to Nazareth, where He had been brought up.*"
LUKE iv. 16

IT was a hard place for Him to visit and to preach in. He had lived there from infancy. The young people knew Him as schoolmate and playfellow, and as the village carpenter. One day He went away from home, and soon there began to come back strange reports about Him. Up in Jerusalem and in other places, it was said, He was performing miracles and preaching with wonderful power, and the people everywhere were thronging to hear Him, and bringing out their sick to be healed by Him. It requires no deep insight into human nature to know how His neighbours would regard all this. In their envy they would sneer at the reports about Him. He was only a carpenter ! Then one day He came home again, and went to the village church and preached. But they could not endure to hear His words, and they were filled with wrath, and rose up and cast Him out of the town, and tried to hurl Him over a precipice to kill Him.

There are some lessons which we ought to gather from this visit of Jesus to His old home. One is that we ought to seek the salvation of our neighbours and friends, not turning our back upon our old home, though we may have grown great and famous elsewhere. Another is that as young people we ought to live so carefully that when we grow up we may be able to stand up in the midst of those who have always known us and bear testimony for Christ. There are some good men now whose preaching would have but little effect where they were brought up, because of the way they lived when they were at home in youth. But Jesus' life had been so pure and blameless that He had no need to blush when He looked His old neighbours in the face and began to preach to them. Every young person should so live that he will never be ashamed to hear again of anything he has ever done.

Church Attendance

" As His custom was, He went into the synagogue on the sabbath day."—LUKE iv. 16.

THERE are many evidences that Jesus had fixed religious habits. Here we have a hint of His attending the synagogue worship on the Sabbath. This had been His custom from childhood, and although He was the Son of God, Lord of earth and heaven, and had been manifested as the Messiah, He still continued to observe the custom. Some people are careless about church attendance. They find fault perhaps with the minister—he does not feed them, they say. They mean that he does not entertain them. Now no doubt Jesus heard a great many dull talks and sermons, but He did not on that account stay away from the synagogue. He went there to worship God, not to enjoy an intellectual entertainment. Others stay away from church, as they say, because there are so many inconsistent Christians who attend, because the church is so imperfect. We know that it was just the same when Jesus was on the earth. There were a great many church members in Nazareth and elsewhere who were very imperfect. Our Lord knew all about men's true character, and He saw the worst there was in them. What He saw in some very prominent church people we may learn from some of His own bitter words against the prominent religionists of His day. Yet this did not keep Him from the services. If He could worship God in a congregation of faulty people, we should be able to do it.

Another thought is that if He, with all the resources of His own Divine nature to draw upon, still needed the means of grace, surely we need them far more. Still another point to be remembered is the importance of forming religious habits, especially the habit of going to church. Here the lesson particularly touches children and young people. Jesus brought this custom from His youth, and never intermitted it in His manhood.

March 23 "**Now is the Accepted Time**"

"*He hath anointed Me......to preach the acceptable year of the Lord.*"—LUKE iv. 18, 19

THEN there must be a year or a time which is not the "acceptable year." We know that this "acceptable year" closed for the Jewish nation when they nailed their Messiah on the cross. They were doomed from that hour. For a number of years things went on as before. There was a measure of prosperity. Their city stood in its splendour, and the people dwelt in their homes in some degree of peace. But the day of their merciful visitation ended for ever when they finally rejected Christ. When Jesus stood on Olivet and looked down upon the city and wept over it, and said, "If thou hadst known, even thou, at least in this thy day, the things which belong unto thy peace; but now they are hid from thine eyes"—when He spoke these words amid the rush of tears, the "acceptable year" closed. After that the doom hung over the beautiful city which in a few years burst upon it in all its woe and terribleness.

This is history, but there is another way to look at this matter. There is an "acceptable year" for each soul. It begins when Christ first comes to us and offers salvation. It continues while He still stands at our door and knocks. It closes when we drive Him away from our door by utter and final rejection, or when death comes and hurries us away for ever from the world of mercy. This "acceptable year" to each one is NOW. Has the reader of these words closed with the mercy and love of Christ? If he has, he knows the preciousness of the "acceptable year of the Lord." If he has not, let him remember that the "accepted time" will soon close. In another place it is called a day—"the day of salvation." A day is short, and when the time of its setting draws on, no power in the universe can prolong it one moment. It would be a fearful thing were the accepted time to end and leave us not saved.

Christ the Great Healer

" This day is this scripture fulfilled in your ears."
LUKE iv. 21

THE words had been written seven hundred years before. Now Jesus reads them and says, " I am the One to whom these golden sentences refer. This scripture is fulfilled before your eyes. I am the Anointed One, and this is the mission on which I came to this world." The whole Old Testament was full of Christ. There were a thousand fingers along its pages, every one pointing to Him. All its types and prophecies and promises were fulfilled when He came, and lived, and died, and was raised up and glorified. It is very interesting to take up Christ's whole public life and ministry, and show how perfectly He lived out the wonderful mission which the prophet here outlined for Him centuries before He came. He preached the gospel to the poor ; He was the friend of the poor. He healed the broken-hearted. Wherever He went the sorrowing and the troubled came flocking around Him. As a magnet draws steel-filings to itself from the heap of rubbish, so there was something in Him that drew the sad to Him.

There are two classes always of the broken-hearted. There are those whose hearts are broken because of sin. There are those who are crushed by affliction. Both these classes came to Christ. Sinners came, and found in Him not a stern, censorious Judge, but a tender, compassionate Saviour. The afflicted came and found true comfort. He loved all men and sympathized with them, and was able to help them. Then He also brought deliverance to sin's captives, setting them free, breaking their chains. He opened blind eyes ; not only the natural eyes to see the beautiful things of this world, but the spiritual eyes as well, to behold the things of heaven and everlasting life. Then He lifted the yoke of the crushed or oppressed, inviting all the weary to Himself to find rest to their souls. Thus His whole life was simply the filling up of this outline sketch.

March 25

The First Disciples

*"Jesus, walking by the sea of Galilee, saw two brethren......
casting a net into the sea ; for they were fishers."*—MATT.
iv. 18

WHEN Christ needs men for important positions He never looks for them among idlers. He always seeks in the ranks of busy people, among those who are at their posts and are faithfully doing their duty. When the Lord wanted a man to be the deliverer of His people, He found Moses tending sheep in the wilderness. When He sought for a man to be king over Israel, He found a shepherd lad watching over his flocks. When He wanted a man for a prophet, he found Elisha at his plough. When Jesus needed men to become apostles, to lay the foundation of the Christian Church, He walked by the sea and sought for them among those who were busiest. No doubt there were many idlers loitering along the shore that day, lounging among the boats and watching those who were at work ; but Jesus did not call any of these to be His apostles. He did not want for His apostles idle men or those whom their neighbours did not care to employ ; so He passed by all the loungers, and kept His eye on the men who were at work. He must have men of activity, men of energy and earnestness, and He knew where to look for them.

We ought not to lose this lesson. If we want Christ to call us to important places we must be busy and active, that when He comes seeking for persons to do His work He will see that we are competent and worthy. We should notice also that Christ often calls those who are engaged in lowly pursuits. If we think our occupation unworthy of us, the way to rise to a better one is to be faithful and diligent where we are, until we are called to a nobler and worthier pursuit. It is to him who is faithful in little things that the charge of greater things is promised. He who does not fill well the lower place is wanted neither by God nor by men for the higher place.

Fishers of Men

" Come ye after Me, and I will make you to become fishers of men."—MARK i. 17

PERSONAL attachment to Jesus is the very beginning of all Christian life. Believing a creed does not make one a Christian. We may believe every word we find in the Bible about Christ, and every word of His that we have in the gospels, and yet not be His disciples. A Christian is one who has joined Christ's party in this world and attached Himself to Christ as a personal follower. All the invitations Jesus gave implied this. He said, " Come unto Me ; " " Come after Me ; " " Believe on Me ; " " Follow Me." He always wanted men to come out from the world and personally identify themselves with Him. Then after they have joined themselves to Him, and He has put His own Spirit into them, He begins to use them. He cannot use them in the saving of souls until they really belong to Him.

We cannot become " fishers of men " just as we become carpenters, or merchants, or physicians. It is not one of the trades or professions to be taken up and learned as trades and professions are. Colleges and theological seminaries cannot make men " fishers of men." They may teach them how to think, how to write, how to speak ; they can furnish them with knowledge of many kinds, can teach them systems of theology, and make them exegetes, logicians, rhetoricians, or orators. But these things do not make men " fishers of men." These acquirements may be helpful to them in their spiritual work if they are consecrated to Christ. But the point to be remembered is, that Christ alone can make any one truly a " fisher of men." Teachers in the Sabbath school should remember this. With all they can learn in normal classes about how to teach, and all they can get in teachers' meetings or from lesson helps regarding the lesson, they need yet to go to Christ to learn to win the souls of their scholars.

March 27

At the Call of Christ

" They straightway left their nets, and followed Him."
MATT. iv. 20

THEIR nets were probably all they had. It was with these that they earned their living. Yet at the call of Christ they gave up all, cut themselves off from their means of support, and in simple obedience and faith went with Him. That is just the way we all should do when Christ calls us. We should obey instantly and without questioning. No matter how much the sacrifice involves, we should make it cheerfully for His sake. Though to obey cuts us off from all our ordinary means of livelihood, and leaves us without provision even for to-morrow, we should not hesitate. Christ takes care of His servants when they are faithfully doing His will. He asks for absolute surrender to Him. He wants us to trust Him while we obey Him unquestioningly.

The faith in Christ which the gospel requires is the utter, unreserved devotement of the whole life to Him, and the unreasoning committal to Him for time and for eternity of every interest and hope. The question what He will do with us or for us, how He will provide for us, should not for an instant be raised. There must be no conditions in the following and the consecration. We may not bargain with Him for an easy time, for " ways of pleasantness," but should simply give ourselves to Him absolutely and for ever, to follow where and to whatsoever He may lead us.

The " straightway " is also important. Many people are for ever postponing duties. But every call of Christ should be answered immediately. Let us get this ringing gospel " straightway " into our lives. Many people obey so laggardly, so reluctantly, and so long after they are called, that half the value of their obedience is lost. Christ wants always instant obeying. There is no to-morrow with Him. To-morrow He may not need us, or we may not be here to do the duty He now asks of us.

"She Ministered unto Them"

"He took her by the hand, and lifted her up; and immediately the fever left her, and she ministered unto them."—
MARK i. 31

THAT is just what Jesus is doing all the time to people sick in body, to those sick in soul, and to those who are down in any way and unable to rise. He does not stand far off when He would help people and call them to come to Him, but He comes to them with a brother's warm heart and ready hand. That is the way we should learn to help each other, by extending a strong, uplifting hand to those that are down. Many fall and perish who would be saved for life and glory if some one would come in Christ's name and help them up. The example of this woman must not be overlooked. Christ had given her back her life, and what should she now do with it but consecrate it to the service of Him who restored it to her? This she did, not in mere words of thankfulness, not in warm and tender emotions of praise only, but in service; she arose and ministered to her Healer and His friends. Her ministry, too, was of the most practical and helpful kind. She did not sigh for some opportunity to do a great service for Jesus; she simply took up the service that came first to her hand, and set about rendering the commonplace attentions of a housewifely entertainer.

There is a whole cluster of suggestions here. Every sick person who is restored, whether in an ordinary or extraordinary way, should hasten to consecrate to the service of God the life that is given back. Surely it was spared for a purpose, and we shall be disloyal to God if we do not thus devote it. A great many persons are always sighing for opportunities to minister to Christ, imagining some fine and splendid service which they would like to render. Meantime they let slip past their hands the very things in which Christ wants them to serve Him. True ministry to Christ is doing first of all and well one's daily duties.

March 29

Communion with God

" *In the morning, rising up a great while before day, He went out, and departed into a solitary place, and there prayed.*"—MARK i. 35

JESUS would always find time for prayer, or make time for it. If His days were full of excitement and toil, He would take time out of His nights for communing with God. At least He never allowed Himself to be robbed of His hours of devotion. There are some Christians who think they are excused from prayer and meditation in secret because they are so busy. Their work presses them so in the morning that they cannot possibly get time to pray. Their cares occupy them so all day that they do not find one quiet moment to go apart with God. In the evening there are so many social or other engagements—meetings, societies, parties—or they are so tired, that prayer is crowded out. The example of Christ speaks its solemn rebuke of all such trifling. We must find time for communion with God, or God will not find time to bless us.

There are some people, also, who claim that they can pray and commune with God just as well in one place as in another. They do their praying while they walk about and while they work. They see no use in going apart to pray. Surely if any one could pray well in a crowd or while engaged in work, Jesus could. No doubt He did hold communion with His Father even in His busiest hours, but this did not meet all the needs and longings of His soul. He left the crowd, left even His own disciples, and retired into places where no eye but God's could see Him, where no human footfall or voice could interrupt the quiet of His soul, and where He would be absolutely alone. Surely if He required such conditions in praying, we do too. We need to find a place for prayer, in which nothing can intrude to break the continuity of thought or devotion. " Enter into thy closet, and when thou hast shut thy door, pray."

"1be went about doing Good"

" He said unto them, Let us go into the next towns, that I may preach there also ; for therefore came I forth."—MARK i. 38

JESUS *went about* doing good. He did not confine His blessings to single localities. He sought to reach as many souls as possible. He did not wait for people to come to Him, but carried the news to their own doors. He thus taught us by example that His gospel is for all men, and not for any particular place or people. He taught us also that we should make the most of our lives and opportunities, scatter the blessings of grace as widely as we can, and tell as many persons as possible the good tidings of God's love. He wants His Church to keep on preaching the gospel to the " next towns " till there is not a town left in which it has not been heard.

Jesus was in this world, for one thing, to show us a pattern of a true life. We should specially study His life as the highest example of consecrated ministry. Here we have a glimpse of the way He sought to do good. He went about, carrying into every place He could reach the blessings of His grace and love. There is something intensely inspiring in the picture which this verse gives us. He seems in eager haste to get to as many places as possible. He has the look and the movement of a man who knows He has not long to stay, and that He has a great deal to do before He goes away. He wants to miss no town, to leave no person unvisited. There surely is much in this stirring picture which we ought to imitate. We are here on an errand of blessing to men. We have something to give to the world, a message from the Father to deliver to His children, benedictions to scatter upon needy lives. Somewhere not very far before us waits the end. What we do we must do quickly. We should hasten on from one to another with the gifts of love, help, and comfort, which our Master has given us to scatter.

March 31

ѣealing Sickness

*" Jesus went about all Galilee......preaching the gospel of the
    kingdom, and healing all manner of sickness."*—MATT.
    iv. 23

IT is sometimes charged that religion is only for people's
souls, that it gives no care to their bodies. But the
charge is without foundation. The most casual glance over
the gospel story shows that Jesus Himself was deeply moved
by the people's sufferings, and was continually putting forth
His power to heal them. Nearly all His great works were
miracles of healing. Then it should be remembered that
the whole system of institutions for the relief of suffering
and for the care of sufferers—hospitals, asylums for all
classes of unfortunate people, and homes for the orphaned
and the aged and the insane—is the fruit of Christianity.
Wherever angels of mercy go among the sick, the wounded,
the suffering, ministering in any way to their comfort, there
Jesus goes about with sympathy and healing. He cares
not alone for men's souls, but for their bodies as well. Any
trouble of ours whatsoever, whether of body, mind, or soul,
moves Him with compassion.

It is a great comfort to know that while we may not expect miraculous healing of our bodily illnesses, we are sure
at least that our Lord is not indifferent to these distresses ;
that He designs to use them for our spiritual benefit ; that
He is ready to give us the grace we need to endure them
patiently and submissively ; and that He is ready to heal
us when His wise purpose in these afflictions has been
accomplished. So we may be sure always of the sympathy, love, and help of Christ in all our sickness. He
sits constantly in every Christian sick-room, and where
faith is strong and clear He gives great comfort and peace.
When He was on earth He did not go very often to the
places of festivity, but whenever there was any one sick
in a home He was sure to go there. Sickness and pain draw
Him to us, and whenever He comes He brings benedictions.

"Make Me Clean"

"Lord, if Thou wilt, Thou canst make me clean."

LUKE v. 12

THIS prayer shows a beautiful faith. The leper had no doubt whatever of Christ's ability to heal him. The only question in his mind was whether He was willing to do it. There might be some reason why the Lord would not wish to answer his request. It would be an unutterable blessing to have this loathsome, terrible leprosy taken away. Jesus could do it if He would, and He would do it if it were best that it should be removed. So we find in his brief prayer acquiescence as well as humility.

This was a prayer, not for spiritual, but for physical blessing, and in such things we never can know what really is best for us. A mother may bend over a dying child and plead with affectionate yearning for its life. God will never blame her for the agonizing persistence of her plea ; yet she dare not pray wilfully. She must end her most intense pleading with the acquiescent refrain, caught from Gethsemane, "Nevertheless, not My will, but Thine be done." It may not be the best blessing to her or to her home to have her child spared.

Or a man may be threatened with loss of property. He turns to Christ for help. "If Thou wilt, Thou canst save me from this sore loss." Yes, He *can*—there is no doubt about that ; but will He ? He will if it is best, for He never chastens but for His people's good. But will it be a blessing to have this calamity averted ? The man cannot tell. Perhaps it may be necessary for him to suffer this misfortune in his temporal estate, that he may not lose his inheritance in heaven. Paul's "thorn in the flesh" is an illustration. He wanted it removed ; but no, it was necessary to keep him from spiritual pride, from being exalted above measure. Prayer should be acquiescent as well as earnest. We do not know what we should pray for, nor if what we desire would really bless us.

April 2

The Master Touched Him

" *He put forth His hand and touched him.*"—LUKE v. 13

NONE of the Jews would have done this. They kept the leper far off. To touch him would defile them. But Jesus was not afraid of defilement. He could as easily have stood afar off and cured the leper by a word, for He sometimes cured miles away. But the man needed a touch from a warm hand to assure him of love and sympathy. The touch left no taint of pollution on the Master, but it left the leprous body clean as a child's.

There are some who want to help others, if at all, at a convenient distance. They work through committees or agents. It is a great deal better to come close to those to whom we would do good. There is a wondrous power in a human touch. A gift to the poor may do good in whatever way it comes ; but if you bestow it yourself, and manifest personal interest and sympathy, its value will be largely increased. You put something of yourself into your gift. The gospel may save the fallen, though coming through the cold air from a lofty pulpit ; but it will be far more likely to save if the sinner feels the touch of a hand of love, and catches the message warm from quivering lips.

There is no danger of receiving defilement even from touching the worst outcasts, if you go to them with the love of God in your heart, yearning to do them good. Do not stand far off and toss the bread of life to them, as men throw gifts into leper hospitals. Do not slip your tract under the door and hurry away as if you were ashamed of what you had done. Go to the homes of the worst people. Give them your hand ; it will not soil it to clasp theirs, and you never can know what a thrill of new life it may start in hearts long unused to tenderness, yet yearning for sympathy. Put heart and inspiration into all you do. You never can know what a thrill of inspiration and life you may give to weary and disheartened ones.

"He could not be hid"

"It was noised that He was in the house."—MARK ii. 1

IT never can be kept quiet long when Jesus gets into any house. He cannot be hid. The neighbours will soon find out that He is there. The people cannot keep the secret. They will let it out in a great many ways. They will show it in their faces. Those who have Christ in their home do not look like other people. There is a radiance or sunniness about them when they come out that tells of an unworldly source of joy. There is something about their speech, too, that lets out the secret ; they cannot help talking about their Guest. So, in spite of themselves, the family in whose house Jesus is will disclose the secret. Fragrant flowers cannot be concealed, and there is a fragrance about Jesus that always reveals His presence. Light cannot be hidden, and there is so much light in Him that it shines out at every window and through every chink and crevice of the house where He abides. Love itself is invisible, but wherever it dwells it produces such effects that its presence soon becomes known. It makes people gentle, kindly, thoughtful, unselfish, and fills them with new desires to do good, and to serve and bless others. And wherever Christ is love is, in all its pervasive, transforming influence.

Some people like to gather beautiful things into their homes—paintings, sculptures, rare things from foreign lands, objects of interest and attractiveness. Some pride themselves on the elegance of their furniture and the fineness of the decorations in their houses. But in no other way can the Christian bring into his home so much beauty, so much joy and comfort, so much true peace, as by making Christ his abiding guest. No matter how quietly Jesus enters, the neighbours will soon know it, and they will also get the benefit and blessing of it ; for from a home where Christ abides there always go forth a fragrant influence and a loving, helpful ministry.

April 4

Divine Power

" The power of the Lord was present to heal them "
LUKE v. 17

IT was not always so. Once we read that Jesus could not do any mighty works at a certain place. It is not said that He *would* not, but that He *could* not. If seems strange that *could not* should ever be written of the omnipotent Christ. Did He then have His weak hours ? Were there times when the power fled from His arm ? But we read on and find that the reason He could not do any mighty works at that time and place was because of the unbelief of the people. Their hearts were shut against Him. He came with rich blessings in His hand to bestow upon them, and finding no reception had to carry them away again with a sad heart. So no doubt the reason the power of the Lord was so graciously present to heal at this time was because the people's hearts were open to take what He had to give. They met His compassion and love with faith, and the Divine power in Him wrought unrestrained.

We ought not to miss this lesson. There is never any want of power in Christ to bless us, and yet we may be near Him and still receive no blessing from Him. He may have come to us eager to impart the rich gifts of strength, comfort, joy, help, wisdom ; and yet He may be unable to bestow them. We ourselves must be in condition to receive what He has to give, or the blessing cannot be bestowed. We can shut up our hearts so close as to keep the mighty Christ outside. Weak as we are, even the Divine omnipotence cannot compel any blessing into our lives. There must be willingness on our part to receive. It is because of our unbelief that the power of God is not always present to heal and to bless. Then whenever we have faith and are willing to receive what Christ will give, His power will be present to heal, and to pour all manner of rich blessings into our hearts and lives. He will never force us to accept His gifts.

Bearing One Another's Burdens

*" They come unto Him, bringing one sick of the palsy, which
was borne of four."*—MARK ii. 3

THAT was a very touching sight, those four strong
men carrying their helpless friend to the Healer.
That is the kind of help we ought always to be willing to
give to one another. There are on all sides of us many
persons who need to be helped. There are lame people to
be assisted over rough places, and blind people to be led
along the way they cannot see themselves, and even paralytics who have to be carried in strong hands. The Christian law of love requires that we shall be ready always to
lend a hand to those who need the aid we can give. We
never can tell how soon it may be our turn to require for
ourselves just such friendly aid as our neighbour requires
from us to-day. If we expect to have people turn aside
from their work to help us in our time of need, we must be
willing to do as much for others who now require help.

There are many ways of doing the neighbourly duty to
others. These four men bore their friend to Jesus. They
could not heal him themselves, but they could carry him to
the One who could heal him. All about us are neighbours
and friends who are spiritual paralytics. We cannot cure
them, but perhaps we can take them to One who can do
for them what we cannot do.

We should notice, too, that there were four of these men
who carried their friend to Jesus. One of them could not
have done it ; two of them could not have carried him with
ease ; even for three the trembling burden would have been
hard to bear. But when all four of these brawny men
united their strength, they bore the man along without
difficulty. So it is in helping sinners to Christ. There is
strength in the union of hearts and hands. When one alone
cannot take his friend to the Saviour, let him call others to
his aid, and let them unite in their efforts on his behalf.

April 6

Faith seen in our Works

" When He saw their faith."—LUKE v. 20

SO far as we know no one had spoken a word to Jesus about the sick man, but there really was no need for words. The pains at which the friends had been to get this poor sufferer into the presence of Christ told of a very strong faith. The best evidence of faith is the effort we make to obtain faith's prize. Abraham proved his faith first of all when he promptly obeyed God's call and left his own home and country to go out he knew not whither, simply following where God might lead. He proved his faith again when he was bidden to offer his only son as a burnt offering, and without a question or remonstrance obeyed. It was after this that God said, " Now I know that thou fearest God, seeing thou hast not withheld thy son, thine only son, from Me." There is no need of words or protestations of faith when there are such acts of faith to attest it.

God can *see* faith. He can see it in the heart where it is exercised, even before there has been any expression of it in word or act ; but here the emphasis lies on the fact that He sees it in act. He is pleased when we show our faith by our works. There are many prayers without words, and God sees them when He does not hear them. There is in the Bible at least one instance of God forbidding spoken prayer and commanding action instead. At the edge of the Red Sea He said to Moses, " Wherefore criest thou unto Me ? speak unto the children of Israel, that they go forward." So we should learn to put our faith into instant act. There are times when we should stop praying, get up from our knees, and hasten out to duty. Praying for a friend in trouble is well, but it is a cheap and selfish way of showing our love if he has needs that we can supply. Praying for missions is right, but it is no acceptable substitute for giving if we are holding the Lord's money in our hands. God wants to *see* our faith.

Strength Bestowed

" *I say unto thee, Arise, and take up thy bed, and go thy way.*"—MARK ii. 11

THAT was surely a very strange command to give to a paralyzed man. He could not rise up. He could not lift up his bed. He could not walk a step. He was as helpless as a corpse. Why did Jesus require of him such an impossibility ? But as we look on the helpless form we see that it at once starts up. The limbs move, the man rises, takes up his bed, and walks away in the presence of all the people. As we watch him going his way, we learn that when Christ gives any command which seems impossible, He always gives strength to perform it. As the man's will began to obey Christ's bidding, power came back into his long-paralyzed body, and he was able to rise up and walk.

It is the same in spiritual life. We have no power in ourselves to do Christ's will, but as we begin to obey the needed grace is given. Young people often say that they are afraid to enter upon a Christian life because they cannot do what will be required. In their own strength they cannot. It would be as easy for them to climb to the stars as unaided to live a noble and lovely Christian life. Human strength in itself is inadequate to life's sore needs. But the young Christian who sets out in obedience to Christ, depending upon Him to open the path of duty, will never fail of needed help at the moment of need. Older Christians also often shrink from duties because they have not the ability to perform them ; but for them, and for all who attempt any work of service in obedience to Christ, it is true that the effort to obey will always bring with it the strength to obey. We should notice too that the strength will not come until we try to obey. If we will not attempt to do our duty, we shall remain for ever poor paralytics; but as we put forth the exertion the life will flow into our souls, and we shall be strong.

April 8

Blessed by Sickness

*" A certain man was there, which had an infirmity thirty and
eight years."*—JOHN v. 5

THAT was a long time to be sick. It is very hard to be
an invalid year after year. This day's reading may
come to some who have been thus afflicted, and we may as
well stop a minute to think about their case. Christian invalids have many comforts, if they will but take them to
their hearts. God makes no mistakes in dealing with His
children. He knows in what school they will learn the
best lessons, and in what experiences they will grow best.
Richard Baxter has a strange note on this passage : " How
great a mercy it was to live thirty-eight years under God's
wholesome discipline ! O my God, I thank thee for the
like discipline of fifty-eight years ; how safe a life is this
in comparison with full prosperity and pleasure ! "

The furnace fires of sickness burn off many a bond of sin
and worldliness. Many now in heaven will thank God for
ever for the invalidism in this life which kept them from
sin. We may be sure that God never calls any of His children apart into the sick-room without a purpose of blessing.
There is some lesson He wants to teach them, some new
glimpse of His love He wants to show them, some beauty in
them He wants to bring out. Sick-rooms should always be
to us sacred places, as we remember that God has summoned us there for some special work upon our souls. We
need to be very careful lest we miss the good He wants us
to receive. It is only those who trust Christ and lie upon
His bosom that are blessed by sickness. Too many invalids grow discontented, unhappy, sour, and fretful.
Sickness ofttimes fails to do good to those who suffer.
There are few experiences in which we so much need to be
watchful over ourselves and prayerful toward God. Be
sure to keep the sickness *out of your heart,* and keep Christ
there with His love and peace.

" Even so send I you "

" I have no man, when the water is troubled, to put me into the pool."—JOHN v. 7

ARE there not many unsaved people in every community who might also say, " I have no man to bring me to Christ " ? There are many lost souls for whom no one is caring. It may be answered that the gospel is offered to all, that all could come if they would. Yet Christians must not forget that the unsaved can receive grace only through the saved ; that those who are forgiven must carry the news of mercy to the unforgiven. The redemption is Divine,—none but Jesus can save ; but the priesthood is human. God's ordinary way of finding sinners and bringing them to the Saviour is through the love and pleading of other saved ones. Christ's commission ran : " As the Father hath sent Me, even so send I you." We are to do for the unsaved just what Christ did when He was here, what He would do now if He were living just where we live, among them,—go to them and ask them if they will be made whole.

Are there not lost ones about us who can say at God's judgment-bar, " The Christians about me would not lead me to the fountain, never even asked me to come to it for cleansing " ? This man waiting at the fountain's edge is a type of many about us,—close to the healing waters, with hungry, unsatisfied hearts, needing but the help of a human hand to lead them to the Saviour, yet never getting that help or that sympathy, and sitting there year after year unsaved. Surely we should not allow any unsaved ones about us to perish without trying in every way to lead them to the cleansing. healing waters. What evidence have we that we are saved ourselves if we are not interested in the salvation of other lost ones ? Let us look about us and see if any of our neighbours could say what this poor man at Bethesda said. Then let us go quickly and lead them to the Saviour.

April 10

"Immediately made Whole"

"Jesus saith unto him, Rise, take up thy bed, and walk. And immediately the man was made whole."—JOHN v. 8, 9

THE man might have said, "Why, I cannot rise. That is the very thing which I have not been able to do for thirty-eight years. Take up my bed! Why, I could not lift a feather; and as for walking, I could as easily fly. I cannot do these things until I am cured." We have all heard people talk thus about starting in the Christian life. They plead their helplessness as reason for their delay. There is a fine lesson for such in this man's obedience. The moment he heard the command he made the effort to rise, and as he made the effort the strength was given. New life came with his simple obedience. Christ never commands an impossibility. When He bids us rise out of our sin and helplessness and begin the Christian walk, He means to give grace and strength to enable us to do it.

The same is true of all that Christ requires of us in His service. People think it "humility" to be timid about duty and about accepting responsibility at Christ's call; but it is not humility at all, it is unbelief and sin. We lie on our poor rugs and say, "I have no strength for this, no wisdom for that," while if we simply arose to obey every call of Christ, He would use us for noble service. This man showed his faith by immediately exerting himself to do what Christ had bidden him do. Had he not done this he would not have been healed. There are many who lie spiritually paralyzed, year after year, just because they are waiting to be healed before they try to rise and walk. There are many who never do any worthy service for Christ, and lie in a condition of uselessness through years, because they think themselves unequal to the duties to which they are called. It is time we learned to step forward instantly, to do whatever Christ bids us do. When we begin to do this we shall find ourselves strong.

The Sabbath

" The sabbath was made for man, and not man for the sabbath."—MARK ii. 27

THE Sabbath was not made for man merely as an arbitrary law which he must observe. It is as much a law of his nature, or in harmony with his nature, as is the night which bids him cease his toil and seek rest and sleep. It was made for man's physical nature. It has been proved many times that the body needs the Sabbath. Then it was made for man's spiritual good, to give opportunity, not alone for physical rest, but for communion with God, when the noise of business and of toil has ceased. It was made for man to promote his welfare in every regard. All history proves that the Sabbath is a blessing wherever it is observed, and that its violation always brings loss and suffering.

Our Lord clearly showed by His example and teaching that the Sabbath is never meant to be a burden or to work oppressively. Though secular work is forbidden on the Sabbath, it is not a violation of the sacredness of the day for us to prepare food sufficient to meet the hunger of our bodies, or to lift out of a pit a beast that has fallen into it, or to heal a man who is sick. There is no great need in these days to say much on this side of the question. Not many people are now disposed to make the Sabbath a burden or a cruel yoke. The tendency is the other way. At the same time it is well to understand just what our Lord taught on this subject. He never sought to make the Sabbath oppressive or a burden. Works of necessity are allowed, even though they may seem to violate the letter of the law. So also are works of mercy, works of benevolence. It will be hard, however, to get out of this great saying of our Lord any excuse for running railway trains, for keeping stores open, or for the hundredth part of the secular goings-on that men want to bring in under the shield of Christ's teaching.

April 12

The Great Physician

" *He had healed many; insomuch that they pressed upon Him for to touch Him.*"—MARK iii. 10

THOUGH the plots of His enemies drove Jesus out of the city, they did not stop His doing good. Though some rejected His love, His heart was not closed. Capernaum lost much when He went out of its gates, but on the throngs that followed Him the gracious blessings fell.

That is ofttimes the way. The gifts of love that Christ bears in His hands are rejected by those to whom they are first offered, but are then carried to others, who receive them with gladness. Persecution generally scatters the seed which it means to destroy. When the first Christians were driven from Jerusalem, it was only to carry the Word into all countries round about into which they fled. They " went everywhere preaching " Opposition should never silence the lips that carry the words of life. If one rejects and scorns us, we must bear our message to another.

The picture of the people thronging here about Christ, pressing upon Him, each one eagerly struggling to touch Him, is very graphic and vivid. A touch was enough. All that touched Him were made whole. Life and health flowed into the diseased bodies when the trembling fingers came in contact with the Healer, even with His garments. So a touch is enough always. Any one who really touches Christ is healed. But we must be sure to touch Him. It is not enough to be in the crowd that gathers about Him. Only those are healed whose faith truly brings them in contact with Him. It is not enough to be in the congregation that worships. One sitting or bowing next to us may receive a great blessing while we receive none at all. It is because he reaches out his hand of faith and touches Christ, while we, as close to Christ as he is, do not put out our hand to touch Him, and therefore receive no blessing.

They Came unto Him

" He......calleth unto Him whom He would : and they came unto Him."—MARK iii. 13

THAT is the way Jesus is doing continually—standing and calling men to come to Him. And here we see the way every one who hears His voice should answer—leave the world's company, step boldly out, cross over the line and take his place by the side of Jesus. There are several things to be said about the way these men responded to Christ's call. They did it freely. Although He had chosen them out of a whole nation, and called them, there was no compulsion laid upon them to go with Him. They could have refused if they had chosen. Christ never makes disciples by force. We must be willing, and must choose to come to Him. Then they responded promptly. There was no hesitation. They said nothing about considering the matter for a while. They did not talk about being unfit or unworthy. They did not tell Jesus they were afraid they could not continue faithful. They did not say, " To-morrow we will go." The moment they heard their names called they answered.

Then their answer was given in a way that could be understood. Whenever they heard the call they stepped out with firm tread, and crossing over the space between the crowd and the Master, they joined themselves to Him. It was not done secretly. They did not wait till they were alone with Him, and then tell Him quietly that they had resolved to accept His invitation. They did not propose to become His disciples, and yet stay among their old friends, and keep on at their old business. They immediately separated themselves from the people about them and went over to Him, putting themselves absolutely into His hands, to be His and to do His bidding so long as they lived. This is the way these men started, and this is the way every one should start whom Jesus calls to be His disciple.

April 14

Transforming Power

"*Simon He surnamed Peter.*"—MARK iii. 16

IN a gallery in Europe are shown, side by side, the first and the last works of a great artist. The first is very rude and most faulty; the last is a masterpiece. The contrast shows the results of long culture and practice. These two names are like those two pictures. "Simon" shows us the rude fisherman of Galilee, with all his rashness, his ignorance, his imperfectness. "Peter" shows us the apostle of the Acts and the Epistles, the rock firm and secure, the man of great power, before whose Spirit-filled eloquence thousands of proud hearts bow, swayed like the trees of the forest before the tempest; the gentle, tender soul whose words fall like a benediction; the noble martyr witnessing to the death for his Lord. Study the two pictures together to see what grace can do for a man.

It is not hard to take roses, lilies, fuchsias, and all the rarest flowers, and with them make forms of exquisite beauty; but to take weeds, dead grasses, dried leaves trampled and torn, and faded flowers, and make lovely things out of such materials, is the severest test of skill. It would not be hard to take an angel and train him into a glorious messenger; but to take such a man as Simon, or as Saul, or as John Newton, or as John Bunyan, and make out of him a holy saint or a mighty apostle—that is the test of power. Yet that is what Christ did and has been doing ever since. He takes the poorest stuff—despised and worthless, outcast of men ofttimes—and when He has finished His gracious work we behold a saint whiter than snow. The sculptor beheld an angel in the rough, blackened stone, rejected and thrown away; and when men saw the stone again, lo! there was the angel cut from the block. Christ can take us, rough and unpolished as we are, and in His hands our lives shall grow into purity and loveliness, until He presents them at last before the throne, faultless and perfect.

Beatitudes

" Blessed......Blessed......Blessed......"—MATT. v. 3-10

THE Blesseds of the Scripture shine all over the inspired pages, like stars in the midnight sky. The Bible is a book of beatitudes and benedictions. God's mercy lies everywhere. Wherever we see Christ He is imparting blessings as the sun imparts light and warmth. While He was here on the earth He was always reaching out His hand to give a benediction to some life that sorely needed it. Now it was on the children's heads, now on the leper, now on the blind eyes, now on the sick, now on the dead, that He laid those gracious hands, and always He left some rich gift of blessing. Then we remember one day when those gentle hands were drawn out by cruel enemies, and with iron nails fastened back on the cross; yet even then it was in blessing that they were extended, for it was for our sins they were transfixed thus on the wood. As we see them thus stretched out as wide as they could reach, the attitude suggests the wideness of the Divine mercy. Thus the arms of God are open to the utmost to receive all who will come to seek refuge. There is room for the worst sinners.

Then it is a striking fact that the last glimpse we have of the Saviour in this world shows Him in the attitude of blessing. He had been talking with His disciples as He led them out, and then He lifted up His hands and blessed them ; and while He was blessing them He was parted from them and received up into heaven. Surely there could be no truer picture taken of Jesus at any point in His life than as He appeared in that last view of Him which this world enjoyed. In heaven now He is still a blessing Saviour, holding up pierced hands before God in intercession, and reaching down gracious hands full of benedictions for our sad, sinful earth. If any life goes unblessed with such a Saviour, it can be only because of unbelief and rejection.

April 16

Humility

" Blessed are the poor in spirit : for theirs is the kingdom of heaven."—MATT. v. 3

THIS beatitude is not pronounced upon the poor in earthly condition; for one may be very poor and yet very proud, or one may be rich in worldly goods and yet be very lowly in spirit. Nor is it on the poor in mind; for mental poverty is not necessarily a state of blessedness, and ignorance is certainly not desirable. It is the poor in spirit, in disposition, on whom the beatitude is pronounced; that is, the lowly in heart, the humble, those who are conscious of unworthiness. Humility is not thinking meanly of one's self, holding one's gifts or abilities as of no account. We are under obligation to recognize our talents and make fullest possible use of them. We are also to recognize our place and our privileges as God's redeemed children—no longer condemned sinners and servile slaves.

What, then, is humility ? It is a spirit that bows reverently before God, and then holds its divinest gifts as not too good or too fine to be used in Christ's name in the service of the lowliest of God's creatures. The Bible everywhere speaks its praises of humility. Christ refers only once in the gospel to His own heart, and then it is this picture that we see : " I am meek and lowly in heart." To be poor in spirit is to be rich toward God, while pride of heart is spiritual poverty Humility is the key that opens the gate of prayer, while to the loud knocking of pride there comes no answer. The proud Pharisee in his prayer found no blessing; but the lowly publican went away with heart and hand full of heaven's divinest gifts. Pride is the cold mountain peak, sterile and bleak; humility is the quiet vale, fertile and abounding in life, where peace dwells. The kingdom of heaven belongs to those who are lowly. They may wear no earthly crown, but a crown of glory, unseen by men, rests even here upon their heads.

Comforted

" Blessed are they that mourn : for they shall be comforted."
MATT. v. 4

WE do not usually regard sorrowing people as blessed. Here, however, is a special beatitude for mourners. Probably Jesus meant particularly penitent mourners. In all this world there is nothing so precious before God as tears of contrition ; no diamonds or pearls shine with such brilliance in His sight. It was Jesus Himself who said there is joy in the presence of the angels of God over one sinner that repents. Truly blessed, therefore, are those who in true penitence grieve over their sins ; a holy light shines from heaven upon all such mourners. They are comforted with God's pardon and peace.

But no doubt the beatitude refers also to those children of God who are in sorrow, from whatever cause. Blessing is never nearer to us than when we are in affliction. If we do not get it, it is because we will not receive it. Some day we shall see that we have gotten our best things from heaven, not in the days of our earthly joy and gladness, but in the times of trial and affliction. Tears are lenses through which our dim eyes see more deeply into heaven and look more fully upon God's face than in any other way. Sorrows cleanse our hearts of earthliness and fertilize our lives. The days of pain really do far more for us than the days of rejoicing. We grow best when clouds hang over us, because clouds bear rain, and rain refreshes. Then God's comfort is such a rich experience that it is well worth while to endure trial, just to enjoy the sweet and precious comfort which God gives in it. But to receive from our sorrows their possibilities of blessing, we must accept the affliction as a messenger from God, and pray for true comfort—not the mere drying of our tears, but grace to profit by our affliction, and to get from it the peaceable fruit of righteousness.

Meekness

" Blessed are the meek : for they shall inherit the earth."
MATT. v. 5

MEEKNESS is not a popular quality. The world calls it a craven spirit that leads a man to remain quiet under insult, to endure a wrong without resentment, to be treated unkindly and then to give kindness in return. Men of the world say that this disposition is unmanly— that it shows weakness, cowardice, a lack of spirit. So it might be if we went to Plutarch's Lives for our models of manliness. But we have a truer, a diviner example for our pattern of manliness than any that this world has produced. Jesus Christ was the only perfect man that ever lived on the earth, and meekness was one of the noblest qualities of His character. He was gentle in disposition, not easily provoked, patient under wrong, silent under reproach. When He was reviled, He reviled not again ; when He suffered, He threatened not. Possessing all power, He never lifted a finger to avenge a personal injury. He answered with tender love all man's wrath ; and on His cross, when the blood was flowing, He prayed for His murderers.

Meekness is then no craven spirit, since in Christ Jesus it shone so luminously. It is Divine to forgive those who have wronged us, to bear long with those who treat us ill, to give the soft answer that turneth away wrath, to bathe in the fragrance of love the hand that smites, to render always blessing for cursing, good for evil. The lesson is hard to learn, for it is directly against nature ; we can learn it only as our lives are transformed into the Divine image, only as Christ enters into our hearts and dwells there. This beatitude shows, too, that meekness is not an impoverishing grace. The meek shall inherit the earth. Those who commit their lives to God, who judgeth right-eously, and leave to Him the adjustment of the inequalities of human treatment received by them, do not suffer in the end.

Spiritual Hunger

*" Blessed are they which do hunger and thirst after righteous-
ness : for they shall be filled."*—MATT. v. 6

IT strikes us somewhat strangely at first that there
should be a beatitude for dissatisfaction. We know
that peace is promised to the Christian, and peace is calm
repose and satisfied restfulness. The words " hunger and
thirst " appear to suggest experiences incompatible with
rest and peace. But when we think a little more deeply
we see that spiritual hunger must form a part of all true
Christian experience. Hunger is a mark of health. It is
so in physical life ; the loss of appetite indicates disease.
So a healthy mind is a hungry one ; when one becomes
satisfied with one's attainments, one ceases to grow.
The same is true in spiritual life. If we become satisfied
with our faith and love and obedience, and our communion with God, and our consecration to Christ, we have
ceased to grow.

Invalids die often amid plenty—die of starvation ; not
because they can get no food, but because they have no
appetite. There are many professing Christians who are
starving their souls in the midst of abundance of spiritual
provision, because they have no hunger. There is nothing
for which we should pray more earnestly and more impor-
tunately than for spiritual longing and desire. It is indeed
the very soul of all true prayer. It is the empty hand
reached out to receive new and richer gifts from heaven.
It is the heart's cry which God hears with acceptance and
answers always with more and more of life. It is the
ascending angel that climbs the radiant ladder to return on
the same bright stairway with blessings from God's very
hand. It is the key that unlocks new storehouses of Divine
goodness and enrichment. It is indeed nothing less than
the very life of God in the human soul, struggling to grow
up in us into the fullness of the stature of Christ. Such
spiritual hunger never fails of blessing.

April 20

The Golden Rule

" Blessed are the merciful : for they shall obtain mercy "
MATT. v. 7

PEOPLE get back in this world just about what they give. If we think the world is hard with us, the probability is that the hardness is in ourselves, and that it is the echo of our own speeches that we hear, the rebound of our own smitings that we feel, the reflection of our own ugliness of disposition and temper that we see, the harvest of our own sowing that we gather into our bosoms. If we are untrue to any one, it is quite likely that some day somebody will be untrue to us. If we are unjust to another, there is little doubt that some time some one will deal unjustly with us. On the other hand, if the world seem to us full of love, it is quite likely that we give the world little but love. People generally treat us as we treat them. The generous man finds people generous. The sympathetic man finds sympathy. The merciful man obtains mercy. The selfish man always thinks this world very selfish.

Hence the Golden Rule rests on a deep principle in life. " Whatsoever ye would that men should do to you, do ye even so to them." What we do to others they will do to us. That is the principle. If we want mercy, we must be merciful ; if we expect sympathy and help, we must give both sympathy and help. We have only to change places with people and then ask ourselves how we would want them to do to us. As a rule people do not give warmth for coldness, courtesy for rudeness, kindness for unkindness. The principle applies even to the Divine treatment of us. In God's judgment we receive according to our deeds. He who obtains forgiveness is he who forgives others. He who finds mercy is he who shows mercy to others. He whom Christ will confess before His Father is he who here before men confesses Christ. So for eternity we shall reap what we have sowed, and gather what we have scattered.

Purity of Heart

" Blessed are the pure in spirit : for they shall see God."
MATT. v. 8

THERE is no beatitude in the Bible for anything unclean. We are told also that there is no room in
heaven for anything that defileth. Therefore if we hope to
enter heaven we must prepare for it here. To a child who
expressed the wonder how he could ever get up to heaven,
it was so far away, a wise mother's reply was, " Heaven
must first come down to you ; heaven must first come into
your heart." The words were very true. Heaven must
really be in us, or we can never enter heaven. And just
as we become pure in heart is heaven entering into us.

But what is heart purity ? It is not sinlessness, for none
are sinless. A pure heart must be a penitent heart that
has been forgiven by Christ and cleansed by His blood.
We have a Bible promise that though our sins be as scarlet
they shall be as white as snow. The pure heart is one, then,
that Christ has cleansed. It is one also that is kept pure
by obedient living and close communion with God. We
are taught in the Scriptures that an important part of true
religion is to keep one's self unspotted from the world. It
is an evil world in which we live ; but if we faithfully
follow Christ, doing His will, keeping our hearts open to
every influence of the Divine Spirit, we shall be kept by
Divine power from the corruption that flows about us. As
the lily remains pure and unstained amid the soiled waters
of the bog in which it grows, so does the lowly, loving,
patient heart of the Christian disciple remain pure in the
midst of all this world's corruption. Over such a heart
God's face beams in perpetual benediction. The vision on
earth of course is never full and clear, but it grows brighter
and brighter as the believer walks ever toward the morning,
and at last it will be unclouded and full in the perfect
day of heaven.

April 22

Peacemakers

" Blessed are the peacemakers : for they shall be called the children of God."—MATT. v. 9

THIS seems to be too much an overlooked beatitude. There are many people who are really strifemakers rather than peacemakers. They do not seek to heal estrangements between others, to prevent quarrels and contentions, and to bring together those who have begun to drift apart. Indeed, their whole influence goes toward widening breaches, intensifying bitterness, and exciting anger and hatred. When they find in any one a germ of suspicion or dislike of another, they stimulate the evil growth. Is it not time that we should get our Lord's beatitude down out of the skies and begin to work it into our lives ? Is it not time that we should become peacemakers in a world whose beauty is marred by so much strife ?

The peacemaking spirit is Divine. No one in heaven finds delight in separating friends. Just so far as we get the peacemaking spirit into our lives do we bear the mark of God's image. To be peacemakers we must first of all strive to live peaceably with all men. " If it be possible, as much as in you lieth," says St. Paul, " be at peace with all men." But, further, we are also to strive to make and promote peace between others. Our ministry is not to be confined to the settlement of great quarrels, but may find even its most fruitful work in the healing of the petty contentions which we discover all about us. Whenever we find one man angry with another, we should seek to remove the angry feeling. The little rifts in others' friendships we should strive to heal. The unkind thoughts of others which we find in people's minds we should seek to change into kindly thoughts. We can do no Christlier service than to seek always to promote peace between man and man, to keep people from drifting apart, and to get them to live together more lovingly.

Let Your Light Shine

" *Ye are the light of the world.*"—MATT. v. 14

EVERY true Christian is a candle shining in this dark world. The Bible speaks of the spirit of man as the candle of the Lord. In the natural state, before regeneration, we are unlighted candles. We are candles, however, capable of being lighted ; for God made us in His own image, though sin has put out the flame or left it only a smoking, smouldering spark. But a thousand unlighted candles in a dark room would not make the room light ; so when we receive Christ into our hearts, the Holy Spirit touches these candles with the Divine flame, and they begin to shine. Thus every believer becomes really a candle of the Lord.

We must remember that we never can shine of ourselves ; that we are light only as we are lighted by the life of Christ in us. We are to let our light shine—that is, we are to keep the wick trimmed, so that the flame shall be always bright ; and we are to keep the windows of our life clean, so that the beams may pour out without hindrance. We are also to be sure always to have reserves of oil to replenish our lamps when they burn low ; that is, we must live in constant communion with Christ, abiding in Him, that we may draw always from his fullness.

Then, each one in his own place, we must give light to other lives, and make the one little spot in this world that is close about us brighter and happier with love and grace. The great lighthouse lamp pours beams far out to sea, but it does not lighten the space around its base. Some people send brightness far away, working for the heathen and doing deeds which benefit the world, while they fail to brighten their own homes and the lives close beside them. We ought not to be such lights as these : while we send our influence abroad as far as possible, we should live so that we shall be benedictions to those who are nearest to us.

April 24

The Old Testament and the New

" I am not come to destroy, but to fulfil."—MATT. v. 17

THERE are not two Bibles in the one. The Old Testament and the New are not two distinct books, but parts of the same. The New Testament does not set aside the Old, but is simply the rich, ripe harvest of which the Old was the sowing and the early growing. The gospel which we have in the New Testament is not a different religion from that which we have in the Old Testament, but the same more fully developed, more clearly taught. In the Old Testament Christ was foretold sometimes in prophetic promise, sometimes in picture and type ; in the New these promises are fulfilled, these pictures and types find their realization, and we see the Son of God walking among men in the beauty and glory of His incarnation.

The blossoms are not destroyed when they fall off and the fruit comes in their place ; the ripe fruit is but the fulfilment of the promise and prophecy of the blossom. The artist's outline sketch is not destroyed when the splendid picture covers the canvas, hiding the first light tracings ; the finished work of art is but the completion, the filling out of the original drawing until in every feature life glows. Christ destroyed nothing of past Divine revelation when He came. He was the warm summer, wooing the slumbering buds and dry roots, and waiting prophecies of life into full, luxuriant growth. He was the great Master, taking the dim sketches and shadows of the Old Testament, and filling them out in His own blessed life and death. So we ought not to lay away our Old Testament as an antiquated book, of no value to us since we have the gospel. The Old Testament is full of precious things. One of the strongest proofs of Christianity is the wonderful fulfilment of Old Testament prophecies in the life, sufferings, and death of Jesus Christ. Let us love the whole Bible ; not one word of it is obsolete.

Promises and Prophecies

" One jot or one tittle shall in no wise pass from the law, till all be fulfilled."—MATT. v. 18

CHRIST referred here primarily to the promises and prophecies of the Old Testament. There are thousands of blessings on the trees in the spring-time that never become fruits ; but there are no lost blossoms on the Old Testament tree. The exact fulfilment of prophecy is an irrefutable evidence of Christianity. But the assurance of these words refers also to every promise of the Scripture. Not the smallest of these shall ever fail any one who trusts them. " No word He hath spoken shall ever be broken." Every pledge God has made He will surely keep. Whenever we find a Divine word we may lay hold of it with perfect confidence, and know that we are clinging to a rock that never can be shaken. " For the mountains shall depart, and the hills be removed ; but My kindness shall not depart from thee, neither shall the covenant of My peace be removed, saith the Lord that hath mercy on thee."

This is true also of the Divine threatenings against sin. Not one of these shall fail to be accomplished upon those who reject God's words of grace and mercy. Christ said, " He that believeth on the Son hath everlasting life ; " and that word will prove true to every one who receives it. But He said also in the same sentence, " He that believeth not the Son shall not see life, but the wrath of God abideth on him ; " and this word shall just as surely be fulfilled as the other. In these days, when so many people hold loose views of God's Word, it is well that we fix it deeply in our minds that whatever God says in the Holy Scriptures He says with authority—that His promises are sure as His own eternity, and that every sentence of His is absolutely irrepealable. " Only words," we sometimes say, as if words were unreal and unsubstantial ; but the words of God are more real and substantial than even earth's great mountains.

April 26

Little Sins

"*Whosoever therefore shall break one of these least commandments, and shall teach men so, he shall be called the least
in the kingdom of heaven.*"—MATT. v. 19

A GREAT many people are careful about breaking large
commandments and committing grave sins, while
they continually and without scruple do little wrong things.
They would not tell a direct lie for the world, but their
speech is full of little falsehoods. They would not take
money from the pocket or drawer of another, and yet they
continually commit small thefts. For example, the grocer
by mistake gives them a penny too much change, and they
do not think of returning it. Through the carelessness of
an official the postage-stamp on a letter is left uncancelled,
and they take it off and use it a second time. They would
not try to blacken a neighbour's name or destroy his character, and yet they repeat to others the evil whispers about
him which they have heard, and thus soil his reputation.
They would not swear or curse in the coarse way of the
street, but they are continually using such words as
"Gracious!" "Goodness!" "Mercy!" and other mild,
timid substitutes for profane oaths. They would not do
flagrant acts of wickness to disgrace themselves, but their
lives are honeycombed with all manner of little mean-
nesses, impurities, selfishnesses, and bad tempers.

We need to remember that little disobediences bring one
down to an inferior place in the kingdom of heaven. Little
sins mar the beauty of the character. Then they are sure
to grow. Ofttimes, too, they are infinite in their consequences. The little rift in the lute widens and by-and-by
destroys all the music. The trickling leak in the dike
becomes a torrent, deluging vast plains. We ought never
to indulge even the smallest faults or evil habits, but should
aim always at perfection. We ought to be satisfied with
nothing less than perfection in character, and perfection
is made up of trifles.

True Righteousness

"*Except your righteousness shall exceed the righteousness of the scribes and Pharisees, ye shall in no case enter into the kingdom of heaven.*"—MATT. v. 20

IN place of abolishing or destroying the law, Jesus put new meaning into it. As He expounded it, it went far more deeply into people's lives than by the religionists of His time it had been understood to go. They had taught that a rigid, external obedience was required; but Jesus told them that if this were all they could not enter the kingdom. Instead of lowering the requirements of the Divine law, He elevated them and gave them a new meaning. He said the righteousness of His followers must be a great deal better than that of the average professors of religion in His day. They had a sound creed, and were punctilious in the observance of the ten thousand minute rules about ceremony, dress, attitude, and devout manners; but their lives were full of hardness, pride, selfishness, and hypocrisies.

Jesus said that unless His disciples had a better righteousness than these orthodox Jews had they would never get into the family of God. The only righteousness that will be accepted by Christ is that which has its origin in the heart, and then produces obedience and holiness in all the life. We ought to apply this truth very closely. Uniting with the Church does not make one a Christian. The careful observance of all the ordinances and rules of the Church is not being good. There must be faith, love, dutiful obedience, submission. Christ demands in His followers a high standard of morality. We are not saved by Christ's righteousness in the sense that we need no righteousness of our own. In place of mere external and formal obedience, the law is written on the heart of the true believer, and he obeys it from within. We should strive to make our obedience so deep and so loyal that our lives will reflect in every feature the radiancy of Christ.

April 28

Angry without Cause

" Whosoever is angry with his brother without a cause shall
be in danger of the judgment."—MATT. v. 22

WE ought to learn to read the commandments with the light of our Lord's explanation upon them. So long as the sixth commandment is interpreted to mean only actual murder, most people get along pretty well with it; they are not troubled in their consciences about its violation. There are not many literal murderers loose in our Sabbath schools and churches, or living in our homes. But when we hear our Lord's interpretation of this commandment, and learn that this literal sense does not exhaust the meaning of the commandment—that we break it, too, when we are angry with a brother—we cannot be quite so sure about our innocence. We have never killed any one, but have we never been angry with another? Elsewhere we read, " He that hateth his brother is a murderer." This does not mean that hatred is as great a crime as murder, but that it grows from the same root and is of the same nature. Murder is only anger full-grown.

The Master's words here should be carefully considered. They condemn all anger against another, all expressions of scorn or contempt. The obedience of this commandment which our Lord requires is, love that thinketh no evil, that cherisheth no resentment, that is patient, gentle, thoughtful, reverent, unselfish. Yet are we not all too apt to allow the passion of anger to take possession of our breasts? Do we not too frequently permit envyings and jealousies and unkind and uncharitable thoughts to enter our hearts and nest there, like evil birds? If we but remembered that the spirit of murder is in all these emotions, we surely would not cherish them for an instant; none of us want the brand of murderer upon us. The way to keep out such feelings is to yield to every gentle and loving impulse of the Spirit—to " overcome evil with good."

Acceptable Worship

" *If thou bring thy gift to the altar, and there rememberest that thy brother hath ought against thee ; leave there thy gift before the altar, and go thy way : first be reconciled to thy brother, and then come and offer thy gift.*"—MATT. v. 23, 24

THERE is something to do before we kneel down to pray in our closet, or begin our worship in the sanctuary, or come to the Lord's table. There ought to be a look inward at our own hearts before the look upward at the face of God. Are we ready to pray ? Are the obstructions out of the way ? Is our heart ready for worship ? The worship that pleases God the best is love in the heart. He has no pleasure in sacrifices and ceremonies and ordinances while the heart is full of bitterness. He cares nothing for our professions of love to Him so long as we hate our brother. " If a man say, I love God, and hateth his brother, he is a liar : for he that loveth not his brother whom he hath seen, how can he love God whom he hath not seen ? "

If, therefore, we want our worship to be acceptable to God, we must be sure to come into His presence with hearts cleansed of all bitterness, wrath, anger, clamour, and all malice. Thus every approach to God in prayer requires self-examination ; and if we can remember that we have wronged any one, or that there is any estrangement or strife, we should seek reconciliation before we pray. At least we must see that our own spirits are thoroughly cleansed of all bitterness before we come to God's altar. This rule is fitted to keep our hearts free from anger. Paul counsels that we should not let the sun go down upon our wrath. No day should be allowed to close with anger in our breasts. We may never see another day, and we should not lie down to sleep cherishing bitterness against any other. The evening prayer should cleanse our spirits of all feelings of anger, as we pray, " Forgive us our trespasses, as we forgive those who trespass against us."

April 30

True Charity

" When thou doest alms, let not thy left hand know what thy right hand doeth."—MATT vi. 3

THERE are some people who want every good thing they do well advertised. If they give money to some good cause, they want to have it noticed in the papers. If they are kind to the poor or relieve some case of distress, they are particular that the matter should be duly published. They take pains that their charities shall not fail to be credited to themselves. But this is not the kind of spirit our Lord enjoined on His disciples. He told them that seeking publicity marred the beauty of their almsgiving ; that instead of announcing to all men what they had done, they should not even let their own left hand know that their right hand had been doing commendable things.

Of course Christ did not mean that we should not be good before people—that we should never give alms save where the act would be absolutely secret. It is the motive that Christ was enforcing. His disciples should never give for the sake of men's praise. Religious acts instantly lose all their value when any motive but the honour of God and the desire for His approval is in our heart. We should not even ourselves think about our charities, but should forget them as the tree forgets the fruits it drops. We should train ourselves therefore to do our good deeds without seeking praise or recognition of men. We should not be so anxious to have our card tacked on every gift we send. We ought to be willing to do good and let Christ have all the glory, while we stay back unknown and unrecognized. Florence Nightingale, having gone like an angel of mercy among the hospitals in the Crimea until her name was enshrined in every soldier's heart, asked to be excused from having her picture taken, that she might be forgotten, and that Christ alone might be remembered as the author of all the blessings which her hand had distributed.

Secret Prayer

" When thou prayest, enter into thy closet, and when thou hast shut thy door, pray to thy Father which is in secret."—MATT. vi. 6

ONE of the most important things we ever do in this world is to pray. No business transacted anywhere so deeply touches the interests of our lives. We ought therefore to learn to pray aright, so as to be sure of answer. We ought to be eager to get every smallest fragment of instruction about prayer.

In our word for to-day we have one of our Lord's plainest and most significant instructions about the manner and the nature of prayer. He is speaking, not of public prayer, as when the minister leads the congregation, but of personal prayer, when the child of God wants to talk to his Father of his own affairs, and lay at His feet his own individual burdens. We should seek to be alone in all such praying. Other presences about us disturb our thoughts and restrict our freedom. So we are to go into our closet and shut the door.

This shutting of the door is significant in several ways. It shuts the world out. It secures us against interruption. It ought to shut out worldly thoughts and cares and distractions, as well as worldly presences. Wandering in prayer is usually one of our sorest troubles. Then it shuts us in, and this also is important and significant. It shuts us in alone with God. No eye but His sees us as we bow in the secrecy. No ear but His hears us as we pour out our heart's feelings and desires. Thus we are helped to realize that with God alone have we to do, that He alone can help us. As we are shut up alone *with* God, so also are we shut up *to* God. There is precious comfort in the assurance that when we thus pray we are not talking into the air. There is an ear to hear, though we can see no presence, and it is the ear of our Father. This assures us of loving regard in heaven, also of prompt and gracious answer.

May 2

"Our Father"

"Our Father which art in heaven."—MATT. vi. 9

THIS is the golden gate of the temple of prayer.
When our Lord taught His disciples how to pray,
it was thus He said they should begin. They were not to
come to infinite power, or to unknowable mystery, or to
inaccessible light, but to fatherhood. This precious name
at the gateway makes the approach easy.

The name assures us of love and care. Does a true
parent have care for a child ? Much more does our Father
in heaven care for His children on the earth. He cares
even for the birds, seeing that they get their daily food. He
cares for the flowers, weaving for them with threads of
light the lovely robes they wear. He surely cares more for
His children. So the precious name assures us that we
shall never be neglected or overlooked in this great
world.

It gives us assurance also of unhindered access to the
Divine presence. The children of a great king are not kept
waiting at their father's door as strangers are. God's children have perfect liberty in His presence. They can never
come at an untimely hour. He is never too busy to see
them and to listen to their words of love and prayer. In
the midst of the affairs of the vast universe He thinks of
His humblest child in this great world, and amid all its
confusion and noise hears and recognizes the faintest cry
that rises from the lips of the least and lowliest of His little
ones. This name interprets also for us the grace and mercy
of our God. We are always conscious of sin. How, then,
can we gain access to a holy God ? Ah ! He is our Father.
We know that even an earthly father does not shut the
door on his erring child. The candle is left burning in the
window through the long dark nights, that the wanderer
out in the blackness and longing to return, seeing the bright
beams may be assured of love and a waiting welcome. Infinitely more gracious is our Father in heaven.

Glorifying God

"*Hallowed be Thy name.*"—MATT. vi. 9

WHILE the name "Father" over the gate of prayer assures us of loving welcome and of all tenderness, thoughtfulness, and care, the words "which art in heaven" remind us of the surpassing glory and majesty of God. We should not rush into His presence as we do into the presence of an earthly parent. We should remember His infinite greatness and holiness, and should come always with reverence. His is a name to be hallowed. "Holy and reverend is His name" Of this, this petition reminds us. It checks the flow of our thoughts and feelings, and bids us approach God with a suitable sense of our unworthiness and of His holiness. It bids us be reverent though bold.

This is a prayer for the glorifying of God in this world. When we pray it we must be sure that we do our part in making His name hallowed. We can do this by our own reverent use of that holy name. Good Christian people sometimes grow very careless in speaking of God. They become so accustomed to using His name in prayer and speech that they utter it as lightly as if it were the name of some familiar friend. I have seen a miner with black, grimy hand pluck a pure flower from the stem, and it seemed a profanation. But what shall we say of our own taking on our sin-defiled lips the holy and awful name of God? We ought to learn to hallow that blessed name in our speech.

Then we should hallow it in our lives. We are God's children, and we bear His name. How may a child honour a parent's name? Only by a life worthy of a parent. We must take heed, therefore, that in every act of ours—in our behaviour, in our whole character and influence—we live so that all who see us shall see in us something of the beauty of God. It would be a sad thing, indeed, if we gave people a wrong idea of God or of the religion of Jesus Christ.

May 4

¶beaven ¶Brought to ¶Us

" *Thy kingdom come.*"—MATT. vi. 10

THIS is a very comprehensive prayer. It pleads for the extension of God's spiritual realm in this world —His power over men's hearts and lives, the subjugation of earth's kingdoms to His sway. It is a prayer that men may be better—that they may put away their sins and amend their lives; that they may take Christ as their King, and yield every thought and desire to Him. It is not a longing to be lifted away to heaven, but a craving that heaven may be brought to us, into our hearts and lives.

We are in danger of thinking too much of other people and the coming of God's kingdom into other hearts and lives as we offer this prayer. The little piece of world for which we are at first responsible is that which lies within our own hearts and lives. While then we pray " Thy kingdom come," we should look within ourselves to see if we have submitted to the reign of Christ.

> " Thy kingdom here ?
> Lord, can it be ?
> Searching and seeking everywhere
> For many a year,
> ' Thy kingdom come ' has been my prayer ;
> Was that dear kingdom all the while so near ?
>
> " Was I the bar
> Which shut me out
> From the full joyance which they taste
> Whose spirits are
> Within Thy Paradise embraced—
> Thy blessed Paradise, which seemed so far ?
>
> " Let me not sit
> Another hour
> Idly awaiting what is mine to win,
> Blinded in wit.
> Lord Jesus, rend these walls of self and sin ;
> Beat down the gate, that I may enter in."

May 5.

Doing the Will of God.

" Thy will be done in earth, as it is in heaven."—MATT. vi. 10.

MANY people always quote this petition as if it meant only submission to some painful providence. They suppose it refers only to losing friends or money, or being sick or in trouble. But this is only a little part of its meaning. It is for the doing of God's will, not the suffering of it, that we here pray.

It is a good deal easier to make prayers like this for others than for ourselves. We all think other people ought to do God's will, and we do not find it a difficult prayer to make that they may do so. But what about ourselves ? There is no other person in the world for whose life we are really and finally responsible but ourself. This prayer, then, if we offer it sincerely, is that we may do God's will as it is done in heaven. We can pray it, therefore, only when we are ready for implicit, unquestioning obedience to the Divine will the moment we know what that will is.

Then sometimes it is a passive doing that is required. God asks of us something that costs pain or sacrifice or earthly loss ; when this is true our prayer may cut deeply into our own hearts. It may mean a giving up of some sweet joy, a losing of some precious friend, the sacrifice of some dear possession, the going in some way of thorns and tears. We should learn always to say the prayer, and then to hold our lives close to the line of the Divine will, never rebelling or murmuring, but sweetly doing whatever God gives us to do.

> " He always wins who sides with God,
>   To him no chance is lost ;
> God's will is sweetest to him when
>   It triumphs at his cost.

> " Ill that He blesses is our good,
>   And unblest good is ill ;
> And all is right that seems most wrong,
>   If it be His sweet will."

Day by Day

" *Give us this day our daily bread.*"—MATT. vi. 11

THIS seems a very small thing to ask—only bread for a day. Why are we not taught to pray for bread enough to last a week, or a month, or a year? For one thing, Jesus wanted to teach us a lesson of continual dependence. He taught us to come each morning with a request simply for the day's food, that we might never feel we can get along without our Father. Another lesson He wanted to teach us was that the true way to live is by the day. We are not to be anxious even about the supply of to-morrow's needs. When to-morrow comes it will be right for us to take up its cares. The same great lesson was taught in the way the manna was given—just a day's portion at a time.

> " Make a little fence of trust
>   Around to-day ;
> Fill the space with loving work,
>   And therein stay.
> Look not through the sheltering bars
>   Upon to-morrow ;
> God will help thee bear what comes
>   Of joy or sorrow."

We should not overlook the word " us." It is plural, and bids us send thought beyond our own individual need and remember God's other children. This should always be a prayer for daily bread for our hungry neighbour as well as for ourself. Then while we thus enjoy our own plenty, we must share with those who have need.

> " This crust is My body broken for thee,
> This water His blood that died on the tree ;
> The holy Supper is kept, indeed,
> In whatso we share with another's need,—
> Not that which we give, but what we share,—
> For the gift without the giver is bare :
> Who bestows himself with his alms feeds three—
> Himself, his hungering neighbour, and Me."

A Forgiving Spirit

" Forgive us our debts, as we forgive our debtors."
MATT. vi. 12

THE first part of this petition is not so hard to say, Most people are willing to confess, at least in a general way, that they are debtors to God, that they have sinned. But the second part is harder to repeat. When some one has done us an injury, and we are feeling hard over it, it is not so easy to ask God to forgive us as we forgive. Perhaps we do not forgive at all, but keep the bitter feeling in our heart against our brother. What is it, then, that we ask God to do for us when we pray, " Forgive us as we forgive " ? God has linked blessing and duty together in this petition. If we will not forgive those who have wronged us, we have not the spirit of penitence to which God grants remission of sins. If we would enjoy the sweet peace of God, we must keep our minds free from all bitterness and anger and all feelings of unforgiveness.

" Forgive us, Lord, because we have forgiven,
　　Not as we have forgiven, is our prayer,—
Earth is so lower far than highest heaven,
　　Man is not even as the angels are,
　　And Thou to angels art as sun to star ;
Measure Thy pity not in our poor scale,
　　But in Thine own which weighs eternities.
We do our little part, we strive, we fail,
　　Our wine of charity has bitter lees ;
　　Our best unselfishness seeks self to please ;
Our purest gold with base alloy is dim ;
　　Our fairest fruit hangs tainted on the tree ;
Our sweetest songs heard by the seraphim
　　Would all discordant and unlovely be,
　　Save for the charity they learn from Thee.
But Thou canst pour forgiveness with a word,
　　O'er countless worlds an all-embracing ray,
Beyond our hopes, our best deserving, Lord ;
　　Forgive us, then, and we in our poor way
　　Shall catch Thy higher meaning as we pray."

May 8

Enduring Temptation.

" Lead us not into temptation, but deliver us from evil."
MATT. vi. 13

IT is impossible to live in this world and escape temptation. In olden times men fled away from active life and from human companionships, hoping thus to evade enticement to evil. But they were not successful; for wherever they went they carried in their own hearts a fountain of corruption, and were thus perpetually exposed to temptation. The only door of escape from all temptation is the door that leads into heaven. We grieve over our friends whom the Lord calls away,—the little child in its sweet innocence, the mother in her ripened saintliness, the young man in his pride of strength ; but do we ever think that we have far more reason for anxiety, possibly for grief, over those who live and have to battle with sin in this world ? Those who have passed inside, in the victorious release of Christian faith, are for ever secure ; but those yet in the sore battle are still in peril.

This petition is a prayer that we may never be called needlessly to meet temptation. Sometimes God wants us to be tried, because we can grow strong only through victory. We have a word of scripture which says : " Blessed is the man that endureth temptation ; for when he is tried, he shall receive the crown of life." Yet we ought never ourselves to seek any way of life in which we shall have to be exposed to the peril of conflict with sin. Temptation is too terrible an experience, fraught with too much danger, to be sought by us, or ever encountered save when God leads us in the path on which it lies. We must never rush unbidden or unsent into any spiritual danger. There are no promises for presumption. " It is written," said the Master, " Thou shalt not tempt the Lord thy God." When God sends us into danger, we are under His protection ; when we go where He does not send us, we go unsheltered.

The Love of Money

" Ye cannot serve God and mammon."—MATT. vi. 24

WE had better look very carefully into the meaning of these words, remembering that it was our blessed Lord who spoke them. *Mammon* means riches. To *serve* means to be the slave of. St. Paul loved to call himself the servant or slave of Christ. Now Jesus says here that we cannot be God's slave and mammon's slave too. We cannot belong to any two masters at the same time. If we are mammon's slave, that ends it—we are not God's. If we belong to God, mammon is not our master. Think, too, what a degrading thing it is for any one bearing the image of God to be the slave of money. To use the word " serve " in its mildest English sense, no man should be even the servant of money. Riches are meant to be a man's slave ; now think how degrading it would be for any man to become servant or slave to his own slave. A man should be ashamed to call riches his master.

Money is meant to be man's servant, and so long as he is its perfect master it may be a blessing to him, and an instrument with which he may do great good. But when he gets down on his knees to it, and crawls in the dust for its sake, and sells his manhood to get it, it is only a curse to him. Thus it is easy to see why any one who serves God cannot serve mammon. God must have all the heart and must rule in all the life. He will not share His throne with the god of gold. God's true servants may have money, and may even be very rich, but they must use their money as a means for honouring God and blessing the world in Christ's name. They must own the money ; the money must not own them. They must carry it in their hands, not in their hearts. This is a very important thing for us to learn. Many Christian people are in danger of forsaking the sweet, blessed service of Christ for the servile, slavish service of mammon.

Anxious Thought

"Therefore I say unto you, Take no thought."—MATT. vi. 25

OF course we *are* to take thought in a true sense. Why were we made with brains if we are not to think with them? It would be as if God bade us not to walk after He had given us feet, or not to talk after giving us tongues. We are to train our minds and to think with them, and think about the future too, laying plans with a long reach into the years before us. It is not forethought that is forbidden, but anxious thought, worry, fear. We shall see as we go on just what we are to do instead of being anxious. At present let us get the simple lesson that we are never to be anxious. This is not a rule with exceptions. It is not a bit of creed that will not work in life. It is a lesson that we are to strive to carry out in all our days, however full they may be of things calculated to distract us.

But why are we to take no thought? The "therefore" helps us to the answer: "Ye cannot serve God and mammon. Therefore take no thought." So, then, taking thought seems to be serving mammon. We say we are God's children, and yet when mammon seems in danger of failing us we get anxious. Practically, then, we trust mammon more than we trust our Father. We feel safer when mammon's abundance fills our hands than when mammon threatens to fail and we have only God. That is, we trust God *and* mammon. Anxiety about the supply of our needs is therefore distrust of our heavenly Father. If we serve God only, we should not worry though we have not even bread for to-morrow; we should believe in our Father's love. Money we may lose any day, for "riches make themselves wings; they fly away as an eagle toward heaven;" but we never can lose God. Nothing can rob us of His love, nor rob Him of the abundance He possesses from which to meet our needs. So if we trust God we ought never to be anxious, though we have nothing else.

May 11.

A Lesson of Trust.

" Behold the fowls of the air......your heavenly Father feedeth them. Are ye not much better than they ? "—MATT. vi. 26.

ARE we to draw the inference that since the birds neither sow nor reap, we should put forth no exertions to provide for our own wants ? No : if we did nothing to earn our own bread we should soon starve. God would not feed us as He feeds the birds. He has bestowed upon us powers by which we can make provision for our own wants ; He feeds us, not by bringing the bread to us, but by making us able to sow and reap and gather into barns. God nowhere encourages that " trust " which idly sits down and waits to be cared for. Little babies, and sick and infirm people, and any who are incapacitated for exertion, may live as the birds do, and may expect to be cared for. But hearty people, with active brains and strong hands, will fare very poorly if they try to live the birds' way.

The point of the illustration lies elsewhere. God's care extends even to birds. There are two reasons, then, why it will more certainly extend to His people. First, they are better than birds. Birds have no souls, do not bear the Divine image, have no spiritual nature, cannot worship nor voluntarily serve God, have no future and immortal life. The God who cares for a little soulless bird will surely care much more thoughtfully for a thinking, immortal, godlike man.

Then the other reason is, that God is our Father. He is the creator and provider of the birds, but not their Father. Surely a father will do more for his children than for his chickens ; a mother will give more thought to her baby than to her canary. Will not our heavenly Father provide more certainly and more tenderly for His children than for His birds ? So from the birds we get a lesson of trust. Every little bird sitting on its bough, or singing its sweet song, ought to lead us to renewed confidence in the care of our Father.

May 12

Useless Anxieties

" Which of you by taking thought can add one cubit unto his stature ? "—MATT. vi. 27

SO it is useless to worry. A short person cannot, by any amount of anxiety, make himself an inch taller. Why, therefore, should he waste his energy and fret his life away in wishing he were an inch taller ? One worries because he is too short, another because he is too tall ; one because he is too lean, another because he is too fat ; one because he has a lame foot, another because he has a mole on his face. No amount of fretting will change any of these things. People worry, too, over their circumstances. They are poor, and have to work hard. They have troubles, losses, and disappointments which come through causes entirely beyond their own control. They find difficulties in their environment which they cannot surmount. There are hard conditions in their lot which they cannot change.

Now why should they worry about these things ? Will worrying make matters any better ? Will discontent cure the lame foot, or remove the ugly mole, or reduce corpulency, or put flesh on the thin body ? Will chafing make the hard work lighter, or the burdens easier, or the troubles fewer ? Will anxiety keep the winter away, or the storm from rising, or put coal in the cellar, or bread in the pantry, or get clothes for the children ? Even wise philosophy shows the uselessness of worrying, since it helps nothing, and only wastes one's strength and unfits one for doing one's best. Then religion goes farther, and says that even the hard things and the obstacles are blessings, if we meet them in the right spirit—stepping-stones lifting our feet upward, disciplinary experiences in which we grow. So we learn that we should quietly and with faith accept life as it comes to us, fretting at nothing, changing hard conditions to easier if we can ; if we cannot, then using them as means for growth and advancement.

Lessons from the Flowers

" Why take ye thought for raiment ? Consider the lilies......
Even Solomon......was not arrayed like one of these."—
MATT. vi. 28, 29

WITHOUT any toiling or spinning on their own part, God clothes the flowers in loveliness far surpassing any adornment which the most skilful human arts can provide. Flowers bloom but a day and fade. We are better than flowers. If our Father lavishes so much beauty on perishing plants, is there any danger that He will not provide raiment for His own ?

Of course it is not implied that like the lilies we need neither toil nor spin. It is all right for lilies just to stand still and grow. That is their mission ; that is the way God made them to grow. But He gave us hands, feet, brains, tongue, energy, and will ; and if we would be cared for as are the flowers, we must put forth our energies to produce the results of comfort. Yet Jesus tells us to consider the lilies, how they grow. We ought to study the beautiful things in nature and learn lessons from them. Here it is a lesson of contentment we are to learn. Who ever heard a lily complaining about its circumstances ? It accepts the conditions in which it finds itself, and makes the best of them. It drinks in heaven's sweet light, air, dew, and rain, and unfolds its own loveliness in quietness and peace.

The lily grows from within. So ought we to grow, having within us the Divine life, to be developed in our character and spirit. The lily is an emblem of beauty ; our spiritual life should unfold likewise in all lovely ways. It is a picture of perfect peace. Who ever saw wrinkles of anxiety in a lily's face ? God wants us to grow into peace. The lily is fragrant ; so should our lives be. The lily sometimes grows in the black bog, but it remains unspotted. Thus should we live in this world, keeping ourselves unspotted amid its evil. These are a few of the lessons from the lily.

May 14

God will Provide

*" Seek ye first the kingdom of God, and His righteousness ;
and all these things shall be added unto you."*—MATT.
vi. 33

WE are to take no thought for our own life, for food
or raiment ; because that is God's part, not ours.
There is one thing, however, for which we are to take
thought, not anxious, but very earnest thought. We are
to take thought about our duty, about doing God's will
and filling our place in God's world.

We ought to get this very clearly in our mind. Too many
people worry far more about their food and raiment, lest
they shall be left to want, than they do about doing well
their whole duty. That is, they are more anxious about
God's part in their lives than they are about their own.
They fear God may not take care of them, but they do not
have any fear that they may fail in fidelity to Him. We
ought to learn well that providing for our wants is God's
business, not ours. We have nothing at all to do with it.
But we have everything to do with our own duty, our allotted
work, the doing of God's will. God will never do these
things for us. If we do not do them, they must remain
undone ; if we do them with fidelity, God will care for us.

The noblest life possible in this world is simple consecration to Christ and to duty, with no anxiety about anything
else. We may not always be fed luxuriously, nor be clothed
in scarlet and fine linen ; yet food convenient for us will
always be provided, and raiment sufficient to keep us warm.
But suppose we are near starving ! Well, we must just go
on doing our part and not worrying ; in due time, somehow, God will provide. Here we have our Lord's own
promise of this. The truth is, too many of us take a great
deal more thought about our support than about our
duty. Then of course we forfeit the promise and may
suffer. How much better the other way—ours the doing,
God's the providing.

One Day at a Time

"Take......no thought for the morrow: for the morrow shall take thought for the things of itself."—MATT. vi. 34

THIS last reason our Lord gives against anxiety for the future is that we have nothing to do with the future. God gives us life by days, little single days. Each day has its own duties, its own needs, its own trials and temptations, its own griefs and sorrows. God always gives us strength enough for the day as He gives it, with all that He puts into it. But if we insist on dragging back to-morrow's cares and piling them on top of to-day's, the strength will not be enough for the load. God will not add strength just to humour our whims of anxiety and distrust.

So the lesson is that we should keep each day distinct and attend strictly to what it brings us. Charles Kingsley says : " Do to-day's duty, fight to-day's temptation, and do not weaken and distract yourself by looking forward to things which you cannot see, and could not understand if you saw them." We really have nothing at all to do with the future, save to prepare for it by doing with fidelity the duties of to-day.

No one was ever crushed by the burdens of one day. We can always get along with our heaviest load till the sun goes down; well, that is all we ever have to do. To-morrow? Oh, you may have no to-morrow; you may be in heaven. If you are here God will be here too, and you will receive new strength sufficient for the new day.

" One day at a time.   A burden too great
    To be borne for two can be borne for one ;
Who knows what will enter to-morrow's gate ?
    While yet we are speaking all may be done.

" One day at a time,—but a single day,
    Whatever its load, whatever its length ;
And there's a bit of precious Scripture to say
    That according to each shall be our strength."

May 16

Judging of Others.

"*Judge not, that ye be not judged.*"—MATT. vii. 1

FEW faults are more common than this judging of others. It would not be so bad if we were disposed to look at people charitably; but we are not. Our eyes are far keener for flaws and blemishes than for marks of beauty. Not many of us are for ever finding new features of loveliness in others; not a few of us can find an indefinite number of faults. If we were ourselves up to the standard whereby we judge others, we should be very saintly people. If we were free from all the faults we so readily see when they appear in our neighbour, we should be well-nigh faultless.

This word of our Lord not only instructs us not to be critical of others and censorious, but it presents the strongest kind of motive against such judging. It makes the appeal to our own interest. Others will mete to us just what we mete to them. None of us like other people to be critical and censorious toward us. We wince under unjust judgments. We resent unkind fault-finding. We demand that people shall judge us fairly. We claim forbearance and charity in our derelictions in duty and for blemishes in our character. Can we expect other people to be any more lenient toward us than we are toward them?

If we would receive kindly judgment from others, we must give the same to them. If we criticise another to-day in a harsh manner, we need not be surprised if we hear some one's harsh criticism of us to-morrow. But if, on the other hand, we speak kindly, appreciative, and charitable words of some one to-day, very likely we shall hear to-morrow some pleasant word that another has said of us. So we make very largely the music or the discord for our own hearts. We get back what we give. We gather the harvest of our own sowing. Then, even in the last judgment, we shall receive from the Judge what we have shown to others.

Finding Fault with Others

*"Why beholdest thou the mote that is in thy brother's eye,
but considerest not the beam that is in thine own eye?"*
MATT. vii. 3

IT is strange how oblivious we can be of our own faults
and blemishes, and how clearly we can see those of
other people. One old writer says : " Men are more apt to
use spectacles than looking-glasses—spectacles to behold
other men's faults than looking-glasses to behold their
own." A man can see a little speck of dust in his neighbour's eye while utterly unaware of the great beam in his
own eye. He observes the most minute fault in his
brother while unconscious of his own far greater fault.

We would say that a beam in a man's eye would so
blind him that he could not see the mote in another's eye.
As our Lord represents it, however, the man with the beam
is the very one who sees the mote and thinks himself competent to pull it out. So it is in morals. No man is so
sharp at seeing a fault in another as he who has the same
or a similar fault of his own. A vain man is the first to
detect the indications of vanity in another. A bad-
tempered person is most apt to be censorious toward a
neighbour who displays bad temper. One with a sharp,
uncontrolled tongue has the least patience with another
whose speech is full of poisoned arrows. A selfish man
discovers even motes of selfishness in others. Rude
people are the very first to be hurt and offended by rudeness in a neighbour.

So it is always. If we are quick to perceive blemishes and
faults in others, the probability is that we have far greater
blemishes and faults in ourselves. This truth ought to
make us exceedingly careful in our judgments, and exceedingly modest in our expressions of censure, for we really are
telling the world our own faults. It is wiser, as well as more
in accordance with the spirit of Christ, for us to find lovely
things in others, and to be silent regarding their faults.

A Self=Righteous Spirit

" Or how wilt thou say to thy brother, Let me pull out the mote out of thine eye ; and, behold, a beam is in thine own eye ? "—MATT. vii. 4

BUT is it not a kindness to a friend to take the mote out of his eye ? If we met a neighbour with a cinder in his eye, would it not be a brotherly thing to stop and take it out for him ? Then why is it not just as true a kindness to want to cure another's fault, even though we have the same fault ourselves ? If we did it in the right spirit it would be. We are bound to seek the welfare of our friends in every possible way, and therefore, if we discover in them things that mar their beauty, we should seek the removal of those things.

But the trouble is we are not apt to look at our neighbour's faults in this loving and sympathetic way. To begin with, we do not know, or at least we do not confess, that we ourselves have beams in our own eyes ; we are not even aware that there are motes in our own eyes. It is the self-righteous spirit that our Lord is here condemning. A man holds up his hands in horror at the speck he has found in his neighbour's character ; and his neighbour, looking up, sees in him an immensely magnified copy of the speck. Will the neighbour be greatly benefited by the rebuke ?

Suppose a bad-tempered man lectures us on the sin of giving way to temper, or a dishonest man on some apparent lack of honesty, or a liar on the wickedness of falsehood, or a bad-mannered man on some discourtesy of ours, or a hypocrite on insincerity, what good will such lectures do, even admitting that we are conscious of the faults ? We are only irritated by the unfitness of such rebukes from those in whom the faults are ten times greater than in us. We wonder how people can have the face to talk about motes in our eyes when huge beams project from their own eyes. Truly *this* is not the way to tell others of their faults.

Begin at Home

" *First cast out the beam out of thine own eye ; and then shalt thou see clearly to cast out the mote out of thy brother's eye.*"—MATT. vii. 5

BEGIN at home—that is the teaching ; not at home in the general sense, with other members of thy family, but very close at home, with thyself. It is a good deal easier, of course, to pull motes out of other people's eyes than beams out of one's own. Yet we are not put in this world to look after other people's faults, to pick the dust out of their eyes, to remove their specks of blemish. Our first business is to get rid of our own faults. At least we are scarcely competent to take the grain of dust out of another's eye while a beam protrudes from our own. We are not ready to do much toward curing our friend of his faults until we have sincerely tried to rid ourselves of our own.

We all know people whose very presence is a silent rebuke of sin. Their lives are pure and holy, and their unconscious influence is a restraint upon all evil. We are ofttimes told that one of the truest tests of a good friendship is that our friend can tell us of our faults and we shall receive it kindly. That depends first on ourselves, and then upon our friend. If we are proud and vain, it will be very hard for any friend, the wisest and gentlest, to speak to us of our faults, save at the peril of the friendship. Then if the friend treats our faults in a conceited and censorious way, it will be equally dangerous. He who would truly help to take the motes out of our eyes must come to us in tender love, proving his generous and unselfish interest in us. He must come to us humbly, not as our judge but as our brother, with faults like our own which he is trying to cure. If he approaches us in this way; conscious of his own infirmity, desiring to be helpful to us, as Christ has been helpful to him, nothing but unpardonable vanity and self-conceit will prevent our accepting his kind offer.

May 20

The Prayer=Promise

" Every one that asketh receiveth ; and he that seeketh find-
eth ; and to him that knocketh it shall be opened."—
MATT. vii. 8

THESE are very positive promises, and yet they must be read intelligently, in the light of other scriptures which explain and qualify the words. It is not all asking that receives ; for there is asking that is not true prayer. Some ask merely in word, with no real desire in their hearts. Some ask selfishly, that they may consume the Divine gift on their lusts. Some ask rebelliously, without submission to the will of God. Some ask without faith, not expecting any answer. Some ask indolently, not ready to do their own part. Some ask ignorantly for things which would not be blessings if they were granted. It is very clear that in these cases those who ask will not receive.

So not literally all who seek find. The seeking must be earnest. There is a remarkable word in one of the old prophets : " Ye shall seek me, and find me, when ye shall search for me *with all your heart.*" The seeking must also be for good things. If our quest is for sinful things, or for worldly good, that would work in us spiritual harm, God will not give us what we seek. Then we must live right. " No good thing will He withhold from them *that walk uprightly.*" The thing itself must be good ; and we must walk in paths of obedience, or there is no promise of reward for our quest.

In like manner it is not to all knocking that God opens the door. There are timid knocks that indicate neither desire nor faith, as when mischievous children ring a door-bell and then run away, not wanting to enter. It is when we knock at the right door, and knock with expectancy and faith and importunity, that the door is graciously opened. Thus in interpreting this wonderful prayer-promise we must read into the words their true meaning. The asking, seeking, knocking, must be true prayer.

"Good Things" from God

" If ye then, being evil, know how to give good gifts unto your children, how much more shall your Father which is in heaven give good things to them that ask Him ? "—MATT. vii. 11

NO father will answer his hungry child's cry for bread with a stone, or give the child a serpent if he asks for a fish. Even sinful parents have in their hearts something of the image of God's own fatherhood. If a true earthly father, with all his imperfection, will not mock a child's cry, but will respond lovingly, how much more will our Father in heaven do for us ?

"How much more ? " is a question none can answer. We can only say as much more as the heavenly Father is more loving, and wiser, and more able to give, than is the earthly father. Yet we must explain this promise also by other scriptures. The gate of prayer is set very wide open in this verse, yet those who would enter must come in the right way and seek " good " things.

While no one who asks for bread will receive a stone, neither will one who asks for a stone receive a stone. And many times do we come to God pleading with Him to let us have a stone. Of course we imagine it is bread, and that it will be food to us. It is some earthly thing, some gift of honour or pleasure, some achievement of ambition, some object of heart desire. It looks like bread to our deluded vision. But God knows it is only a cold stone—that it would leave us starving if we were to receive it ; and He loves us too well to listen to our piteous cries for it, or to be moved by our earnestness or our tears to give it to us. When we ask for a stone He will give us bread. Thus it is that many requests for earthly things are not granted. Yet the prayers are not unanswered. Instead of the stone we wish, God gives us the bread we need. We do not always know what is bread and what is a stone, and we must leave to God the final decision in all our prayers.

Our Duty to Others

" All things whatsoever ye would that men should do to you, do ye even so to them."—MATT. vii. 12

THIS is a wonderfully comprehensive rule of action. It bids us consider the interests of others as well as our own. It bids us set our neighbour alongside of ourself, and think of him as having the same rights as we have, and requiring from us the same treatment that we give to ourself. It gives us a standard by which to test all our motives and all our conduct bearing on others. We are at once in thought to change places with the person toward whom duty is to be determined, and ask, " If he were where I am, and I were where he is, how should I want him to treat me in this case ? " The application of this rule would instantly put a stop to all rash, hasty actions ; for it commands us to consider our neighbour and question our own heart before doing anything. It would slay all selfishness ; for it compels us to regard our neighbour's interests as precisely equal to our own. It would lead us to honour others ; for it puts us and them on the same platform.

The application of this rule would put a stop to all injustice and wrong ; for none of us would do injustice or wrong to ourselves, and we are to treat our neighbour as if he were ourself. It would lead us to seek the highest good of all other men, even the lowliest ; for we surely want all men to seek our good. The thorough applying of this Golden Rule would end all conflict between capital and labour ; for it would give the employer a deep, loving interest in the men he employs, and lead him to think of their good in all ways. It would also give to every employee a desire for the prosperity of his employer and an interest in his business. It would end all strife in families, in communities, among nations. The perfect working of this rule everywhere would make heaven ; for the will of God would then " be done on earth, as it is in heaven."

Two Roads and Two Gates

" *Enter ye in at the strait gate.*"—MATT. vii. 13

ALL truly valuable things cost much. Such a glorious privilege as the Christian's, therefore, cannot be gotten without effort. To open the way, and to purchase for us the privilege of becoming children of God, the Son of God had to come from heaven in condescending love and give His own life. Jesus said, too, that any who would reach the glory of His kingdom must go by the same way of the cross by which He went. He said that he who will save his life—that is, keep it from self-denial and sacrifice —shall lose it ; and that only he who loses his life, gives it out in devotion to God and to duty, shall save it.

In one of His parables Jesus speaks of salvation as a treasure hid in a field, and a man who learns of the treasure and its hiding-place sells all that he has and goes and buys the field. In another parable our Lord presents the same truth under the figure of a merchant seeking goodly pearls, who, finding one pearl of great price, sells all he has and buys it. We must, in a very deep sense, give up all we have to get Christ and the blessings that come with Him.

Here the truth is put in another way. There are two roads through this world, and two gates into the future world. One of these ways is broad and easy, with descending grade, leading to a wide gate. It is not hard to go on this way. The other road is strait, and leads to a narrow gate. To go this way one has to leave the crowd and go almost alone, and leave the broad, easy way, and go on a hard, rugged path, and enter by a gate too small to admit any bundles of worldliness, or self-righteousness, or any of the fashionable trappings of the old life. If we would get to heaven, we must make up our minds it can be only by this narrow way of self-denial. All the world is not flowing into heaven ; the crowds are going somewhere else.

May 24

In Sheep's Clothing

" Beware of false prophets, which come to you in sheep's clothing, but inwardly they are ravening wolves."—MATT. vii. 15

THERE is something fearful in the eagerness of the devil to destroy souls. He sends his agents and messengers in forms and garbs to deceive the simple-minded and unwary. He even steals the dress of God's own servants and children, hoping thus to gain the confidence of believers and then destroy their faith and lead them away to death. The world is full now of just such agents of Satan. They profess to be Christians, but in their hearts they are disloyal to Christ and to His cause and kingdom. They win the confidence of the sheep by passing off for sheep themselves; but the sheep's covering is only worn outside, while underneath is the heart of a hungry, bloodthirsty wolf.

We need to be on our guard perpetually against the wiles of the devil. Eternal vigilance is the price of spiritual safety and of Christian peace. Many young people, especially of those who are intelligent and gifted, fall under the influence of those who have caught smatterings of sceptical talk which they drop in the form of sneers or mocking queries in the ears of their confiding listeners. They laugh at the simple cradle-faiths these young Christians hold, and ask with wise air, " Do you still believe these old superstitions?" Then they go on to cast doubt or to start questions about this or that difficulty in the Bible, or they caricature some Christian doctrine and hold it up in such light as to make it look absurd.

Thus they poison the minds of these earnest young believers, weaken their faith, and fill them with perplexity. Pastors and teachers of intelligent young people are continually called to try to undo the destructive work of those wolves in sheep's clothing; but ofttimes it is impossible to undo it. Wrecked cradle-faiths are hard to restore.

Doing the Father's Will

*" Not every one that saith unto Me, Lord, Lord, shall enter
into the kingdom of heaven ; but he that doeth the will
of My Father."*—MATT. vii. 21

IT is not enough to believe in Christ intellectually, even
to be quite orthodox in creed. It is not enough to
seem to honour Christ before men, praying to Him and
ascribing power to Him. It is a sad thing that Jesus tells
us here—that some who have thus seemed to be His friends
on earth, and who have publicly confessed Him, shall fail
at last to get into heaven.

Such a word from our Lord's lips cannot but startle us.
We stop and ask, " Are we sure that *we* shall be admitted
to heaven ? Why are these confessors of Christ kept out ?
What are the conditions of entrance ? " To these questions the answer is so plain that there is no possibility of
mistake if we read the Lord's words with honest care. He
tells us that those only shall enter heaven who on earth do
the will of the Father. No confession, therefore, is true
which is not confirmed and verified by a life of obedience
and holiness. " Simply to Thy cross I cling " is but half
of the gospel. No one is really clinging to the cross who
is not at the same time faithfully following Christ and doing
whatsoever He commands. No one can enter into heaven
into whose heart heaven has not first entered on this earth.
We shall do God's will in heaven if we ever get there ; we
must do it here, or we shall never do it there.

Some people have the impression that salvation sets
them free from the law ; it does as a ground of salvation,
but it does not as a rule of duty. We pray, " Thy will be
done in earth, as it is in heaven ; " if the prayer be sincere
it must draw our own lives with it in loving obedience and
acquiescence to the Divine will. Our confessions of Christ
must be confirmed by the earnest doing of the Father's
will. All other confession is only an empty mockery.

May 26

The Safe Foundation

" Whosoever heareth these sayings of Mine, and doeth them, I will liken him unto a wise man, which built his house upon a rock."—MATT. vii. 24

ALL turns on the doing or not doing of Christ's words. Both these men heard the words, but one of them obeyed as well, and thus built on the true and immovable foundation. Both men built houses very much alike so far as the superstructures were concerned. But there were two kinds of ground. There was a valley, which was dry and pleasant in the summer days, when the men were looking for building sites. Then there were high, rocky bluffs. One man decided to build in the valley. It would cost less. It would be easy digging. It was more convenient, for the bluffs were inaccessible. The other man built on the high ground. It would cost more, but it would be safer.

The two homes went up simultaneously, only the one in the valley was finished long before the other was. The families moved into their new residences, and were quite happy for a time. But one night there was a storm. The house in the valley was carried away with its dwellers; the house on the bluff was unharmed.

The pictures explain themselves. He who built in the valley is the man who has only knowledge and profession, but who really has never built on Christ as a foundation. The other man, who built on a rock, is the man who has true faith in Christ, confirmed by loving obedience. The storms that burst are earth's trials which test every life, and then the tempests of death and judgment. The mere professor of religion is swept away in these storms, for he has only sand under him; he who is truly in Christ is secure, for no storm can reach Christ's bosom. It will be a terrible thing to cherish a false hope of salvation through life, and only find out in eternity, too late to build again, that we have no foundation under our hopes.

Christ the Great Counsellor

"*John calling unto him two of his disciples, sent them to Jesus.*"—LUKE vii. 19

HE was in perplexity about certain matters. There were some things that were worrying him, that he could not make out himself, and he sent to Christ to ask Him about them. That is just what every one of us should do when there arise perplexities of any kind in our lives or affairs—we should carry them straight to Jesus. Even the children have their disappointments and trials. They have discouragements. Now, they ought not to worry about these matters. Of course they cannot always understand them ; how could they expect to understand everything in such a vast world as this ? But is it not a great thing to know that Jesus understands it all ? He knows what He is doing.

So the true way for us is just to do what John did— tell Jesus whenever anything appears to go wrong or when anything happens we cannot understand. That is the rule Paul gives for keeping clear of anxiety. "Be careful [or anxious] nothing ; but in everything by prayer and supplication with thanksgiving let your requests be made known unto God." Then He promises that if we only do this we shall never have worry—" The peace of God shall keep your hearts and minds."

The meaning of all this is that we should never carry a worry of any kind even for a moment, but whenever any matter begins to perplex us we should go instantly and tell Jesus all about it, and leave it in His hands, that He may manage it for us.

The leaving it is the hardest part. We can easily take it to Him, but we are so apt to pick it up again and carry it back with us, and keep it, just as if we had not taken it to Him. We should learn to tell Jesus of our perplexities and sorrows, and then commit all to Him without further anxiety. This is faith, and is the way to find peace.

Loss of Faith

" Art Thou He that should come ? or look we for another ? "
Luke vii. 19

JOHN was in prison, in the castle Machærus. It certainly was not a very cheerful place to be in. We ought scarcely to be astonished at his temporary loss of bright faith. Yet a good many people think it strange that the grand, brave John could really have been in doubt, and scarcely believe it. " It is not possible," they say, " that such a great, heroic man should ever waver in his confidence." They forget that John lived just in the dim dawn of the gospel, before the full day burst upon the world. He had not the thousandth part of the light that we have in our day ; and yet do we, with all our light, never get depressed ? The truth is, there is not one of us who is not sometimes disheartened without a hundredth part of the cause John had.

But that is always the way. We are amazed at every person's blindness, or dullness, or unbelief, but our own. Other people's failures look very large to us, but we never see our own at all. We wonder how Moses once, under terrible provocation, lost his temper and spoke a dozen hasty and impatient words ; while we can scarcely get through a single sunny day without a much worse outbreak upon a far slighter provocation.

We wonder how the beloved disciple, with all his sweet humility, could once show an ambition for a place of honour, while we ourselves are for ever scrambling for preferments. We say, " Isn't it strange that people would not believe on Christ when they saw all His power and love ? " Yet we do not believe in Him any more fully than they did. We can scarcely believe that John Baptist grew despondent when his trials were so great, though most of us are often plunged into gloom by the merest trifles. Many Christian people get more despairing over the loss of a few pounds, or a little pain, than John did in his really great trials.

Needless Doubts

" Look we for another ? "—LUKE vii. 19

JOHN did not doubt the Messiahship of Jesus that day beside the Jordan, when from the cloven heavens the radiant dove descended upon Him and the Father's voice was heard in loving approval. Nor did he doubt in any of the bright days that followed. It was only when it grew dark for John himself that he doubted.

That is just the way yet with many people. When everything is bright and sunny they think they have surely found Christ, and they believe He is their friend, and their hearts are full of joy. But when troubles come and things begin to go against them, they wonder whether, after all, they have really found the Saviour. They begin to question their own experiences. " Am I really a Christian ? Was that really conversion when I thought I was saved ? or is there some other experience that I must yet have ? " Christ does not do just the things they thought He would do for them. Their religion does not support them as firmly as they supposed it would. If they are indeed Christians, why does Christ let them suffer so much and not come to relieve them ? So they sink away down into the Slough of Despond, sometimes losing all hope.

See how unnecessary was John's doubt. Jesus was indeed the Messiah. John's active work was done, and he was now to glorify God by suffering and soon by martyrdom. Just as needless is all anxiety of Christian people in their times of darkness. Of course we must have some earthly trials. Christ does not carry us to heaven on flowery beds of ease. We must expect to bear the cross many a mile. The true way for us is never to doubt Jesus. Suppose there are clouds, the sun still shines behind them undimmed. Suppose we have failures, trials, and disappointments ; Jesus is the same loving friend as when there was not a speck of trouble for us in all the world.

May 30.

Jesus Always Answers.

" Then Jesus answering."—LUKE vii. 22.

JOHN was perplexed, and sent from his prison to ask Jesus if He were indeed the promised Messiah. Jesus patiently answered the messengers. He always answers. Many of our prayers to Him are mixed with doubt ; many of them are filled with complaints and fears and murmurings. Still He never grows impatient with us. He never shuts His door upon us. It must grieve and pain Him to have us doubt Him. Joseph wept when his brothers sent a message to him, after their father's death, asking him to forgive them, when he had forgiven them years before, and had proved it by a thousand kindnesses ; it almost broke his heart to think how they had misjudged him.

Yet that is the way many of us do with Jesus. After all the sacrifices He has made on our behalf, and the blessings His love has bestowed upon us, when some shadow falls upon our heart we wonder whether Christ loves us or not, whether or not He has forgiven us, whether or not He will take care of us in the future. We are half the time perplexed about something—full of worries ; and these doubts, fears, and anxieties get into our prayers. They take the joy out of our worship, and the faith out of our supplications, and give a sad tone to our devotions.

Does Jesus never get tired of such prayers ? No, no ; He listens, and hears all the discords made by the murmurings. His heart must be pained by them too ; but He answers us nevertheless. He is very patient with us—He never chides ; He remembers how frail we are, and sends the sweetest answers that His love can give. It is wonderful indeed how rich and gentle our Saviour is. Verily

" There is no place where earth's sorrows
    Are more felt than up in heaven ;
There is no place where earth's failings
    Have such kindly judgments given."

The Footprints of Christ

" *Go your way, and tell John what things ye have seen.*"
LUKE vii. 22

JOHN wanted to know whether Jesus really was the Messiah or not. Jesus did not present arguments to prove that He was the Messiah, but pointed the messengers to the work He was doing. The best evidence of the divinity of Christ is not any number of proof-texts gathered from all parts of the Bible and arranged in order, but the *works* that Christ has done and is doing every day. An atheist asked an Oriental how he knew there was a God. The man answered by inquiring, " How do I know whether it was a man or a camel that passed my tent last night ? " He knew by the footprints. Then he pointed to the setting sun and asked : " Whose footprint is that ? "

Look at the footprints of Christ, and see whether they are a man's or God's. Whose prints are those by the gate of Nain, by the grave of Bethany, coming away from the tomb of Joseph of Arimathæa ? Whose prints are those by the doors of sorrow, along the path where the leper, the blind, the lame, the demoniac waited for Him ? Or look around at what you see now—churches, missions, hospitals, asylums, sweetened homes, cleansed sinners, renewed lives, comforted mourners : whose prints are these ? These works, wrought by Christianity, are the best evidences of Christianity. Christ wants to be judged, not by His claims, but by His works. The world is full to-day of the proofs of Christ's divinity.

In like manner we must prove that we must belong to Christ, not by getting certificates of Church membership, but by showing in our daily lives the unselfishness, the sympathy, the self-denial, the kindness, the love that were the highest proofs in Christ's own life of His Divine mission. We must be able, when persons ask us if we are Christians, to say : " Look at my life and my works, and judge for yourselves."

June 1

Waverers

" A reed shaken with the wind."—LUKE vii. 24

THE picture is of a man wavering and unstable, easily swayed and bent from uprightness. That is what a good many men are. A reed grows in soft mud by the water's edge. Then it is so frail and delicate that every breeze bends it and shakes it. Jesus did not intimate that John was a man of that stamp, but meant just the reverse. John was *not* like a reed shaken with the wind. He was a man whom nothing could bend or sway. Rather than preach soft words to please Herod, and keep quiet about sins that the king was committing, John charged home the sins without quailing, losing his head at last as reward.

Yet there are some persons who are like reeds. Instead of being rooted in Christ, their roots go down into the soft mud of this world, and of course they are easily torn up. Then they have no fixed principles to hold them upright and make them true and strong ; and they are bent by every wind, and moved and swayed by every influence of fear or favour. The boy that cannot say no when other boys tease him to smoke, or drink, or do a wrong or mean thing, is a reed shaken by the wind. The girl who is influenced by frivolities and worldly pleasure, and drawn away from Christ and from a beautiful life, is likewise a reed bent and swayed by the wind.

They are growing everywhere, these reeds, and the wind shakes them every time it blows. Who wants to be a reed ? Who would not rather be like the oak, growing in soil as solid as a rock, which no storm bends or even causes to tremble ?

There is one apparent advantage in being like a reed : one seems to escape persecution. John would hardly have met the fate he did meet if he had been easily shaken. People who are like reeds do not often lose their heads on the martyr's block. But they are in danger of losing their souls ; and that certainly is worse.

The Friend of Sinners

" A woman in the city, which was a sinner, when she knew that Jesus sat at meat."—LUKE vii. 37

IT is wonderful how genuine goodness draws to itself the unfortunate, the troubled, the friendless, the outcast, the fallen. Wherever Jesus went, these classes always found Him out and gathered about Him. It was because He was the true, disinterested friend of all men. They found sympathy in Him. He would listen to their story. Though He was the sinless One, there was yet no air of " I am holier than thou " about Him. He was just as gentle to an outcast sinner as to a spotless Nicodemus. No matter who reached out a hand for help, He was ready to grasp it. One of the truest things ever said of Jesus was the prophetic word concerning Him, " A bruised reed shall He not break." He dealt always most gently with sore spirits and with bruised hearts.

Those who want to be useful in this world must have the same qualities. There is a kind of human " holiness " that draws nobody to itself, but rather repels ; genuine holiness, however, wins its way everywhere into men's hearts. The secret of it all is in living " not to be ministered unto, but to minister ; " in considering one's self not too good to serve the unworthiest of God's creatures. If we stay in this world *to be served*, we shall be of no manner of use. But if we live to minister to others, yearning to be of service to every one we meet, our life will be something worth. The hungry-hearted and the soul-needy will be drawn to us, and God will love to put work into our hands.

We need, too, to train ourselves to exceeding gentleness in dealing with human souls in their spiritual crises. Many earnest people, in the excess of their zeal, do incalculable harm to those whom they greatly desire to help. People with sore and bruised hearts usually need loving sympathy and strong, kindly friendship much more than they need theology.

June 3

A Broken Spirit

"*Stood at His feet behind Him weeping.*"—LUKE vii. 38

THOSE who are familiar with the story of Paradise and the Peri will remember how the banished Peri sought to gain admittance at the closed gate of Paradise. The angel told the nymph that there was one hope—that the Peri might yet be forgiven who would bring to the eternal gate the gift that was most dear to Heaven.

The Peri wandered everywhere, sweeping all lands with her swift wings, searching for some rare and precious thing to carry up to the barred gate. Amid scenes of carnage she found a hero dying for liberty ; and

> "Swiftly descending on a ray
> Of morning light, she caught the last,
> Last glorious drop his heart had shed,
> Before its free-born spirit fled."

With this she flew up to the gate ; but, precious as was the boon, the crystal bar moved not. Next in her quest the Peri came upon a dying lover, over whom his betrothed hung ; and stealing the farewell sigh of that vanishing soul, again she sought the gate of bliss : but even to this precious boon the bar swung not.

Again she wandered far, and came at last upon a wretched criminal, stained by countless deeds of shame and blood, but now weeping in bitter penitence. The Peri with joy caught up the holy tear of contrition as it fell, and swiftly bore it away to heaven ; and the door flew open, admitting her to the blessedness within.

This beautiful Oriental legend is not untrue to heavenly fact. The Bible tells us the same thing. " The sacrifices of God are a broken spirit : a broken and a contrite heart, O God, Thou wilt not despise." No offerings we can bring are so precious as contrite tears. No song on earth rings with such music up in heaven as the penitential cry, " God be merciful to me a sinner ! "

Free Forgiveness

" When they had nothing to pay, he frankly forgave them both."—LUKE vii. 42

ALL of us are in debt. Of course there are a difference in the amount of our debts. Some have sinned far more than others. But whether our debt be little or much, we have nothing at all with which to pay it. We could not more easily pay the fifty than the five hundred pence. He forgave them *both*. It is just as easy for God to forgive the greatest sins as the smallest. He *forgave* them. That is the only way we can ever get clear of our sins.

A king owed a large sum to one of his nobles, but could not pay it. The nobleman made a great feast in honour of his king. A fire of perfumed woods burned on the hearth. During the feast the host brought out all the king's notes and cast them into the fire, thus obliterating beyond possibility of restoration every evidence of his indebtedness. That is the way God does with our sins. Into the fragrant flames of Christ's sacrifice He casts them all, and they will never be heard of more.

There is a story of a half-witted boy whose idea of forgiveness was beautiful. He said that Jesus came and *with His red hand* rubbed out all his sins. A quaint man used to carry a little book, which he took very often from his pocket, and which he called his " biography." It had only three leaves, and there was not a word written on any of them ; yet he said the book told the whole story of his life. The first leaf was black : that was his sin ; that was his condition by nature. He would shudder when he looked at it. The second was red : that was the blood of Christ ; and his face glowed when he gazed upon it. The third was white : that was himself washed in Christ's blood, made whiter than snow. His book told the whole story of every redeemed life. Between the black of our sins and the white of redemption must always come the red of Christ's blood.

June 5

peace with pardon

" *Thy faith hath saved thee ; go in peace.*"—LUKE vii. 50

SAVED! This poor, shame-soiled, sin-ruined thing, that the Pharisee would have thrust out of his house into the street—*saved !* Never to go back any more to her old life ! An heir of heaven now, destined to walk the heavenly streets in white ! There is an old legend that Mohammed once in passing along the way touched a plant of mallows, and it became a geranium, and has ever since been a geranium, pouring fragrance everywhere. No matter about the legend, but Christ did something far more wonderful on the day of our story. He touched this sinful soul, and it was transformed into beauty. That woman has been in glory for eighteen centuries. That is what Christ does for every one who creeps to His feet in penitence and faith.

Peace came with the forgiveness. There could be no peace until she was forgiven. No one has any right to be at peace while the guilt of sin remains uncancelled. But when Christ has forgiven us we should be at peace. Why or of what should we then be afraid ? What is there for us to fear in this world or the next ?

There is a story of one in the olden days who had committed a capital crime. He was the king's friend and favourite ; and when his trial came on, although the case went sorely against him, he manifested no fear. The evidence accumulated. There was no loophole of escape from conviction. His friends had no hope, yet they marvelled at *his* calmness—he was at perfect peace. He was convicted, and was about to be sentenced ; still there was in his features no trace of alarm. At the last moment the secret was revealed. He drew from his bosom a paper, and handed it to the judge. It was the king's pardon. With that in his possession he had no cause for fear. And with our King's pardon, no matter how guilty we are, we have no need to be afraid, and may be at peace.

Right Enthusiasm

" When His friends heard of it......they said, He is beside Himself."—MARK iii. 21

EVEN our Lord's relatives did not understand Him. His life was so unworldly that it could not be measured by the ordinary standards. Here they could account for His unconquerable zeal only by concluding that He was insane. We hear much of the same kind of talk in modern days when some devoted follower of Christ utterly forgets self in love for his Master. People say, " He must be insane ! " They think every man is crazy whose religion kindles into any sort of unusual fervour, or who grows more earnest than the average Christian in work for the Master. Some of Paul's friends thought he was crazy when he went sweeping over land and sea to carry the gospel to every city. But his answer was, " No, I am not crazy ; the love of Christ constraineth me."

That is a good sort of insanity. It is a sad pity that it is so rare. If there were more of it there would not be so many unsaved souls dying under the very shadow of our churches ; it would not be so hard to get missionaries and money to send the gospel to the dark continents ; there would not be so many empty pews in our churches, so many long pauses in our prayer-meetings, so few to teach in our Sabbath schools. It would be a glorious thing if all Christians were beside themselves as the Master was, or as Paul was.

It is a far worse insanity which in this world never gives a thought to any other world ; which, moving continually among lost men, never pities them, nor thinks of their lost condition, nor puts forth any effort to save them. It is easier to keep a cool head and a colder heart, and to give ourselves no concern about perishing souls : but we are our brothers' keepers, and no malfeasance in duty can be worse than that which pays no heed to their eternal salvation.

June 7

A Beacon Light

" *He that shall blaspheme against the Holy Ghost hath never forgiveness.*"—MARK iii. 29

FEW words in the Bible have caused more anxiety and fear than these. Learned men do not agree in their idea as to what it is to blaspheme against the Holy Ghost. But no matter about the exact meaning of the words ; they stand here as a warning against a terrible danger. They are like a red light hung over a perilous rock. While we may not know just what constitutes the sin, it certainly is our duty to keep as far from its edge as possible.

And surely all wilful and determined resistance to the influence of the Holy Spirit is a step toward this point of awful peril. This utterance of our Lord should lead us to treat with the utmost reverence every appeal, persuasion, or bidding of the Holy Ghost, never to resist, but always to yield to His every influence. We have no other Friend in this world who can guide us home. If we drive Him away from us for ever, we shall be left in the darkness of eternal night. How long we may continue to reject Him and not go beyond the line that marks the limit of hope we know not ; but the very thought that there is such a line somewhere ought to startle us into instant acceptance of the offered guidance.

> " Oh, where is this mysterious line
> That crosses every path,—
> The hidden boundary between
> God's patience and His wrath ?
>
> " How far may we go on in sin ?
> How long will God forbear ?
> Where does hope end, and where begin
> The confines of despair ?
>
> " An answer from the skies is sent :
> ' Ye that from God depart,
> While it is called To-day, repent,
> And harden not your heart.' "

Christ's Relations

"Whosoever shall do the will of God, the same is My brother, and My sister, and mother."—MARK iii. 35

THIS seems too good to be true. To be the brother or the sister of Jesus—did you ever try to think out what it means ? Then for every Christian to be taken by Christ into as close and tender a relationship as His own mother sustained to Him—did you ever try to think that out, remembering that you are the one taken into this loving fellowship ?

Thousands of women have wished that they could have had Mary's honour in being the mother of Jesus. Well, here it lies close to their hand. They cannot have Mary's distinction in this world, but they can have a place just as near to the heart of the Christ as she has. How strange it is that sinful creatures can be taken thus into the very family of God, and have all the privileges and joys of the children of God ! We cannot understand it, but let us believe it and think of it until it fills our hearts with warmth and gladness. We do not begin to realize the blessedness and glory of being a Christian. There is a picture which, seen in one light, shows a poor, weary pilgrim, lying on a miserable pallet in a dreary garret ; but seen in another light the same picture shows a saint of God, an heir of glory, arrayed in white robes, surrounded and carried up by angels to heavenly glory. The first view is that which human eyes see in the Christian ; the other is the reality —that which heaven sees.

But we must not overlook the first part of this verse, that tells us who are received into this close relationship— " whosoever shall do the will of God." At every point as we go on, we catch more and more distinctly the teaching that obedience to God is part of the faith that saves. We must do God's will, and follow Christ with loving fidelity, if we would obtain the privilege of being the brothers and sisters of Christ.

June 9

Always on Duty

"*A certain Pharisee besought Him to dine with him: and He went in, and sat down to meat.*"—LUKE xi. 37

OUR Lord was not ashamed to be the guest of publicans and sinners, but neither did He reject the invitations of the rich and influential. He was ready to go wherever there was an opportunity of doing good, even to social feasts and large dinner-parties. Of course we are safe in following His example; but we must read on a little farther, and then we shall see that He always used these opportunities as occasions of doing good.

We may go to any place where we can do the part of a messenger of God to other souls. We are never to be off duty as Christians, and as Christians we must be always Christ's servants, ready to bear blessings from Him to others. We are to be sure, before we accept an invitation to any place, that our Master has an errand there for us. Then when we go, we are to improve the occasion for doing good in some way to some who are there. Christ never went to any such places of amusement as offer their temptation to young people in these days; and yet this same principle applies to these. "Is it right for me to attend the theatre or the dancing-party?" Well, can you go there as a Christian? Can you confess Christ there? Can you talk of Him to others? Can you ask His blessing on your going? Can you go as His messenger, sure that He sends you there? It is time we began to look at these matters very honestly and frankly. If we are Christians, we are to be Christians seven days in the week and everywhere.

Then we are to be Christians always on duty. A young clergyman who had been reproved by his bishop for certain unministerial conduct, sought to excuse himself by saying that he was not on duty at the time. The bishop replied, "A clergyman is never off duty." This is true of every Christian. Wherever we go we represent our Master.

Covetousness

*" Take heed, and beware of covetousness : for a man's life
consisteth not in the abundance of the things which he
possesseth."*—LUKE xii. 15

THIS is one of the red flags our Lord hung out which
most people nowadays do not seem much to regard.
Christ said a great deal about the danger of riches ; but
not many persons are afraid of riches. Covetousness is
not practically considered a sin in these times. If a man
breaks the sixth or eighth commandment, he is branded as
a criminal and covered with shame ; but he may break the
tenth, and he is only enterprising. The Bible says the love
of money is a root of all evil ; but every man who quotes
the saying puts a terrific emphasis on the word " love,"
explaining that it is not money, but only the love of it,
that is such a prolific root.

To look about one, one would think a man's life *did*
consist in the abundance of the things he possesses. Men
think they become great just in proportion as they gather
wealth. So it seems, too ; for the world measures men by
their bank-account. Yet there never was a more fatal
error. A man is really measured by what he *is*, and not
by what he *has*. You may find a shrivelled soul in the
midst of a great fortune, and a grand, noble soul in the
barest poverty.

The first thing is to gather into our life all the truly
great and noble things of character. Here are two texts
to ponder, because they settle this question : " Whatsoever
things are true, whatsoever things are honest, whatsoever
things are just, whatsoever things are pure, whatsoever
things are lovely, whatsoever things are of good report......
think on these things "—" Add to your faith virtue ; and
to virtue, knowledge ; and to knowledge, temperance ; and
to temperance, patience ; and to patience, godliness ; and
to godliness, brotherly kindness ; and to brotherly kindness, charity."

Heart=Hardening

" And when he sowed, some seeds fell by the wayside."
MATT. xiii. 4

HOW are human hearts beaten into a highway ? A child's heart is sensitive to every impression. But as it grows older, the thousand influences, feelings, emotions, imaginations, treading over it continuously, trample it into hardness. Every time a young man feels conviction of sin and does not turn from the sin, his heart is left a little less tender. Every time he feels that he ought to do a certain thing and does not do it, allowing the good impulse to pass, he is left a little less sensitive to good impressions afterward.

The same effect is produced by the common experiences of life. The wheels and carts of business go lumbering over the heart. We ought to have our hearts fenced in, and allow none of these heavy wagons to pass over them. A business man ought to keep his heart soft and warm in the midst of all his business, tender as a little child's, humble, teachable, loving, trusting. He ought to have a sanctuary in his inner life into which no unhallowed foot, none but the priestly foot of heavenly guests, should ever pass. But too many make their hearts an open common, till they are beaten into a callousness that nothing can impress.

Another way is by the feet of sinful habits. There was an old legend of a goblin horseman that galloped over men's fields at night ; and wherever his foot struck, the soil was so blasted that nothing would ever grow on it again. So is it with the heart over which the beastly feet of lust, of sensuality, of greed, of selfishness, of passion, are allowed to tread. There is an impression that it does young people no harm to indulge in sin for a time, if they afterward repent. No more fatal falsehood was ever whispered by the tempter into any ear. The heart that is trodden over by vile lusts or indulgences of any kind is never the same again.

Rootless Graces

" *Some fell upon stony places.*"—MATT. xiii. 5

THERE is a thin covering of soil on the rock. The seed sinks in a little way, and the heat radiating from the rock causes it to shoot up at once. This represents a class whose religion is emotional. At first they give great promise. They are easily moved by any appeal. The feelings work immediately to the surface. Such persons always seem most affected by sorrow. They weep inconsolably ; but their grief is soonest over. In like manner they appear to be most deeply affected by religious appeals. They begin a Christian life with an earnestness that puts older Christians to shame. They attend all meetings ; they weep as they sing and pray ; they talk of Christ to their friends ; their zeal is wonderful. " Immediately it sprang up, because it had no depth of earth."

But such quick growths lack root, and cannot endure the heat of summer. The sun soon scorches them, and they wither. In spiritual life, also, the analogy holds. Emotional religion is not apt to be permanent. It bursts up into great luxuriance to-day, but we are not sure that it will be found to-morrow in healthy life. Too often the enthusiasm is but transient. In the heat of trials, temptations, toil, or sorrow the rootless graces wilt down and die.

Usually the religious life that is most permanent is that which springs up naturally, and grows slowly to strength and luxuriance. It has good soil, and the roots go down deep into the earth, and are unaffected by the frequent changes in temperature, by heat or cold, by rain or drought.

If any one finds that his spiritual graces are rootless, and that there is a hard rock in his heart underneath the surface, he should seek at once to have the rock broken by penitence and prayer, that the plants of righteousness in him may have opportunity to grow.

What of the Root?

" Because they had no root, they withered away."

MATT. xiii. 6

A ROOT is very important in a plant or a tree. One may take a green branch from a living tree and set it in the ground, and for a little while it may seem to be living ; but soon, under the sun's heat, it will wither. It has no root. The root is not a very beautiful part of a tree—it is hidden away out of sight, and nobody praises it ; yet it is essential to the tree's life. In like manner there is a hidden part in every Christian's life. It does not seem to bless the world in any way. It is the heart-life—faith, love, communion with God in His Word and in prayer. No one praises a Christian's inner, closet life ; it is secret, and no one sees it : yet it is the root of the whole strong, beautiful life which men do see and praise, and whose ripe fruits feed their hunger.

Our Lord says the trouble with these shallow-soil people is that they have no root in themselves—that is, there is not in their heart that root-principle of Christian life which consists of faith in Christ and love to Him. Where there is such a root no persecution can tear it away, no outward circumstances can affect the permanence of its life. It is not kept alive by any external influences. Its source is in the heart. It feeds on heavenly food. Temptations and persecutions only make the true Christian purpose all the stronger.

But it is not so with this superficial religion. It has no inward life of its own. It is not produced by an unconquerable love in the heart for Christ. It depends simply on external excitement—revival meetings, some favourite preacher, some special form of worship, the influence of some friend—something, at least, in the outer circumstances which keeps the emotions in play for a time. But it has no root in itself ; and in such a religion there is nothing to carry a life very far through experiences of trial.

Uhat are the Thorns?

" Some fell among thorns, and the thorns grew up, and choked it, and it yielded no fruit."—MARK iv. 7

THE thorns had been chopped off, but their roots were still in the ground. Then as the seed began to grow, so did the thorns ; and growing faster and more rankly than the wheat, they soon choked it out, so that it came to nothing in the end. What are these thorns ? Our Lord says they are " the cares of this world, and the deceitfulness of riches." " Cares " are anxieties, distractions, worries. Martha was in danger of having the good seed in her heart choked out by her distracting thoughts about her household affairs. Many a promising Christian life has been dwarfed and stunted from the same cause. " The deceitfulness of riches : " thousands of spiritual lives have been starved into ghostly leanness by the desire for riches. " The lusts of other things entering in, choke the word." We have all seen people who began well ; but as cares multiplied or riches increased, their zeal waned. We need, however, to look to our own hearts, and we shall probably have enough to do if we keep out all the thorns and weeds in the one little garden committed to us.

Jesus did not say these people are not Christians, but that they " bring no fruit to perfection." The distractions of this life, the deceitfulness of riches, the lusts of other things, entering in, choke the spiritual life, stunting its graces. They lose the sweet comforts of a healthy faith. The fruits of the Spirit in them are shrivelled. They may go on working in the church, preaching, teaching, praying, but the life is wanting. What is the lesson ? This : we need to watch without ceasing these hearts of ours, and let no weed or brier grow there for a day. Sometimes God Himself does the weeding. He lifts out of the bosom the earthly object that is absorbing all the heart's love. The process is sore, but the results are full of blessing.

June 15

Golden Grain

" The sower soweth the word."—MARK iv. 14

THE human heart is only the soil. Its natural products are thorns and briers. These grow without sowing and without cultivation. We do not need to be taught in order to be wicked. But if good things are to grow in our hearts, they must be sown and cultivated. The seeds must be brought from heaven. This is just what has been done. The words of the Bible are Divine seeds. They have a wondrous power in themselves. Like natural seeds, they grow when planted, and produce plants of righteousness. Bare like the desert, or rather grown all over with rank weeds and briers, like neglected gardens, until the Sower comes are our hearts by nature; yet if we receive the good seed with faith and love, our lives are changed, and are made to blossom like the rose.

There is another thought : all of us may be sowers of this good seed. We must take heed that we really sow the " word." There is no other seed that will yield the harvest of spiritual life. The words of God have life in them. " The words that I speak unto you," said the Master, " they are spirit, and they are life." If we get these heavenly seeds into people's hearts, we shall not look in vain for fruits.

It is a holy privilege to be permitted to help the great Husbandman in the sowing of this precious seed. We can carry the golden grains with us, and drop them wherever we go. This we can do by being full of the Word, thus having something to give for every experience. We can sow the seed by the judicious giving of tracts and leaflets. We can do it by writing letters to carry to others some truth suited to their need. Then we can live so sweetly that our daily influence will be a scattering of heavenly seed all about us. Then some day we shall stand before the great Husbandman, our bosom full of golden sheaves.

Hidden Lights

" Is a candle brought to be put under a bushel, or under a bed ? "—MARK iv. 21

NO one would think of doing such a thing. People always set a lamp where it will give the most light. It would be very absurd to cover it up so that its beams could not pour out. Yet that is just what a great many people do with their Christian life. It is a very striking figure this that our Lord uses when describing Christians. He calls them lights, lamps, candles, which He lights with the fire of His own life when they believe on Him. There is much difference in the brightness of the light in different believers. Some are only little tapers ; others are great lights. But even a taper makes one spot a little brighter.

The point of our Lord's teaching here is that the light is not to be hidden or covered up, but permitted to shine. Yet some people do indeed put their candle under a bushel. They carry it so that it never gives light to others. Sometimes they hide it away under an imagined modesty or humility. They do not want to " put themselves forward " —it would seem presumptuous. Sometimes it is the " bushel " of timidity or bashfulness under which they hide their light. One cannot rise to say a word in the prayer-meeting ; another cannot even conduct family worship in the midst of his own household ; another cannot talk to a neighbour about his soul ; another cannot stand up to make a public confession of Christ before the world ; another cannot go to call on a poor family or sick person, or to offer consolation to one in sorrow—all because they are " too backward." Some again hide their candle under a very imperfect life. Their faults obscure the light of the religious knowledge they possess, as a dirty glass chimney dims a lamp's shining. There are a great many lamps hidden away under bushels which ought to be shining to some purpose.

June 17

Profitable Bearing

" *Take heed what ye hear.*"—MARK iv. 24

THIS is a very important counsel. " Take heed what ye hear." The things we hear enter into our souls and become part of our being ; they give form and colour to our character. There have come infinite blessings from the printing-press. There are thousands of good books, whose pages are like leaves from the tree of life, for the healing of the nations. But there are also thousands of evil books, whose pages reek with poison, and scatter influences of moral and spiritual death. With all this great mass of books, good and bad, it is vitally important that we take heed what we hear. We would not eat poisoned food ; why should we take poison into our souls ?

If we open our ears to the evil things that are continually spoken on all sides, and that come to us on vile printed pages, our hearts will become foul and unclean, and our lives will be debauched. We should shut our ears to all that is unholy. Many a now utterly ruined life dates the beginning of its debasement from the moment when an impure word was whispered in a listening ear, or when a vile book or paper was secretly read. On the other hand, every beautiful life has been made beautiful by what it has heard. We are saved by words. Pure, true words are transforming.

The Bible is simply a book of words ; but every word contains a revelation of some beautiful thing in character or attainment which we should strive to reach. We should always gladly, because we may always safely and profitably, hear the words of God. Then we should open our ears to the voice that speaks in every good book. We should take heed what we hear. Then we must not forget the Master's other counsel, " Take heed *how* ye hear." We should hear thoughtfully, reverently, obediently, letting the good words of God into our heart, that they may transform our life.

"After Many Days."

"The earth bringeth forth fruit of herself."—MARK iv. 28.

YET not without certain other influences upon it. If the sun does not shine upon it, and if there is no rain from heaven, the seed will never germinate, however rich the soil. The human heart is the soil in which the seeds of truth grow; but it must have the sunshine and rain of Divine grace upon it before it will produce any spiritual fruit.

A gentleman tore down an outbuilding that had stood for many years in his yard. He smoothed over the ground and left it. The warm spring rains fell upon it, and the sunshine flooded it; and in a few days there sprang up multitudes of little flowers, unlike any that grew in the neighbourhood. Where the building had stood was once a garden, and the seeds had lain in the soil without moisture, light, or warmth all the years. So soon as the sunshine and the rain touched them they sprang up into life and beauty.

So ofttimes the seeds of truth lie long in a human heart, growing not, because the light and warmth of the Holy Spirit are shut away from them by sin and unbelief; but after long years the heart is opened in some way to the influences of the Divine Spirit, and the seeds, living still, shoot up into beauty. The instructions of a mother may lie in a heart, fruitless, from childhood to old age, and yet at last may save the soul.

When we have sown the heavenly seed, we should continually pray that God would pour His Spirit, like rain and sunshine, upon the heart where it lies to quicken it into life. Then, for ourselves, we should seek always to keep our hearts open to every invigorating influence of the grace of God. We need to pray constantly for the rain to come down, else our hearts will lie bare and sterile, though filled with the Divine seeds.

June 19

Progress

" First the blade, then the ear, after that the full corn in the ear."—MARK iv. 28

WE understand this well enough in nature, but do we in spiritual life ? The beginnings of Christian life are very feeble and imperfect. We must not expect in young converts the maturity of character we look for in older Christians. Grace begins in a small way. We have no right to look at once for the ripened fruits of Christian experience. But the wheat does not stop at the tender blade ; it shoots up into a strong stalk, at last into ripeness. Christian lives should grow ; they have no right to stay always at the starting-point. They should grow in knowledge, in power, in purpose, in achievement, until they put forth all the fruits of the Spirit, and grow into the ripeness of Christian experience.

We are to notice here also that while the growth is secret its results are manifest. The processes of spiritual life are invisible, but the results are not. If a Christian is growing in grace, we shall know it by his life. He will wear more and more of the image of Christ, and the " mind of Christ " will appear more and more in his disposition and conduct.

Another thought suggested here is that the beginnings of Christian life in young Christians ought to be most gently nurtured by those who are their spiritual overseers. The tender blades cannot endure a frost. Young converts cannot endure the sharp trials and temptations of this world. A clergyman is reported as saying, " I do not dare to bring too many children into my Church—not because I do not believe in their sincerity and piety and fitness for Church membership, but because there is no provision for their growth and nurture after they are in the Church." Could any sadder confession be made ? Something must be wrong with the Church when this is true. Let the words stand for the pondering of those whom they concern.

Dropping Seeds

" The kingdom of heaven is like to a grain of mustard seed ......the least of all seeds : but when it is grown, it...... becometh a tree."—MATT. xiii. 31, 32

MANY great histories of blessing may be traced back to a very small seed. A woman whose name is forgotten dropped a tract or little book in the way of a man named Richard Baxter. He picked it up and read it, and it led him to Christ. He became a holy Christian, and wrote a book entitled " A Call to the Unconverted," which brought many persons to the Saviour, and among others Philip Doddridge. Philip Doddridge in turn wrote " The Rise and Progress of Religion," which led many into the kingdom of God, among them the great Wilberforce. Wilberforce wrote " A Practical View of Christianity," which was the means of saving a multitude, among them Legh Richmond. In his turn Legh Richmond wrote the book called " The Dairyman's Daughter," which has been instrumental in the conversion of many thousands.

The dropping of that one little tract seemed a very small thing to do ; but see what a wonderful, many-branched tree has sprung from it ! This is only one illustration of marvels of grace coming from the most minute grains of the heavenly seed. One seed planted in a heart, dropped by some very humble worker, perhaps unconsciously, may not only save a soul for an eternity of blessedness, but may start a series of Divine influences which shall reach thousands of other lives. A simple invitation from his brother brought Simon to Jesus ; and what a tree sprang from *that* seed !

Let us go on, day by day, dropping seeds into as many hearts as we can. We may not always know what comes of them, but from any one of them may spring a history of blessing which shall reach thousands of souls. The branches of the tree from one seed may spread over all lands.

June 21

"The Other Side"

"He saith unto them, Let us pass over unto the other side."
MARK iv. 35

CHRIST is continually saying the same to us, though with varying meaning in His words. He is ever calling us to pass over some line into new fields, with their new experiences, new privileges, new duties, new conflicts, new joys.

He says it to the impenitent when He graciously invites them to become His disciples. He wants them to cut loose from this world, from sin and all their old dead past, and rise up and go with Him to the better life which lies beyond. He invites them to His Father's country, into His Father's family. It is a land of blessing and of beauty, of plenty and of great riches. True, there is a sea that must be crossed to reach it. No one can reach the glorious country on " the other side " without passing over this sea, and no one can pass over without encountering tempests. There are fierce temptations, sore self-denials, mighty struggles, and many losses and sorrows, before we can reach heaven ; but the reward is so great that we should be ready to endure any hardship or suffering to win it.

Then Christ gives the same call and invitation to His people when they reach the end of earthly life and when He comes to take them home. Before them then rolls the sea of death, dark and full of terrors to the natural sense. They shrink from crossing it. Yet there is no reason why they should. On " the other side " glory waits. There is the Father's house with the many mansions. And however dark and terrible may seem the narrow sea that has to be crossed, there is no danger ; for Jesus Himself accompanies His people, and none of them can perish. But if we would have this final invitation to come over to the other side into the heavenly glory, we must accept the first call to come over out of the old life of sin into the new life of holiness.

Life's Storms

" There arose a great tempest in the sea."—MATT. viii. 24

THE disciples had not put out to sea of their own suggestion. Had they done so without Christ's bidding, they would not have had the same reason to expect protection and deliverance. The lesson we learn here is this—that storms may arise even when we are in the plain line of duty. We should not be discouraged by the difficulty or trouble that comes, and conclude that we are in the wrong path.

We see, too, that Christ's presence with His disciples does not keep the storms away. There are no promises in the Bible that Christian people shall not meet trials. Religion builds no high walls about us to break the force of the winds. Troubles come to the Christian just as surely as to the worldly man. There are the storms of temptation ; these sweep down with sudden and terrific power from the cold mountains of this world. Then there are storms of sickness, of disappointment and adversity, of sorrow, that make the waves and billows to roll over the soul.

On the Sea of Galilee travellers say that a boat will be gliding along smoothly over a glassy surface, unbroken by a ripple, when suddenly, without a moment's warning, a tempest will sweep down, and almost instantly the boat will be tossed in the angry waves. Thus many of life's storms come. Temptations come when we are not looking for them. So disasters come. We are at peace in a happy home. At an hour when we think not, without warning, the darling child we love so much lies dead in our arms. The friend we trusted, and who we thought could never fail us, proves false. The hopes cherished for years wither in our hands in a night, like flowers when the frost comes. The storms of life are nearly all sudden surprises. They do not hang out danger-signals days before to warn us. The only way to be ready for them is to be always ready.

June 23

Faithless Fear

" They awake Him, and say unto Him, Master, carest Thou not that we perish ? "—MARK iv. 38

THESE words imply that the disciples thought Jesus was indifferent to them in their danger—that He was neglecting them by sleeping while they were exposed to such peril. But how unjust was this reproach ! They were never safer than they were that moment, in the midst of the wild tempest. The bark that bore the Lord could not sink in the sea. Faith should have trusted in the darkness.

Yet do we never, at least in our hearts, make the same complaint of our Lord ? When we are in some sore trial, and the trial grows very sore, and He does not come to deliver us ; when we seem about to be engulfed by the waves of adversity, and no relief comes down from Him— do we never say, " Jesus does not care though I perish " ? When we pray long and with importunity for the lifting away of some heavy cross, or the lightening of some sore burden, and no answer comes, does the thought never arise in our minds that Jesus does not hear us, or that He does not come to us ?

But such complaint is never just. Sometimes He may seem not to care. The disciples had some lessons to learn. One was, how helpless they were in themselves in the world's dangers. Another was, that Christ alone could deliver them. They could not learn these lessons save in the storm with the Master asleep. So there are similar lessons that we never can learn until Christ withholds His help for a time. And sometimes He hides Himself for a season just to teach us faith. But He is never indifferent to us. He never neglects or forgets us. His heart ever wakes and watches, and at the right moment He comes and brings deliverance. We should learn to trust our Lord so confidently that in any hour of danger we can nestle down in His bosom, without fear or anxiety, and let Him take care of us.

The Hearer of Prayer.

" *And He awoke.*"—MARK iv. 39 (Revised Version).

THE roar of the storm He did not hear in His sound sleep; but the moment there was a cry from His disciples for help He instantly awoke. What a revelation of heart have we here! He is never asleep to His people when they call Him. Amid the wildest tumults of this world He ever hears the faintest cry of prayer. Nor is He ever too weary to listen to the supplications of human distress.

We have another illustration of this same quickness to hear prayer in the hours of our Lord's sufferings on the cross. His life was fast ebbing away. His own agony was intense beyond description. Around Him surged a storm of human passion. Curses fell upon His ear. But amid all this tempest of hate He was silent. To all these bitter insults and keen reproaches He answered not a word. Then amid the derisions and jeers of the multitude there broke a voice of prayer. It came from one of the crosses beside Him. It was the penitential cry of a soul—" Lord, remember me." And in all the tumult of the hour He heard this feeble supplication. In His own agony He gave instant answer. Doubt not that this Jesus always hears prayer. His love is ever on the watch, ready to catch the faintest note of human distress.

Though aroused so suddenly in the midst of such scenes of terror, Jesus awoke calm and peaceful. Dean Trench says : " It is such cases as these—cases of sudden, unexpected terror, met without a moment of preparation— which test a man what spirit he is of, which show not only his nerve, but the grandeur and purity of his whole nature." Here we have an illustration of what Christ's peace was, and of what He meant when He said, " *My* peace I give unto you." It was thus He moved through all the turbulent scenes of His earthly life.

June 25

Christ in the Storm

" *He......rebuked the wind, and said unto the sea, Peace, be still.*"—MARK iv. 39

HE spoke to the storm and to the tossing sea as if they were intelligent creatures—just as a man would speak to his servants. The truth we learn here is that He is Lord of nature ; that the elements recognize His voice, and obey Him even in their wildest moods. If we only fully believed this, it would bring a great deal of peace to our lives. No tempest ever breaks from the control of Him who is our Lord and Redeemer. No wave ever rolls any farther than He permits. There is nothing in this world that is not under the sway of the hand that was nailed on the cross.

There is a story of a Christian army officer at sea with his family in a storm. There was great terror among the passengers, but he was calm. His wife, in her consternation, chided him, saying that he ought to be concerned for her and the children, if not for himself, in such danger. He made no reply, but soon came to her with his sword drawn, and with a stern countenance pointed it at her heart. She was not the least alarmed, but looked up into his face with a smile. " What ! " said he, " are you not afraid when a drawn sword is at your breast ? " " No," she replied, " not when I know it is in the hands of one that loves me." " And would you have me," he asked, " to be afraid of this tempest when I know it to be in the hand of my heavenly Father, who loves me ? "

Thus even in the wild tumults of nature we should be at peace, since our Saviour is Lord of nature. Some one tells of being at sea in a terrible cyclone, and of seeing a little bird fly down, when the storm was at its height, and light on the crest of a wave, where it sat as quietly as if it had been perching on some green bough in the quiet forest. So should the believer in Christ repose in quietness and confidence in the wildest terror.

June 26

"Depart from Us."

" They began to pray Him to depart."—MARK v. 17

THIS is one of the saddest sentences in the Gospels. We can scarcely conceive of any person asking Jesus to go away. He had come to their coast to bring them rich blessings. His hands were full of golden gifts. He had power to heal the sick, to open blind eyes, to make the lame walk, to scatter all kinds of blessings among the people. He had begun His work of grace as soon as He landed by curing their most terrible case of demon-possession. He would have gone on performing other works of mercy and love if they had not besought Him to depart. It was probably all because of the loss of the swine. If that was the way Christ's work was going to affect them, they did not want Him to go any farther.

Some people feel the same way when a work of grace begins in their community. They are opposed to Christianity because it interferes with their business. Rum-sellers and saloon-keepers oppose revivals, because when the devil is cast out of men they stop drinking and card-playing, and so these men's business suffers ; they are against Christianity because Christianity is against them. So all of us are apt to want Christ to depart from us when He interferes with our cherished plans. We need to be careful lest we send Christ altogether away from us.

For He did not stay after these people asked Him to go away. He would not stay where He was not wanted. He carried back the gifts He had come there to leave. The sick remained unhealed that He would have healed, and the lame continued lame, and the demoniacs remained possessed, and the dying whom He would have restored passed away. Does any one now ever ask Christ to depart when He comes with blessings ? Does Jesus never turn away from any heart now because He is not wanted, because He is rejected ?

June 27

They that are Sick

" *They that are whole have no need of the physician, but they that are sick.*"—MARK ii. 17

THAT was the answer of Jesus to the murmuring about His presence among the disreputable people at Matthew's feast. The Pharisees thought He was compromising Himself in sitting down at the table with such characters. Their insinuated inference was that He must belong to the same class Himself. But Jesus gave them a wise and good answer. These wicked and sinful ones were the very classes that needed Him most. It was just with Him as with a physician The physician does not go about visiting the people who are in excellent health. Those who are well do not need the physician, but the sick and plague-stricken need him ; and the sorer their sickness, the worse their diseases, the more do they require his presence and his service.

No one would ever find fault with a physician for going into sick-rooms, and into hospitals, and into plague-infested districts. No one would ever suggest that he must have a low and vitiated taste because of the kind of people among whom he spends his time. It was just the same with Him, Jesus said. He had come to this world expressly to save sinners. Surely, then, He could not be blamed for going where sinners were ; and the worse the sinners the more reason there was why He should be found there. Good people, like those who criticised Him, did not need His services ; but wherever He found a poor, lost sinner, there was one of the persons He had come to help and save.

One suggestion is that, like their Master, Christ's disciples should try to carry the gospel to the lowest classes. We should not mingle among the wicked as companions ; but when we strive to save them we are becoming Christ to them. Another lesson is that no sinner need ever despair of hope, since the worse he is the more surely is Christ willing to save him.

Joy in the Lord

" Can the children of the bride-chamber fast while the bride-groom is with them ? "—MARK ii. 19

THIS was our Lord's answer to those who thought His religion was too sunny and joyous—that it had not fast-days enough in it. They thought that religion was genuine only when it made people sad, and that its quality was just in proportion to its gloom. But Christ's reply showed that mournful faces are no essential indicators of heart-piety. Should His disciples be mournful and sad when He was with men, filling their lives with the gladness of His presence ? Should Christians profess to be heavy-hearted, wearing the symbols of grief, when they are really filled with joy, and when there is no occasion for sorrow ? Why should one who has been saved by the Lord Jesus, and who is rejoicing in full assurance of hope, go about in sackcloth and ashes ? Is there any piety in a sad face ? Does God love to see His children always in mourning ? Is human joy displeasing to our Father ?

All these questions are answered here in our Lord's words. He does not wish His disciples to go mourning and fasting when they have no occasion for such exercises. His words are a defence of Christian joyfulness. Christ wants His friends to be glad. There is an utter incongruity in a sad and mournful Christian life. By its very nature true religion is joyous. Our sins are forgiven. We are adopted into God's family. We are heirs of God, and joint-heirs with Christ. The covenant of love arches its shelter over us all the while. All things in this world work together for our good, and then glory waits for us beyond death's gates. With all this blessed heritage, why should we be mournful and sad ? While we enjoy the smile of Christ, the consciousness of His love, the assurance of His forgiveness, and the hope of heaven and eternal life, what should make us sad ? We should have radiant faces.

June 29

A New Garment

" *No man seweth a piece of new cloth on an old garment.*"
MARK ii. 21

CHRIST did not come into this world to patch up an old religion, merely to mend a hole here, and beautify a spot there, and add a touch to this part or that; He came to make all things new. And when He saves a sinner, He does not propose merely to mend him up a little here and there, to cover over some bad spots in him, and to close up rents in his character by strong patches of the new cloth of grace. Gospel work is not patchwork. Christ does not sew on pieces; He weaves a new garment without seam throughout.

So we may try from without to make human character lovely; but there is sin in its very fibre, and the blemishes will ever work out and mar all. The only way is to have a new heart, and then the beauty will be real and will endure. A mother lost by death a lovely and precious child—her only child. To occupy her heart and hand in some way about her vanished treasure, and thus fill the empty hours, she took up a photograph of her child and began to touch it with her skilful fingers. Soon, as she wrought, the features became almost lifelike. The picture was then laid away for a few days, and when she sought it again, the eyes were dimmed and the face was marred with ugly blotches. Patiently she went over it a second time, and the bewitching beauty came again. A second time it was laid away, and again the blotches appeared. There was something wrong in the paper on which the photograph had been taken. There were chemicals lurking in it which in some way marred the delicate colours, and no amount of repainting could correct the faults. So is it in human lives. No outside reform is enough, for all the while the heart is evil within, and it sends up its pollution, staining the fairest beauty. The change that is permanent must be wrought in the heart.

At the Point of Death

" *There cometh one of the rulers......and besought Him greatly, saying, My little daughter lieth at the point of death.*"—MARK v. 22, 23

THERE is nothing like trouble to drive people to Christ. So long as things go on prosperously, many men do not ask any favours of Him ; but when sickness or great need comes, He is the first to whom they turn. This is one of the most obvious uses of trouble. God stirs up many an earthly nest in which His children are reposing too softly, that they may be compelled to try heavenward flights. There are many in heaven now who would never have left the old earthly life had not God sent troubles, sorrows, and adversities.

This father said his little daughter was " at the point of death." This is one point to which every one must come. The paths of earth run in very diverse ways, but they all pass at last the " point of death." It is a point that lies hidden from view ; no one knows the day or the hour when he will come to it, and yet somewhere along the sunny years it waits for every one. Sometimes this point is struck in early youth. Here it is a little girl of twelve that lies " at the point of death." Even the children should think about dying, not as a sad and terrible thing, but as a point to which they must come, and for which they should prepare.

It is a touching sight to see this father falling at Christ's feet. The strongest men break down when their own children are sick or in danger. A man may seem very cold and stern as he carries his load of business, or makes his struggle with the world, or presses toward the goal of his ambition. You think he has no tenderness in him—that he is a man of iron or rock. But let one of his children be stricken down, and your man of iron melts like wax. Behind his stern aspect and all his severity there is a warm spot in his heart where he is gentle as a woman.

The Touch of Faith

" Jesus......turned Him about in the press, and said, Who touched My clothes ? "—MARK v. 30

HOW did He know that one touch amid all the jostlings of the crowd ? The multitude were close about Him, pressing up against Him. The disciples even thought it strange that He should ask such a question. The people could not help touching Him. Ah, but there was one touch different from all the rest ! There was a heart's cry in it, a piteous, earnest supplication. It was not like the jostling of the crowd, an accidental or a thoughtless touch, the mere touch of nearness ; there was a soul in it. So, amid all the rude pressure of the multitude, He recognized it.

In every church-service all are near to Christ, but all are not blessed. All press up against Christ, but some go away as they came, carrying with them sores unhealed, weakness unstrengthened, heart-hunger unfilled. Others, sitting close by, receive rich help. The first, though near, reach out no hand of faith, while the others touch the hem of Christ's garment.

The ordinances of the Church may be compared to telegraph-wires, through which messages are all the while passing. You may climb up and put your ear to the wire, or hold it in your hand ; but you will not hear a word of all the important messages that are flashing through it. But let an operator come with his instrument and attach it, and he hears every word. So in the ordinances we touch the invisible wires that bind heaven and earth together. Along these wires messages are flying—up from earth to heaven, prayers, praises, heart-cries, faith-filled desires ; down from heaven to earth, answers of comfort, cheer, joy, and help, blessings of pardon, healing, life, peace. But many know nothing of all this—no flash of healing, new life, joy, or help comes to them ; they are close, but have no faith-attachment. The others touch by prayer and faith.

The Child of Jairus

" While He yet spake, there came......certain which said, Thy daughter is dead."—MARK v. 35

SO it seemed that Jesus had tarried too long on the road. To us it appears that He ought not to have stopped at all to heal or talk with the woman. The child of Jairus was dying, and there was not a moment to lose. Why did the Master not hasten on and get to her bedside before she died ? But when we read the story through to the end, we are glad that He did stop to heal and help the woman.

One thing we learn from this incident is, that Jesus is never in a hurry. He is never so much engrossed in one case of need that He cannot stop to give attention to another. He is never so pressed for time that we have to wait our turn. No matter what He is doing, He will always hear instantly our cry for need.

A little child's idea of God's listening to her was that when she began to pray God bade all the angels be quiet, saying, " I hear a noise—a little girl's noise ; " and then all the angels kept perfectly still till she said Amen. The angels need not be hushed for God to hear the humblest little one pray ; yet the child was not far wrong.

Another thing we learn from this delay is, that Jesus never comes too late, never waits too long. It certainly seemed that He had tarried too long this time ; but when we see how it all came out, we are sure that He made no mistake. True, the child died while He lingered ; but this only gave Him an opportunity for a greater miracle. He waited that He might do a more glorious work. There is always some good reason for it when Christ delays to answer our prayers or come to our help. He waits that He may do far more for us in the end. So we have one more lesson on letting our Lord have His own way with us, even in answering our prayers. He knows best when to answer, and what answer to give.

July 3

Not Dead, but Sleeping

*" Why make ye this ado, and weep? the damsel is not dead,
but sleepeth."*—MARK v. 39

THE Christian should not sorrow as others do. Christ has brought the truth of immortality out into clear light. We ought to familiarize our minds with the Christian conception of death. Christ wrote no whiter lines anywhere than He wrote over the gateway of the believer's grave. We ought to learn to look at death in the light of Christ's teachings. Too many Christians, however, never seem to have entered into the blessedness of the Saviour's victory over the grave. Here, in the account of this miracle of the raising of the ruler's daughter, we have a beautiful illustration of the way our Lord would have us look at death.

When we lament over our dead He says, " They are not dead, but sleeping. Why do you make all this bitter lamentation ? " Our Christian friends who have died have only passed away out of our sight. They have not ceased to be. Even their bodies only sleep. And as a mother in the morning calls her children and awakes them, so Christ will some day call up from their graves all who sleep in Him.

Sleep is not a terrible experience ; it renews and strengthens the weary body. So the sleep of death is a time of rest and renewal. The calling of this child back from death, and her restoration to her friends, represented what Christ will do for all His people at the end. He will restore friend to friend, and bind up again the broken fragments of households.

There is one point, however, in which the raising of this young girl does not illustrate the final resurrection of believers. She was brought back to resume the old life of toil, struggle, temptation, and sorrow, and to die again. But in the final resurrection believers shall rise to a new, glorious, and immortal life, without sorrow or sin, in the fullness of life, joy, and blessedness.

Words of Wonder

" Many hearing Him were astonished, saying, From whence hath this man these things?"—MARK vi. 2.

THEY could not help being astonished, for Christ's words were full of wisdom. "No man ever spake like this man," they said. Yet, although they were astonished, they did not yield Him their confidence and their love. The outcome of their amazement was only scornful and unbelieving rejection. It is ofttimes the same yet. People cannot help confessing that Christ is wonderful—that He is the most glorious character the world ever saw ; that His teachings are infinitely above all human teachings ; that His power is majestic ; that His love passes all thought. Yet while they grant all this they do not give Him the homage of their hearts. It is as if a drowning man in the sea were to be amazed at the beauty and the completeness of the lifeboat that came to offer him rescue, and should yet sneeringly reject the rescue and stay in the waves to perish.

" From whence hath this man these things ? " they asked in derision and contempt. They knew Him. Some of them had been His playmates and schoolmates in earlier years, and then later His workmates. They knew that He had never been to any but the village school, where they had all attended. How came it that this plain, untaught young man had such wisdom as He now seemed to have, and did such works as were reported of Him ? They could not explain it, and so treated the whole matter with contempt.

We may ask the same question to-day in sincerity of those who reject Christ. Here is a man who spoke the wisest words ever spoken on this earth, and who did the most wonderful works ever performed. Yet He was only a village carpenter, and had only a village school education. How do you account for His wisdom and His power ? " Whence hath this man these things ? " Can it be that He is no more than human ?

July 5

Only a Carpenter

" Is not this the carpenter ? "—MARK vi. 3

CERTAINLY ; yet that refutes nothing. It only helps to prove the claims of Jesus to be the Son of God. If He had been a learned rabbi or philosopher, it might have been said that He had received His wisdom from men ; but as He was only a poor village carpenter, He must have been taught of God.

There are other thoughts which this question suggests. It tells us how wisely Jesus spent His youth and early manhood—not in idleness, but in useful toil, no doubt helping thus to provide for His mother and her family. The example has its inspiring lesson for every young man growing up in the home of his childhood. He should make the years bright with earnest work and the conscientious use of every moment of time.

There really are no pictures of the Christ ; yet there are on the pages of the evangelists pictures of the Christ in certain attitudes, which have their deep meaning for us. Once we see Him with a whip in His hands driving the temple-profaners from their unlawful work. Another time we see Him with a basin and towel. Again we see Him on the cross dying. All these pictures are richly suggestive. Here we see Him as a carpenter, with the saw and the chisel in His hands, and this picture is rich in meaning.

It teaches us that there is no disgrace in working at a trade, since the Son of God wrought as a carpenter. No hands are so beautiful as working hands. Marks of toil are brighter insignia of honour than jewelled rings and delicate whiteness. The picture shows also the condescension of Christ. Though He was rich, He became poor, and even toiled for His daily bread. It assures us, therefore, of His sympathy now with those who toil. It is a pleasant thought that the hands that now hold the sceptre once wielded the hammer and the saw.

The Secret of Power

" Then He called His twelve disciples together, and gave them
power and authority over all devils."—LUKE ix. 1

THE first thing is always to come to Christ Himself. We can do nothing until we have been to Him. We should take every commission from His lips, and go out always with the blessing of His touch upon our heads. It is related of one of Wellington's officers that when commanded, during a battle, to do some perilous duty, he seemed to hesitate. He did not for a moment shrink from the hazardous service, but he said to the Duke, " Let me, before I go, have *one grip of your all-conquering hand*, and then I can do it." There is no duty too perilous, no toil too heavy, no task too responsible, if, as we start, we have the inspiration of Christ's hand-grasp and His cheering words.

Christ alone can give power for the work He bids us do. His followers are to have authority over devils. Any one who tries to cast out devils in his own strength, whether the devils be in himself or in some other, will meet only miserable failure. A man may rule nations and conquer kingdoms, and yet be unable to eject one devil from his own breast. Alexander conquered the world, but he was overthrown by the devils of appetite and passion. Men are for ever foolishly trying to battle unaided with the evil of their own natures; but they fail in the struggle.

The same is true of power over devils in others. Once the disciples, in Christ's absence, tried to cast out an evil spirit, and could not do it. Yet they ought to have been able, in Christ's name, to cast out the demon. Jesus said afterward that the reason they could not do it was that they had not faith. He wants every follower of His to have power over all forms of evil in this world ; not miraculous power, such as He gave the apostles, but real power. And if only we have faith in Him, He will always give us power.

July 7

What We can do for Others

"*He sent them to preach.*"—LUKE ix. 2

APOSTLES are not the only persons to whom Christ gives this same commission. He wants every one that He saves to go out and preach the gospel to others. Christian boys and girls can preach by living a sweet and beautiful life at home, at school, among companions. Beautiful living is the most eloquent of all preaching. There is a story of one who became a Christian ; and when asked under whose preaching he had been converted, he replied : "Under nobody's preaching, but under Aunt Mary's practising." Every one ought to preach by faithful practising.

But there are other ways. There is in the Bible a story of a little captive maid, far away from home, who told in her master's house what the God of her own nation could do ; and her words led to the healing of one leper at least. We can all tell something about Christ—what He has done for us, what He can do for others ; and our words may fall upon some ear that will be glad to hear them, and upon some heart that will turn to Him with hungry faith and prayer.

This is a missionary text, and there are a thousand ways in which we can help to give the gospel to the world. What a pity it is that we should keep to ourselves anything so precious, that has such power to bless the world, and that men, women, and children everywhere need so much, as the gospel of Jesus Christ ! Think of a rich man in the time of famine, when his neighbours are all starving, keeping his great, full barns locked up, and not dealing out bread to the hungry ! We who have found Christ have bread for human souls, not only enough for ourselves, but enough for all about us ; for giving out does not waste this bread of life. All around us are perishing sinners whom we may save. Shall we keep to ourselves that for want of which souls are dying ?

home Missions

" Whatsoever house ye enter into, there abide."—LUKE ix. 4

THE place to carry the gospel is right into people's homes. We must take it down along the streets and alleys, and over the fields and hills, entering every door, and telling the old, old story by the firesides and at the household tables. It should be the aim of every church to reach every house in its parish with the gospel. Christians should go themselves to this work, and not merely send a hired carrier to put tracts under the people's doors. Tracts are good ; but we should take them ourselves, and add to them the gifts of our own warm love and eager sympathy and interest. We should get the sweet gospel into every home by telling it from our own lips.

Did you ever think what a wondrous blessing it is to a home when the salvation of Christ comes to it ? Think what a dark and sad place a godless home is, with no prayer, no recognition of God's love and mercy, no shelter, no comfort in sorrow, no hope in death. Then think what Christ brings when He is admitted. Peace comes with Him, for sin is pardoned. God's love builds a shelter over the home ; for they are His children who dwell there now. There is communication direct from heaven, a ladder running up, with angels upon it and God above it. There is comfort in sorrow, help in trial, strength in weakness, hope in dying.

For illustration of the two homes—the godless and the godly—we can picture an Egyptian and a Hebrew home on that night when the angel of death came to slay the firstborn. The blood on the door-post made the difference. Christ's blood on the door of a home is a shelter from every woe. Would it not be a great thing if we could carry Christ's gospel into every home about us where Christ has not already been received ? Do you know a home where there is no prayer ? Will you not try to open that door for Jesus ?

July 9

The Missionary Spirit

*" They departed, and went through the towns, preaching the
gospel, and healing everywhere."*—LUKE ix. 6

A GREAT many people do not do this. They come to
Christ and hear His command, but they do not go,
or at least they do not preach and heal. They do not
carry to other homes and to other lives the sweet blessings of mercy and health they have themselves received.
Surely this is very ungrateful to Christ, when we remember all He has done for us. Then it is also very selfish,
when we have found such joys, not to try to share them
with others who need them.

Christ wants to get the gospel into every home in the
world ; and the way He wants to do this is through the
hearts and hands of those whom He has already saved. If
we do not carry the good news, the lost will not receive it
at all. It is told of a boy who was converted that at once
he started to walk—for he was poor, and could not buy a
ticket on the railroad—away to a place in the West, more
than a thousand miles from his home, to tell his brother
about Christ. History relates that the early Christians,
many of them, were so eager to carry Christ's gospel
everywhere that they even hired themselves out as servants
or sold themselves as slaves, that they might be admitted
into the homes of the rich and great among the heathen,
to live there, and thus have opportunity to tell in those
homes of the love of Jesus and of His salvation.

It would have great power in shaping our lives for usefulness for us to consider ourselves under a Divine commission to advance the kingdom of our Lord by bringing
others under its holy sway. So long as we merely regard
ourselves as sinners saved by grace, with no further responsibility, we shall be of very little use. But when we become conscious that we are apostles, every one of us, sent
to witness for Christ, we shall become blessings.

Herodias's Revenge

" The daughter of Herodias danced before them, and pleased Herod."—MATT. xiv. 6

IT was deemed disgraceful even in that country and in those days for a woman to show herself at all in a hall of revelry and carousal. Then to perform such a dance in such a place for the entertainment of the revellers was regarded as a most debasing and shameful act. The dance was indecent, and only those who had lost all sense of modesty and womanly propriety would so debase themselves. That a mother should send her own daughter into such a scene to perform such a part seems almost incredible. The act reveals the kind of home life and the ideas of womanly purity that prevailed in the court of Herod ; also the strength of Herodias's passion for revenge upon John. She would even send her own daughter to play this shameful part, in order to accomplish her purpose.

While this picture is before them, young girls should learn that they cannot be too careful of their behaviour and bearing in public. A young woman's reputation is a precious jewel, which she should prize above all wealth or pleasure. If she lose it, neither wealth nor pleasure will be of much avail to her afterward. Her name once sullied, never can be altogether white again.

Sometimes young girls think their parents unreasonable in the restraints which they put upon them with regard to appearance or conduct in public ; but some day they will see how wise and loving is such restraint. It may very fairly be questioned whether young ladies can take part in certain fashionable dances of to-day, and not pass beyond the bounds of pure womanly delicacy and propriety. At least, heart-purity is so holy a thing, and so easily tarnished, and the harm when done is so irreparable, that one had better deny one's self many a fascinating pleasure rather than risk the loss of anything so precious.

July 11

A Royal Coward

" For the oath's sake, and them which sat with him at meat, he commanded it to be given her."—MATT. xiv. 9

HEROD called himself a king, and yet see what a poor slave he was, what a craven coward! He was sorry he had made the oath, exceedingly sorry. His conscience was not altogether dead. He did not want to kill John. He was afraid of public opinion, which he knew would condemn him. He was afraid of avenging wrath. Then he hated himself for having been caught by Herodias in her plot to have her long-cherished revenge. Yet he was so much a slave that, although he claimed to be a king, he had not the courage to refuse such a request.

True, he had made an oath, but no promise or oath is binding which requires one to sin. Of course, Herod did very wrong to make such a reckless oath, not knowing what his promise would involve. After he had made it he was bound to keep it, at whatever cost to himself, provided nothing sinful was involved. If Herodias had asked for half his kingdom, he would have been bound to grant her request; but he was under no obligation to grant any desire which required him to commit sin.

It was not the oath, however, that really influenced Herod. He had not the courage to do the heroic thing he ought to have done. He was afraid of the ridicule of his guests; and he was so under the power of Herodias that he dare not refuse what she demanded. It was his weakness that wrecked him. Rather than be a moral hero he stained his hands in holy blood; and the stains are not yet washed out.

There are some things we have no right to swear away. Things that are our own we are always to do with as we have sworn. According to the Scriptures, a good man, having sworn to his own hurt, changes not. But no oath binds any one to give away another man's life. This is not his to give.

Death of John the Baptist

" And he sent, and beheaded John in the prison."
MATT. xiv. 10

THIS seems a sad end for this glorious man's life. After a few months of faithful preaching he was cast into a dungeon, where he lay for a year, and where he was beheaded as a felon. To us it is very mysterious. Why did God permit such a fate to come upon so faithful and noble a servant? Our Lord Himself said that no greater man ever lived than John. Why then was his life allowed to go out in such darkness?

We know, first, that it was no accident. There are no accidents in this world over which our loving Father presides. John would not have chosen such a life-plan for himself, so brief, with such a tragic ending; few of us would choose just the life we live in this world. There are no chances, no accidents. "Our ways are those of the Lord's choosing—ways sadder, perhaps, but safer; rougher, perhaps, but surer; narrower, perhaps, but better than those of our own dreaming."

John finished his work. If there had been anything further for him to do he would not have been left to die so ignominiously, to gratify the revenge of a wicked woman. His work was done when Christ began to preach. Then when he died, it was for faithfulness to the truth. It is not long years that make a complete life. A life is complete, whether long or short, that fulfils the purpose of its creation; and the longest life is incomplete and a failure if it does not do the work for which it was made. It is better to die in youth with a life unspotted than to live on to old age in sin and crime. It was better to die as John died, than to live on as Herod and Herodias lived.

> " He liveth long who liveth well,—
> All else is being flung away;
> He liveth longest who can tell
> Of true things truly done each day."

July 13

Tell Jesus

" The apostles gathered themselves together unto Jesus, and told Him all things."—MARK vi. 30

THAT is just what we should always do when we have been trying to do any service for our Lord. We should do it as well as we can, and then go and tell Him what we have done. At the close of each day we should go to Him and tell Him of all that we have done or tried to do during the day. We should tell Him how we have lived, how we have done our work, how we have endured temptations, how we have treated our friends and those with whom we have been associated, how we have performed our mission as His servants, what words we have spoken for Him, what efforts we have made to do good or to give comfort or help, and how we have met the calls upon us for sympathy and aid.

We must not forget to tell Him about the day's failures. Did we lose our patience ? Did we yield to temptation ? Did we neglect to speak the word for the Master that we ought to have spoken ? Were we unkind to any one ? We must tell Him of the efforts to do good which seemed to come to naught. Ofttimes we are like the disciples who had toiled all the night and caught nothing. At many a setting sun we come, weary and sad, with empty hands. Then sometimes we are tempted to stay away from the Master and make no report : what have we to report ? nothing but a fruitless day. But we should not, therefore, keep away from Him who sent us forth. Jesus had days in His own life that seemed fruitless, and He can understand our sadness when we come with no sheaves.

So let us tell Him all. That is the kind of evening secret prayer that will bless us. It will make us very watchful all day if we remember that we must report to Jesus all we say, or do, or fail to do ; it will keep us in more intimate relations with Him. Then His sympathy will strengthen us for better service each day.

Quiet Resting=Places

" He said unto them, Come ye yourselves apart into a desert place, and rest a while."—MARK vi. 31

HOW thoughtful Jesus is for the comfort of His disciples! He never wants to overwork them. He provides seasons and places of rest for them all along the way. One of these " quiet resting-places " is the night, coming after each day of toil. Then our emptied life-fountains are refilled. Another resting-place is the Sabbath, after the week of anxious battle and strife. Then it is that we should seek the renewal of our spiritual life by communing with God, by lying on our Lord's bosom. The Lord's Supper is another resting-place. The Master leads us into the upper room to sit with Him at His table, to feast our souls on the provisions of His love and grace.

Then there are many other quiet places to which our Lord invites us to come apart with Him to rest a while— the sweet hours of prayer, alone, or in the house of God, the communings with friends, the sacred hours we spend in home joys. Sometimes the Master calls us to rest a while in a sick-room, away from the noise and struggle of the busy world. It may be in pain or in suffering, and there may be no bodily rest ; but our souls are resting, and we are learning lessons we never could have learned in the midst of life's exciting toil.

One thing about all these " rests " to which Jesus invites us, is that we are to rest *with Him*. He never says, " Go ye apart and rest," but ever His word is, " Come ye apart." The resting is always to be with Him. It is His loving presence that makes the blessedness of the rest. There is no true soul-refreshing for us anywhere, even in the most sacred ordinances, if we do not find Christ there. It is lying on His bosom when we are tired or sorrowing or penitent that rests us. Rest apart from Christ brings no refreshing. So we must be sure that we go apart *with* the Master.

Divine Compassion

"*Jesus......saw much people, and was moved with compassion toward them, because they were as sheep not having a shepherd.*"—MARK vi. 34

HERE we have a window through which we catch a glimpse of the heart of Jesus. Every scene of sorrow touched Him. It is a great thought that the heart of the Son of God is actually moved at the sight of human distress or want. It was this compassion that brought Christ from heaven. It was because our Father loved the lost world that He gave His Son to save the world. Does God care now if we are in suffering or in need ? " Like as a father pitieth his children, so the Lord pitieth them that fear Him." Does Jesus, since He has gone up into glory, have any such compassion for human sorrow on the earth ? "We have not an High Priest who cannot be touched with the feeling of our infirmities."

It is worth while to notice what kind of trouble it was that so stirred the compassion of Jesus at this time. It was because He saw the people as sheep not having a shepherd. It was not their hunger, nor their poverty, nor their sickness, but their spiritual need that so deeply touched His compassions. There were no wise, gentle, thoughtful pastors watching over the higher interests of their immortal natures, feeding them with heavenly bread, protecting them from the wolves of sin and lust, and leading them in right paths.

We learn here that no condition is so sad as that of spiritual neglect. Soul peril is far more pitiable than bodily danger or distress. Nothing moves the Divine heart so deeply as a soul exposed to the world's enmities, wandering from the fold amid sin's pitfalls and uncared for. Happy are those people, old and young, who are safe in the Good Shepherd's keeping ! If we have " the mind of Christ," we also shall be moved with compassion for all souls that have no shepherd.

The Barley Loaves

" *He......took the five loaves.*"—MATT. xiv. 19

WE are not surprised that a disciple asked, of the five loaves and two fishes, " What are these among so many ? " What a little way they will go in feeding such a multitude ! Surely Christ can feed the hungry people without these poor little black loaves.

Still, Jesus bade the disciples bring the loaves to Him, and He used them. Is it not strange that the mighty Christ should need us and our little barley-loaves to feed people's hunger ? Yet He does: He wants our gifts; and then He wants our ministry in dispensing the gifts. He passed the bread to the multitude through the hands of the disciples : He passes salvation through His saved ones to the unsaved.

" Only one talent small,
    Scarce worthy to be named :
Truly He hath no need of this,—
    O soul, art thus ashamed ?
He gave that talent first :
    Then use it in His strength ;
Thereby—thou know'st not—He may work
    A miracle at length.

" Many the starving souls
    Now waiting to be fed,
Needing, though knowing not their need
    Of Christ, the living Bread.
Oh ! hast thou known His love ?
    To others make it known ;
Receiving blessings, others bless !
    No seed abides alone.

" And when thine eyes shall see
    The holy, ransomed throng
In heavenly fields, by living streams,
    By Jesus led along,
Unspeakable thy joy shall be,
    And glorious thy reward,
If by thy barley-loaves one soul
    Has been brought home to God."

" Toiling in Rowing "

*" He saw them toiling in rowing ; for the wind was contrary
unto them."*—MARK vi. 48

JESUS always sees our toils and distresses in this world.
We do not see Him, and sometimes we think He has
forgotten us ; but that is never true. He is never
indifferent for a moment. On the heights of Sedan, while
the battle was in progress, stood a group of men watching
the struggling armies in the plain below. In this group
was the American general Sheridan, who watched the
mighty strife with the keen eye of a soldier. King William
was also there ; but his interest was different from Sheridan's. His son was in the thick of the fight, and he
watched the battle with the eye of a father as well as of a
king.

Christ looks down upon our struggles in this world.
He sees us toiling ; all our battles and strifes He beholds.
He sees us in the waves and in the storm. He sees us, not
with the eye of the calm spectator merely, but with the
eye of tenderest love. This is a great thought ; if we can
only get it into our hearts, it will give us wondrous courage
in the hour of toil, sorrow, or struggle. Jesus knows when
the battle is hard, when the night is dark, when the temptation is more than we can bear.

Here the winds were contrary, though Christ sent His disciples out to sea. We learn that even when we are doing
the things God has bidden us do, we may encounter opposition and sore difficulty. We may even be beaten back
and find the resistance too great for our strength. Many
of the Lord's disciples have to make their voyage over
very stormy seas on their way to glory. For some people
duty is hard ; indeed, a true, noble, positive, aggressive
life must always be in the face of opposition and contrary
winds. " The law of head-winds in life is doubtless in the
secret love of God. When the voyage is over, perhaps we
shall be let see the charts, and know why it had to be."

Never Forgotten

" About the fourth watch of the night He cometh unto them, walking upon the sea."—MARK vi. 48

IT was a long night for the tempest-driven disciples ; they were in great distress. But Jesus was only trying them ; He had not forgotten them. From His mountain seat, unseen by them, He was watching them. He saw their struggle and danger. He put up prayer for them. Then at length He came to rescue them.

It is the same in every Christian's life. Sometimes Christ seems to have forsaken His people. For a long while they are left to struggle alone and to be driven back by contrary winds. They call, and get no answer. The night wears away, and it is almost morning. Then at last He comes.

When people are in sore trouble of any kind they are like those disciples that night out in the midst of the sea. No human aid can reach them. Human friends eagerly want to help, and they come to offer sympathy and consolation. But in such hours the most helpful of us are only like men standing on the shore of a dark and stormy sea, while our friends are far out on the wild waves. We cannot go to them to give help or rescue. Our little boats cannot ride in the mad surges. All we can do is to stand on the shore, as it were, and look with pitying eye and heart at the struggling ones in the angry sea. That is the very best that the richest human love can do. A father stood on the shore opposite the wild cataract, and with anguish unutterable saw the boat that bore his own son swept into the angry torrents, and could do nothing.

Thus it is in all life's deep needs. It is in such hours that we realize the blessedness of Christ's power to help. He can go out on any wave, into the wildest sea, to reach those who are driven and tossed. He can carry help to all who are troubled. He can comfort in any sorrow, and give victory in any strife.

Christ Walking on the Sea

" When they saw Him walking upon the sea, they supposed it had been a spirit, and cried out."—MARK vi. 49

IT seems strange to us that the disciples should ever have been afraid of their own Master. They had been in great distress all the night because He was not with them. There was nothing they had desired so much all those long, dark hours as that He would come to them. Yet now, when He came, they were in terror at sight of Him. It was because they did not know it was He that His presence so affrighted them.

It is ofttimes just so with us. We are in some need or danger, and Jesus does not come to us. We call upon Him, and most earnestly desire His coming ; yet He comes not. At length He comes ; but it is not as we expected, in lovely visage and gentle mien, but in form of terror. It is in some great trial that He comes. Death enters our door and carries away a loved one. We experience some loss or some misfortune—at least it seems to us loss or misfortune. We cry out in terror. We do not know it is the Christ, veiled in the dark robe, that has come. We do not know that this is the answer to our prayer for His presence and His help. We are affrighted at the form that moves over the waters in the dark night. We think it is new danger, when really it is the very Divine love and Divine help for which we have been longing and pleading.

We ought to learn that Jesus is in every providence that comes to us. He does not come in the sunshine only ; quite as frequently it is in the shadow that He draws nigh. It is our duty as Christians to train ourselves to see Christ in each event. Then, whether it be sorrow or joy that knocks at our door, we shall give it like loving welcome, knowing that Jesus Himself is veiled in whatever form it is that enters. Then we shall find that when we welcome Him in the sombre garments of pain He has always a rich blessing for our lives.

Peace in Storm

" *He went up unto them into the ship ; and the wind ceased.*"
MARK vi. 51

WHEN Jesus comes to us our trouble ceases. At His bidding the wildest storm instantly becomes a calm. The trouble itself may not go away from us, but it is no longer a trouble when He is with us. The wind may not cease to blow without and beat upon our lives, but He makes peace within. It is far better to have so much grace that our hearts shall be calm and quiet in the fiercest storm, than to have the storm itself quieted, while our hearts remain restless as ever. Peace within is far better than any mere calm without.

In a gallery in Italy there are two pictures side by side by different artists. One represents a sea tossed by storms. Dark clouds hang over it, and the lightning-bolts pierce the sky, and the wrathful waves roll in fury. In the seething waters a dead human face is seen. The other represents a sea similarly storm-tossed ; but in the midst of the angry waters is a rock, and in the rock a cleft with green herbage and flowers, and amid these a dove quietly sitting on her nest.

These two pictures tell the whole story of human life in this world. The first is the story of life without Christ, unblessed by His presence and peace. There is storm everywhere, with no quiet shelter. The other picture paints the peace which Christ gives. There is no less storm. The waves roll as high. But there is peace. The rock represents Christ ; it is in the cleft of the rock that the peace is found.

> " Rock of ages, cleft for me,
> Let me hide myself in Thee."

It is in the redemption and atonement of Christ alone that we can have peace. " In Me ye shall have peace." If, therefore, we take Christ into our barques on the storm-swept sea, we shall glide on in safety through earth's tempests to glory's shore.

July 21

One Thing Needful

" Labour not for the meat which perisheth, but for that meat which endureth unto everlasting life."—JOHN vi. 27

WE should call a man very foolish who, in building a great and costly house, should look only after the outside, spending large amounts of money in exterior decoration, while he left the interior in a rough, unfinished state, the walls unplastered, the rooms filled with rubbish and without furniture or decorations of any kind. No one can get comfort from a beautiful exterior in his home and from fine grounds, if within all is bare and rude. The wise man will think more of the inside than of the outside of the house in which he is to live. He will provide beauty, warmth, and comfort, and thus make a true home for himself, in which he may dwell in peace and in real enjoyment.

Still more foolish is the man who thinks only of the needs of his physical nature, and gives no thought to the needs of his immortal soul. He is looking after the outside, and neglecting the inner life. He is providing for his body, which will soon perish, and giving no care to his soul, which will endure for ever. He is planning only for the present, and neglecting the interests that are eternal. How pitiable is such a life, deliberately turning away from all the best, holiest, most beautiful, and most enduring things, and seeking only the poor, miserable, worthless things that are only loads, impediments, not enriching him who has them !

Our Lord's counsel is, that we should look first after our spiritual necessities. It is a fearful mistake to toil all one's days for bread and raiment, or for wealth and honour, and never do anything for the inner life. At the end there will be nothing left to show for all the toil and pain and sacrifice. If we look after the interests of our souls, then when this life is ended we shall find ourselves in possession of eternal life. A good motto for life is, "Live for the immortal things."

The Work of Faith

" This is the work of God, that ye believe on Him whom He hath sent."—JOHN vi. 29

PEOPLE are puzzled to know how they can eat spiritual bread. They cannot see it, nor take it into their hands. When they are told to work for the meat which giveth eternal life, they ask how they can do it. Here Christ says that the way to work for the spiritual food is to believe on Him.

Of course believing on Christ must be taken in its fullest sense. Merely believing that bread will satisfy hunger will not in itself satisfy any hungry man ; he must eat of the bread, its nourishing qualities being thus assimilated in his system. And merely believing that Christ is able to meet all our soul's needs will not in itself bring to us spiritual satisfaction. Christ must be received into our lives.

There are different ways of believing. One may read in a book on astronomy that the sun is some ninety million miles away. He believes the statement, but it has no particular effect on his living to-morrow ; it is not calculated to have any effect of this kind. But when he reads that whosoever believeth on the Lord Jesus Christ shall be saved, the truth is meant to bless him by leading him, first of all to entrust himself to Christ for salvation, then to follow Him as his Master, then to have his unholy life transformed into beauty like Christ's. So it is with all spiritual truth. The mere receiving it is not enough ; it must be assimilated, as food is assimilated in the body. The bread of to-day is the labourer's strength, the orator's eloquence, the artist's skill to-morrow. The Bible verses of the morning must become the Christian's joy, or refuge, or inspiration, or warning, or transforming influence, in the day's struggles and toils. It should be noticed also that we are not to get this spiritual food by working for it, but by believing on Christ. We live by faith.

July 23

"The Bread of Life"

"The bread of God is He which cometh down from heaven."
JOHN vi. 33

NO bread that grows on the earth will furnish food for a human soul. In all our worldly strivings and ambitions we are thinking only of our perishing part, we are looking only after the poor, frail tabernacle, while we are allowing the dweller within to die of hunger. Recently, in a well-furnished house in a city, a family was found starving for bread. There are many souls starving in bodies that are luxuriously cared for. A soul cannot feed on grains and fruits. The finest luxuries of earth will never quench a soul's hunger.

Manna is called once in the Bible "angels' food," but this was only a poetical designation, referring to its falling from the sky. Manna did not really come down from heaven. It was not angels' food. It was food for bodies, not for spirits. Angels could not have lived on it. Imagine an angel taking up his abode in some millionaire's palace on the earth. Would he care for the magnificent things filling every apartment? Would he sit down and feed at the rich man's luxurious table? And souls and angels are much alike in their needs; both are spirits, unable to subsist on material food. Yet many people live as if their souls could be clothed in earth's finery, and fed and satisfied with earth's dainties.

Bread for souls must literally come down from heaven. It is the nature of the soul to feed upon immortal things. Its hungers and cravings are for pardon of sin, for peace, for communion with God, for holiness of character, for Christ-likeness, for restoration to the Divine favour. The bread for these spiritual hungers must come down from heaven. It must come in the form of mercy, of grace, of love, of Divine friendship, of gifts of life. Such food is found on no table on earth; it grows in no earthly clime; it can come only from God. It is for God, the living God, that our souls hunger and thirst.

Spiritual Food

" *I am the bread of life : he that cometh to Me shall never hunger.*"—JOHN vi. 35

HOW is Christ bread ? We understand what the bodily needs are which common bread satisfies. What in the soul corresponds to these cravings ? The most intense of the soul-cravings is for pardon. All men sin, but sin satisfies no one. Nor has the world any power to give peace to a troubled conscience. We cannot forgive our-selves, and no man can really forgive us. How is Christ bread to *this* hunger ? He was the Lamb of God, taking away the sin of the world ; and because He bore our sins He is able to forgive us. We remember how on earth the guilty crept to His feet when they saw Him, and looking up into His face heard the word which gave them peace.

Another craving is for holiness. The world has no art by which human souls can be restored into moral beauty. Men can restore paintings, and buildings over which the fire has swept can be erected again into more than their original nobleness ; but there is no human hand that can replace the glory of a ruined soul. Yet this craving Christ satisfies through the Holy Spirit, who enters the heart of every one who believes, and builds up anew the holy beauty which sin has destroyed.

Another of the soul's cravings is for life, spiritual life here, and then everlasting life. Again, earth has no bread to meet the hunger. The searches for hope are among the most pitiable of this world's experiences. But those who receive Christ *have* eternal life. He has opened the doors clear through into the glory beyond. He said, " Whoso-ever liveth and believeth on Me shall never die." He is the hope of glory to every one that receives Him. Said a martyr as he was led to execution : " I have only two stiles to get over to reach my Father's house—one, the steps up the scaffold ; the other, the ladder let down·from heaven."

July 25

A Welcome for All

" *All that the Father giveth Me shall come to Me ; and him that cometh to Me I will in no wise cast out.*"—JOHN vi. 37

WE need not worry ourselves trying to harmonize the two parts of this verse ; we can believe them both, and find great comfort and joy in them. Together they bring to every Christian a glorious and double confidence. Surely it is a blessed thing to know that God has thought about our salvation and planned for it, and then given us to Christ to be His.

If this be true, it is easy to understand the other part of this verse. Of course Christ will not cast out any whom His Father gives to Him. They are His own ; He knows them by name, and loves them, for He died for them. Surely He will not pass by one of His own when He finds him lying by the wayside or among the thorns, wounded, bleeding, dying, but will take him up and bear him home in safety. We need not give ourselves any anxiety about the former part of this sentence ; the latter part is all that really concerns us. If we truly come to Christ, we are here assured that He will in no wise cast us out : but we *must come.* Then we shall find room enough, and a most loving welcome.

" No father's house is full,
E'en though there seems no resting-place for more ;
Forgiving arms and doors do open wide,
If one repentant child implore
Outside.

" No mother's heart is full,
Unless it be with longing, burning wild—
Heart throbbings that no cheerful face can hide—
The wish to clasp her sinning child
Outside.

" God's flock is never full :
Fear not to enter boldly at His door ;
None ever were refused who there applied ;
He hath abiding-place for more
Inside."

Our Security

*" This is the Father's will which hath sent Me, that of all
which He hath given Me I should lose nothing, but should
raise it up again at the last day."*—JOHN vi. 39

THERE is not a shadow of doubt in the Christian's
hope. There is not a broken link in the chain that
binds the believer to eternal blessedness. There is not a
step wanting in the ladder that reaches up from the depths
of sin to the heights of glory. " Whom He foreknew, He
also foreordained to be conformed to the image of His Son
......and whom He foreordained, them He also called : and
whom He called, them He also justified : and whom He
justified, them He also glorified." These are the links in
the Christian's hope as St. Paul saw them ; in the words
of to-day's text we have the same links as they appeared
to our Saviour's eye.

The assurance is, that Christ will never lose any soul
that entrusts itself to Him for salvation. " Yet Christians
die, just like other people," says some one. Yes ; but they
are not then lost ; their spirits pass at once into glory with
Christ, and their bodies will only rest in the grave until the
resurrection. An old Christian sailor put it well. When
asked if he was not afraid when the storms were very high,
he answered that according to the Bible God held the waters
in the hollow of His hand ; and even if the ship were
wrecked, and he should fall into the sea, he would but drop
into his Father's hands. That is what death is to a Christian, however and wherever he may die—breathing his
soul into the hands of God.

The grave seems dark, but we have Christ's own pledge
here that not one of His own shall be lost or left in the
grave. No matter where we die, or where our bodies lie,
we have the Saviour's word—which we had better receive
in simplicity, without questioning or doubt — that He
" will lose nothing, but will raise it up again at the last
day."

Pharisaism

" The Pharisees.......except they wash.......eat not."
MARK vii. 3

THE religion of the Pharisees consisted not in love to God, and in disposition, character, and conduct, but in certain ceremonial rites which they observed with great scrupulousness. They washed their hands before meals, because ceremonial uncleanness in the hands communicated itself to the food Yet they took no pains to wash their hearts of evil or uncharitable thoughts and feelings toward others. They washed when they came in from their shops because worldly business defiled them ; but they were not careful in their dealings with others to be just, honest, and true. They saw that every pot and kettle, every vessel, and all household arrangements, were ceremonially cleansed ; but they did not stop to look within their own hearts to see if all was clean there for the indwelling of God's Spirit.

We all need to watch against making our religion consist in forms of worship. We may pray many times a day, and read a regular number of chapters, and go through many and laborious devotions, and yet not have a particle of true religion. We are truly religious just in the measure in which we have the spirit of Christ in our disposition, heart, and character. " The kingdom of God is not meat and drink, but righteousness, and peace, and joy in the Holy Ghost."

Loving God and our fellow-men is the sum of all duty. Unless we have this twofold love in our hearts, manifested in life and character, our profession of religion is vain. Not a word should be said against external cleanliness ; a clean heart should make the life clean to the tips of the fingers, and in all tastes, feelings, habits, words, and actions. But clean hands and well-scrubbed floors and shining dishes and careful ceremonial observances will never please God, if in the heart there be no love for Him and no love for men. " Blessed are the pure in heart : for they shall see God."

July 28

" Corban."

*" Making the word of God of none effect through your tradi-
tion, which ye have delivered : and many such like
things do ye."*—MARK vii. 13

IT is a good thing to dedicate one's property to God.
But when we have done this we must take good heed
that we use it in the ways marked out for us by the Divine
commandments. It will not do to cover miserliness and
greed by a pretence that we have given our money to God,
and therefore cannot use it for charitable purposes.

For example, if a man has needy parents, one of the
first uses of consecrated money is to provide for their
wants. He may say that he is gathering means to build
an orphanage, or an asylum for infirm old men or old
women, and that he has consecrated his property to this
great charity ; but if meanwhile he allows his own aged
parents to suffer, his consecration of property is not acceptable to God. He who sets aside the fifth commandment
that he may use his money for the poor is playing a miserable farce before God. No amount of service in the work
of the Church avails when one is neglecting the duties he
owes to his own family.

The case is still worse when, as under the Rabbinical
rules, the money or property was never really used at all
for God, the plea of " Corban " being only a pretext to
evade the requirements of filial duty. The consecration of
money to God implies always the use of the consecrated
money in the service of God as He may call for it. God
does not want money hoarded up ; He wants it going
about doing good. We apply the parable of the talents to
everything but money, when there surely is nothing to
which the parable applies more certainly than to money.
At least we may never pretend that we have given our
money to God, and therefore cannot give it away. Giving
it away for wise use is the very thing God wants us to do
with it.

July 29

Ⱳhat Defileth?

" Not hat which goeth into the mouth defileth a man ; but that which cometh out of the mouth, this defileth a man."
MATT. xv. 11

THERE are many applications of this principle. The food we eat does not affect our moral character. No external ceremonies really touch the soul. Indeed, nothing in this world has any power to defile a heart while it remains outside and is not allowed to enter. A man may be a coal-miner, always black and grimy, and always working in dirt, and yet he may have a soul white and unspotted. This is true of living amid temptations. So long as we keep them outside, they have no power to injure us.

Luther says somewhere that we cannot prevent the birds flying about our heads, but we can prevent them building their nests in our hair. We cannot prevent a great many evil things buzzing around us continually, but we can keep them from entering our hearts and nesting there. And so long as we do this, the worst things in the world cannot lay a spot upon our souls.

The Saviour says further, that it is what comes out of the mouth that defiles. So, then, there may even be evil in the heart which does not defile unless it is allowed to shape itself in thoughts, words, or deeds. The suggestion of wrong-doing is not a sin until the suggestion is accepted and entertained. Temptation to sin is not itself sin. Jesus was tempted. Suggestions of evil were made to Him by Satan ; yet He never sinned, because these suggestions never found any lodgment in His heart, and therefore never found any expression in word or act, or even in thought. So temptations come to us from without. These things we cannot help ; we are not responsible for them ; there is no sin in merely having these suggestions. But the sin begins the moment we open the door to one of these sinful solicitations. That which *cometh out* defileth.

Ibe is Ibere

" He could not be hid."—MARK vii. 24

THE fame of Christ had gone out too widely over the whole country for Him to travel anywhere without being recognized. No doubt there was something in His appearance and bearing that distinguished Him from other men and soon revealed Him. There must have been a rare sweetness in His face, the outpouring of the great love of His heart. There was no halo upon His features, as artists represent Him in their pictures; yet there must have been a glow of grace that revealed Him to sad and hungry hearts.

But really Christ never can be hid. He can be in no place in this world very long and His presence not be recognized. You may hide sweet flowers so that they cannot be seen, but soon the fragrance will disclose their hiding-place. So the sweetness of the Saviour's life and love will always tell when He is near. When He enters a human heart He cannot be hidden; for soon His Spirit begins to breathe out in all the words, actions, and life of the new follower. When He enters a home He cannot long be hidden, for the home is changed—worldliness, bitterness, and sin giving place to prayer and praise, to the spirit of love and gentleness, and to purity and holiness. When He enters a community He cannot remain concealed. The stories of missionary work illustrate this. Cannibal islands are changed into God-fearing, man-loving settlements. Christ will always reveal His presence in this world.

The same is true also of all faithful discipleship. A Christian cannot be hid. If the love of Christ is in his heart, people around him will soon know it. They will see it in his bearing, in his disposition, in the way he honours God, in the way he treats his fellow-men. When a man can hide his religion, he has not much of it to hide. True religion breathes out in fragrance, shines out in light.

Silence not Denial

" But He answered her not a word."—MATT. xv. 23

THERE is something very remarkable in this silence of Christ. Usually He was quick to hear every request made to Him by a sufferer. Scarcely ever had any one to ask twice for a favour. His heart was sensitive, as is a mother's heart to her child's cries, and instantly responded to every petition for help. Yet now He stood and listened to this woman's piteous pleading and answered her not a word. Like a miser with hoards of gold, at whose gates the poor and suffering knock, but who, hearing their cries of need and distress, keeps His gates locked and is deaf to every entreaty, so Jesus stood unmoved by this woman's cries, though He had all power in His hands.

Why was He thus silent ? It was not because He could not help her, for His arm was never weak. The best of us have our weak hours, our days of emptiness, when we have nothing wherewith to help; but His fullness was never exhausted. It was not because He was so engrossed in His own approaching sorrows that He could think of no other one's sorrow, for even on the cross He forgot Himself to show kindness to others. Evidently the reason for His silence was to try this mother's faith, and to draw it out into still greater strength. He was preparing her to receive in the end a better blessing than she could have received at the beginning.

Our Lord sometimes yet seems to be silent to His people when they cry to Him. To all their earnest supplications He answers not a word. Is His silence a refusal ? By no means. Ofttimes, at least, it is meant only to make the suppliants more earnest, and to prepare their hearts to receive richer and greater blessings. So when Christ is silent to our prayers, it is that we may be brought down in deeper humility at His feet, and that our hearts may be made more fit to receive heaven's gifts and blessings.

Crumbs from the Master's Table

" The dogs eat of the crumbs which fall from their masters' table."—MATT. xv. 27

BOTH the humility and the quick, eager faith of this woman appear in this response. She was not offended by the figure our Lord had used. She was willing to be as a little dog under the Master's table. The children were first served, and then the pieces they let fall belonged to the dogs. All she asked was the portion that ordinarily went to the dogs. And even the crumbs from that table were enough for her, more than the richest dainties from any other table.

Thus both humility and faith were shown in her answer ; and in both she is an example to us. We should come to Christ with a deep sense of our unworthiness, ready to take the lowest place. It is such a precious thing to be permitted to take even the crumbs from the Master's table, that we should exult in the privilege. The crumbs of His grace and love are better than the richest feasts of this world.

" Not worthy, Lord, to gather up the crumbs
    With trembling hand that from Thy table fall,
A weary, heavy-laden sinner comes
    To plead Thy promise and obey Thy call.

" I am not worthy to be thought Thy child,
    Nor sit the last and lowest at Thy board ;
Too long a wanderer, and too oft beguiled,
    I only ask one reconciling word."

Yet we are not fed with crumbs ; we are seated at the full table, with the richest provisions before us. The prodigal, returning, asked only to be made a servant, as he felt unworthy to be restored to a son's place. But father-love knew no such half-way restoration as that. The white robe, the ring, the shoes, were given to him, insignia of sonship. God puts the lowliest and unworthiest at once into the children's place, and feeds them abundantly.

Divine Sympathy

*" Looking up to heaven, He sighed, and saith unto him,
Ephphatha."*—MARK vii. 34

HOW it must have saddened the heart of Jesus to walk
through this world and see so much human misery!
There is a story of a sculptor who wept as he saw at his
feet the shattered fragments of his breathing marble, on
which he had spent years of patient, loving toil   Jesus
walked through this world amid the ruin of the noblest
work of His own hands.   Everywhere He saw the destruction wrought by sin.   So His grief was twofold—tender
sympathy with human suffering, and sorrow over the
ruinous work of sin.

It is a precious thought to us that we are so dear to
Jesus that the beholding of our grief touches and stirs His
heart.   What a wonderful revelation it is to us that we are
thought of by Him, and that He cares enough for us to be
moved to sorrow by our woes and sufferings!

Then Christ's help does not end in the thrill of sympathy.
That is about as far as human help usually goes.   People
stand over us when we are in misfortune or trouble, and
heave a sigh, and then pass on.   Sometimes this is all they
can do.   Human sympathy in suffering is a wonderful
help: but the assurance of Divine sympathy is infinitely
more uplifting.   Then Christ gives real help.   He was
moved with compassion as He saw the widow of Nain in
her lonely sorrow, and restored her dead son to her.   He
wept with Mary and Martha, and then raised their brother.
He sighed as He looked on the misfortune of this deaf
man, and then opened his ears.   He is " touched with the
feeling of our infirmities," and then gives " grace to help
in time of need."   Not only does He pity us when He finds
us deaf to all the sweet voices of love and grace, but He is
ready to open our ears.   We have only to bring to Christ
our infirmities, and He will take them and give us back in
place souls with all their lost powers restored.

Deaf and Dumb

" *His ears were opened, and the string of his tongue was loosed, and he spake plain.*"—MARK vii. 35

IT is a great thing to have deaf ears opened. In many places in the Bible we find the words, " He that hath ears to hear, let him hear." This suggests that there are people who have no ears, and also that there are those who, having ears, hear not. He who cannot hear is a great loser. The world is full of harmonies of sound. The deaf man misses all the pleasure which others derive from the songs of the birds, the tones of human speech, the charms of music. It is a great thing when closed ear-gates are opened.

Then souls have ears—ears fitted to hear the voice of God and the harmonies of heavenly music. Yet there are many who are utterly deaf to these spiritual utterances. They hear God neither in the voices of Nature, in the whisperings of conscience, nor in the sacred words of Holy Scripture. Christ is able also to open these spiritual ears, that our souls may listen on this earth to the music of heaven.

Then it is a great thing also to have our tongues loosed. that we may talk of these things to others. Some people, however, who seem to have their ears opened, still have their tongues tied. They do not speak of God's love. They have such an impediment in their speech when they talk of spiritual things that they stammer and hesitate and break down altogether, although on other themes they can talk plainly and fluently. There are Christian men who are eloquent when they talk of business, of science, of farming, or of whatever may most occupy their thoughts and hands ; but the moment the subject of religious experience is approached, their eloquence forsakes them. They are tongue-tied Christians. What a blessing it would be to them if Christ would some day loose the string of their tongue, that they could speak plainly !

Aug. 4

"The Lord will provide"

"They have now been with Me three days, and have nothing to eat."—MARK viii. 2

THIS word of Christ shows first how earnest the people were in their desire to be with Christ They had been three days with Him, and even when their provision was exhausted they would not leave Him. They would rather stay with Him hungry than leave Him to go away to seek bread. It would be a good thing if there was such devotion to Christ in these days. Some people can scarcely sit through one short hour with Jesus in the church, or spend a few minutes with Him morning and evening, communing with Him. If we had real spiritual hunger, we should not weary so soon of waiting upon Christ.

Another thought suggested by these words is, that Christ will take good care of those who are earnestly following Him. The reason for this multitude being so long in the wilderness was their desire to be with Jesus ; and it was this fact specially that stirred His compassion when He saw them growing hungry. "They came here to find Me, and they have lingered here, forgetting their own needs, that they might be near Me. I will not allow them to suffer, but will provide for them." We may draw the lesson that Jesus will take care of those who are enduring hardness for His sake. He may not always save them from suffering, but He will always watch over them and provide for them in the best way. His heart is just as tender now in the midst of heaven's glory, and as thoughtful of His friends in their need, as it was when He was on the earth.

We must not overlook the fact that it is care for the people's bodily wants that we find here in our Lord. We are constantly in danger of limiting our faith in Christ to spiritual things ; but He looks just as lovingly after the supply of our physical wants as after the needs of our souls.

ᕼelp in Time of ᕼeed

" *Having eyes, see ye not ?.....do ye not remember ?* "
MARK viii. 18

THERE is nothing unreasonable in expecting a man with two eyes, when walking through an art gallery, to see the beautiful pictures that hang upon the walls. Why were his eyes given to him, if he is not to see with them ? And it was nothing unreasonable that our Lord looked for when He expected the disciples to understand His spiritual teachings. They had eyes with which they might have seen spiritual things, yet they failed to use them. Many people never learn to see much with their natural eyes. They walk over the fields in summer days and never see a lovely thing ; while in every wild flower and in every grass-blade there is beauty enough, if perceived, to fill the dullest heart with rapture. It is still more true in spiritual things : we walk in a world full of the glories of God's love ; yet how much do we see of this ineffable splendour ? At best, in this world we see only through a glass, darkly. Should we not train our eyes to see ?

Then there was another wonderful faculty which the disciples did not use. This was memory. " Do ye not remember ? " They *did* remember the facts of the miracles very definitely, but the spiritual lessons they did not recall. They had forgotten the spiritual meaning of the miracle. This is the way all of us are too apt to do : we remember the things God has done for us in the past, but we fail to draw the lessons from these experiences which they are meant to teach us ; we fail to profit by the experience. Every deliverance in time of danger, every help in time of need, ought to write upon our hearts its new lesson on trusting in the Lord. When we come again to similar points of need or danger, we ought not to be afraid, but, remembering how God helped us before, should believe that He will give us the same help in the new experiences.

Aug. 6

Led Apart

" He took the blind man by the hand, and led him out of the town."—MARK viii. 23

THAT was a very gentle thing to do. Look closely at the picture—Jesus leading a poor blind man along the street. What thoughts does it start in our minds ? The blind man represents each one of us in our sinful state—in the midst of a world of beauty, but seeing nothing ; groping in the gloom, unable to find the way alone ; doomed to perish for ever in the darkness, unless some one take us by the hand and lead us. As Jesus came to this man in his blindness, so He comes to each one of us, offering to take us by the hand and be our guide, to lead us, through the gloom and the dangers, home to light and glory. We can never stumble in the darkness if He leads us.

The blind man entrusting himself, without fear or questioning, to be led by this Stranger, and quietly and confidingly going with Him, is a picture of what true faith in Christ always does. It is in this way that we are to commit ourselves to Christ. It is not enough to lay our sins on Him ; we must entrust our whole life to His guidance. We can never find the way ourselves in this world's paths, but we may entrust ourselves with unquestioning confidence to Christ's leading.

> " I do not try to see my way,
>   Before, behind, or left, or right ;
> I cannot tell what dangers gray
>   Do haunt my steps, nor at what height
>   Above the sea my path doth wind :
>   For I am blind.

> " Yet not without a guide I wend
>   My unseen way, by day, by night ;
> Close by my side there walks a Friend,—
>   Strong, tender, true : I trust His sight ;
> He sees my way before, behind,
>   Though I am blind."

"What Think Ye of Christ?"

" But whom say ye that I am ? "—MATT. xvi. 15

IT is to us a great deal more important question what we think personally about Christ than what the world thinks about Him. We may be able to state the doctrines of all the creeds of Christendom concerning His person, and yet the question remains : " Whom do *you* say that I am ? What think *you* of Christ ? "

It is vitally important that we have right views of Christ. Who is He ? Is He Divine, or only human ? If He is only human, we may get much profit from His teachings and from His example, but that is all. In our days of struggle and temptation we cannot turn to Him for personal help. The holiest saints in heaven cannot impart to us any strength in our weakness. They cannot reach down their hands to lead us, to defend us, to help us over the hard places. If we fall, they cannot lift us up again. We can get no help from John or from Paul. If Jesus was no more than a good and holy man, He can do nothing for us now excepting through His teachings and His example ; but if He is Divine, He can be to us all that we need as friend, helper, guide, comforter, refuge. So we see that it does matter what we believe concerning the person of Christ. Doctrines are important.

Then, when the doctrinal question has been answered, there are other questions that come still more closely home : " What is Christ to you personally ? Is He only in your creed ? Is He only a person about whom you believe a great many blessed and glorious things ? Is He in your thoughts only as the mighty Saviour of all who believe on Him ? Is He anything to you personally ? Is He your Saviour, your Friend, your Helper ? " These are the questions that tell just where we stand with regard to Christ and eternal life. Opinions about Christ, though ever so true and orthodox, are not enough , only living faith in Him saves.

Aug. 8

The Shadow of the Cross

" *He began to teach them, that the Son of man must suffer,......
be rejected,......be killed, and after three days rise again.*"
MARK viii. 31

PETER had made a noble confession of his faith in
Christ as the promised Messiah, and now Jesus tells
him what that Messiahship meant—how He was to fulfil His
mission. It was not as the disciples expected. They were
looking for His manifestation as an earthly king, but He
tells them that the way to His throne was through suffering and by the cross.

It is to be noticed that while the way He marked out lay
through darkness and sorrow, at the end there would be
glory—" after three days rise again." Thus there was to
be no failure in His mission. An apostle said to believers
in Christ : " Ye must through much tribulation enter into
the kingdom of heaven." The tribulation was hard, but
they would go *through* it ; and beyond was the kingdom of
heaven. In the Twenty-third Psalm there is a verse often
quoted : " Yea, though I walk through the valley of the
shadow." In these words there is a suggestion of gloom
—but the Christian is going *through* it ; then comes " the
house of the Lord for ever." So here the dying of the
Saviour seemed to be failure ; but the rising again meant
glory, victory, and eternal blessedness. He was simply
going *through* death, as the appointed way to His throne.

This quiet announcement by our Lord of what was in
store for Him reminds us of an element of sorrow in
Christ's life from which we are mercifully spared. He
knew beforehand every inch of His path of woe. The
shadow of His cross lay upon His soul through all the
years. We sometimes rashly say that we wish we could
see our future ; but really it is a most gracious provision
of our own life that we cannot see an hour before us. To
know the future would only darken the present and unfit
us for duty. It is better far that it is hidden.

Peter Rebuked

" He turned, and said unto Peter, Get thee behind Me, Satan."
MATT. xvi. 23

IT was Peter's love for Christ that made him rebel so at the thought of such a fate for Him. In his love he sought to hold the Master back from so throwing away His life. But in doing this he was acting the part of Satan in seeking to tempt Jesus from His great work of sacrifice. This way of the cross was not an accident ; it was the way marked out for Christ : to swerve from it would be to fail in His mission.

Our best friends may become our tempters in the same way. In their love for us they may seek to keep us from entering paths of duty which will lead to sacrifice. Mothers may seek to restrain their children from going to foreign fields. Any of us, in the warmth of our affection for our friends, may seek to dissuade them from perilous or costly service which it may be their duty to undertake. We need to guard ourselves at this point. The path of true success does not always lie along the sunny hillside ; sometimes it goes down into the dark valley of self-sacrifice. And if we try to hinder any from entering upon hard duties, urging them to choose easier ways, we may be doing Satan's work. We may be plucking the crown from the brow of our friend by holding back his feet from the way of the cross.

We all need to guard, too, against the counsels of friends who would restrain us from costly or perilous service. In matters of duty we must know only one guide, and follow the call of only one voice. We are not set in this world to have a good, easy time ; we are not set here to consult our own inclinations at all. We are here to go where Christ leads ; to follow Him to sacrifice and to death if He leads us in these paths. We dare not allow ourselves to be turned aside by any tenderness of human love. It is the way of duty, however hard, that takes us home.

Aug. 10

Self=Denial

" If any man will come after Me, let him deny himself."
MATT. xvi. 24

THERE are few things at which people play more wretched farces than in their efforts at self-denial. Very few seem to have the remotest conception of what it is . One does without meat on Fridays, eating fish instead, and thinks he has denied himself in a most commendable way. Another gives up social dissipation for forty days in Lent, and is complacent over the merit of great self-denial. Others make themselves miserable in various ways, inflicting pain. making useless and uncalled-for sacrifices, as if God were pleased when they suffer. But these things do not constitute self-denial. There is no merit or virtue in giving up anything, suffering any loss or pain, or making any sacrifice, merely for its own sake.

True self-denial is the renouncing of self and the yielding of the whole life to the will of Christ. It is self coming down from the life's throne, laying crown and sceptre at the Master's feet, and henceforth submitting the whole life to His sway. It is living all the while, not to please ourselves, not to advance our own personal interests, but to please our Lord and do His work. It is denying to ourselves anything that is sinful in His sight. It is the glad making of any sacrifice that loyalty to Him requires. It is the giving up of any pleasure or comfort for the good of others which the living out of His spirit may demand. The essential thing is that self gives way altogether to Christ as the motive of life.

Nothing, therefore, is true self-denial which is done merely as self-denial. True self-denial, like all other traits of Christlikeness, is unconscious of itself, wists not that its face shines. We deny ourselves when we follow Christ with joy and gladness, through cost and danger and suffering, just where He leads.

No Cross, No Crown

" *And take up his cross, and follow Me.*"—MATT. xvi. 24

THE cross is to be *taken up*, not simply borne when laid upon the shoulder. This implies willing, cheerful suffering for Christ. Some people endure trials, but always with repining. The spirit of these words requires cheerfulness in suffering for Christ. Half the trial is gone if we meet it in this glad spirit.

Notice again, it is *his* cross and not some other man's that each one is to take up. It is the particular cross that God lays at our own feet that we are to bear. We are never to make crosses for ourselves, but we are always to accept those which are allotted to us. Each one's own cross is the best for him. Sometimes we think our lot is peculiarly hard, and we compare it with the lot of this or that other person, and wish we had his cross instead of our own. But we do not know what other people's crosses really are. If we did we might not want to exchange. The cross that seems woven of flowers, if we put it on our shoulders we might find filled with sharp thorns under the flowers. The cross of gold that seems so bright we should find so heavy that it would crush us. The easiest cross for each one to bear is his own.

There is a way to get the crosses out of our life altogether. A father explained it thus to his child. Taking two pieces of wood, one longer than the other, he said : " Let the longer piece represent God's will, and the shorter your will. If I lay the two pieces side by side, parallel to each other, there is no cross ; it is only when I lay the shorter piece across the longer that I can make a cross. So there can be a cross in my life only when my will falls athwart God's, when I cannot say, ' Thy will be done.' If my will sweetly acquiesces in His, there is no cross." The way to take out the crosses is therefore always gladly to accept, through love to Him, whatever trial, pain, or loss God sends.

Aug. 12.

Lost, yet Found

" *Whosoever will save his life shall lose it : and whosoever will lose his life for My sake shall find it.*"—MATT. xvi. 25

IT seems to be saving one's life to be governed by self-interest, to avoid self-denial and sacrifice, to live to gather about one and into one's hands as much as possible of the things that give comfort, pleasure, or power. But if this be the motive, the life is really thrown away. That is the deep meaning of our Lord's words. Self-*seeking* is self-*losing*. We have not really learned how to live at all until we have learned to live for Christ. What we keep for ourselves we lose ; it is only what we give away that we really keep. Selfishness is not only sin ; it is also spiritual death.

The way to save one's life, says the Master, is to lose it. Christ Himself lost His life, poured it out in loving self-sacrifice for the good of others. It seemed a waste ; but was it a waste ? He found it again in greater glory. Paul lost his life for Christ, renounced everything for His sake, suffered everything, and gave his very life at the last ; but did he lose anything by his self-sacrifice ? A young girl, beautiful, cultured, honoured, with a lovely home and many friends, turned away from ease, refinement, and luxury, and went to teach the freed slaves. She lived among them, and gave out her rich young life in efforts to help them up and save them. One day she sickened and died, and her friends said : " Oh, what a waste of precious life ! " But was it a waste ?

All who follow Christ truly make this choice between saving and losing their life—that is, between making self-interest and Christ the motive in living. In following Christ we may never be called actually to make great sacrifices ; but that we are ready to make them, even to the utmost, is implied in our covenant of discipleship. Yet this losing is saving ; it is sowing the golden wheat in the ground—losing it for the time—to reap therefrom a rich harvest by-and-by.

An Unanswered Question

*" What is a man profited, if he shall gain the whole world,
and lose his own soul ? "*—MATT. xvi. 26

THAT is putting the case in its most favourable light.
The whole world is the largest possible gain. But
suppose a man gets it, it cannot keep him from trouble ; it
cannot give him peace of conscience ; it cannot comfort him
in sorrow ; it cannot make a soft pillow for him when he
is dying ; it cannot purchase heaven for him when he is
gone. All he can do with the world, after he has it, is to
keep it until he dies ; he cannot carry any of it with him
to the other life. " How much did he leave ? " asked
one, referring to a millionaire who had just died. " Every
cent," was the reply. He left all. So it is easy to see that
there is no profit, but rather a fearful and eternal loss, in
gaining even all the world at the price of one's soul.

Then think for how much smaller price than " the whole
world " many people sell their souls. Some do it for a few
hours' guilty pleasure ; some for a political office ; some for
money ; some for honour which fades in a day. In a
newspaper this advertisement appeared : " *Wanted*—A
nice cottage and grounds in exchange for a lot of choice
liquors." No doubt many people answered the advertisement. Men are continually giving home and property and
peace and love for strong drink. They are selling their
souls also in many other ways for pitiable trifles. They
are bartering their heavenly birthright for a mess of pot-
tage.

What shall a man give in exchange for his soul ? Ah !
that's the trouble. When the soul is lost, there is no way
of recovering it. When we have made our choice, and
lived our life, whether right or wrong, there is no possibility of changing the results. Life is given to us only
once ; and if we live it wrongly, there is no chance to live
it over again. A soul lost cannot be gotten back ; no
money will redeem it.

Christ's Special Friends

"*Jesus taketh Peter, James, and John.*"—MATT. xvii. 1

THESE three disciples belonged to the inner circle of our Lord's friends. There must have been something in them that peculiarly endeared them to Him. We know that Peter was a leader among the apostles, and also a bold confessor; that John was "the disciple whom Jesus loved;" and that James was the first of the band to die as a martyr. It is very encouraging to look at Peter, a man with so many faults, and who made so many mistakes, at last shamefully denying Christ, and yet remember that he was one of our Lord's closest friends, admitted to such high privileges. It gives encouragement to us that with all our faults we may yet be very dear to Christ.

It does not seem so strange that John was allowed to enter the inner circle. His disposition was gentle and amiable, very much like the Master's. Yet it is probable that John owed his sweetness and gentleness of character to his being with Jesus. He was not always a man of love. There is a Persian fable of a piece of clay made fragrant by lying on a rose; the perfume of the rose passed into the clay. So it is with John. He crept into his Master's bosom, and lay close to His heart; and his Master's spirit of love and gentleness passed into his life and transformed it. Thus we have a lesson, too, from John: constant and loving communion with Christ will change us into His likeness.

The lesson from this choosing of three out of the whole band for peculiar privileges is that while Jesus loves all His friends, there are certain ones whom He takes into closer confidence than the others. There are degrees of nearness to Him, even in this world. Should we not strive to be among those who, by disposition and by service, win their way to the closest places? We must remember that those who *serve* most are chiefest.

ḣeavenly Messengers

" There appeared unto them Moses and Elias talking with Him."—MATT. xvii. 3

THESE two heavenly messengers were conversing with Jesus; they were talking with Him about His death. Several thoughts are suggested by this. One is, that the death of Jesus was part of the Divine plan. It was no disaster, no defeat. It was understood in heaven that He was to die on a cross.

Another thought is, that Moses and Elijah had been sent to talk with Jesus, as He was now about to turn His face toward Jerusalem, that they might strengthen Him for the sad journey and for the bitter sorrows at the end of it. Before Jesus went to the wilderness there was a vision of glory, and a voice spoke, uttering the Divine approval, to strengthen Him to endure His temptation. Now again, when He is setting out for His cross, there is a vision and a voice, to prepare Him for the darkness and the agony.

In these heavenly visits we have a hint of the employment of the redeemed in heaven. These two men are sent all the way to earth to comfort and cheer a weary spirit in its mission of suffering. May it not be that all the saved shall thus be employed in glory ? It is delightful to think that we shall be sent from world to world on errands of love. The idea that in heaven we shall do nothing for ever but rest on green banks and sing praises to God receives no encouragement in the Scriptures. We are to be like Christ; and He is never idle, but ever busy in loving service. We shall be as the angels ; and they are ministering spirits, sent forth to minister to the heirs of salvation. " His servants shall serve Him " is one description of the employments of heaven. It will still be nobler there to minister than to be ministered unto. They will still be chief there who serve. Our poor work here is only a training for work in heaven and for ever.

Duty after Privilege

" *Lord, it is good for us to be here :......let us make here three*
tabernacles."—MATT. xvii. 4

WE should know that it was Peter who said this, even
if his name were not given ; it is just like Peter.
He wanted to hold the heavenly vision on the mountain-
top, and not go back any more to the cold, struggling life
of earth. It seemed such a heavenly place that he did not
want to leave it. It certainly was good to be there ; but
they could not stay there long and yet be faithful to their
duty and their mission. There was work waiting in the sad
world below which they must hasten to do. There was a
poor demoniac at the foot of the mountain whom the disciples could not cure ; the Master was sorely needed there.
Then farther off were Gethsemane, Gabbatha, and Golgotha
for Jesus ; He must make an atonement for the world.
Then for Peter there was Pentecost, with many years of
earnest service, and martyrdom in the end.

Devotion is good. It is very sweet to commune with
God in the closet, in the church, at the sacramental table ;
but we must not spend all our time in these holy exercises.
While the raptures thrill our souls we must not forget that
outside there are human wants crying for help and sympathy ; and we must tear ourselves away from our warmest
devotions and most exalted experiences to go down to
answer these cries. Religion is not for enjoyment only ;
God gives us spiritual enjoyment that we may be strong
for all loving service.

" Hark, hark ! a voice amid the quiet intense !
  It is thy duty waiting thee without.
Open thy door straightway, and get thee hence ;
  Go forth into the tumult and the shout ;
  Work, love, with workers, lovers all about ;
Then, weary, go thou back with failing breath,
  And in thy chamber make thy prayer and moan.
  One day upon His bosom, all thine own,
Thou shalt lie still, embraced in holy death."

Bright Clouds

" *A bright cloud overshadowed them.*"—MATT. xvii. 5

THE cloud was a symbol of the Divine presence. One of the writers says the disciples were afraid as they saw the cloud come down over the Master and the heavenly visitants. God still comes to us often in thick clouds, and we are afraid too. But the cloud meant no harm to the disciples. No cloud means any harm to a disciple when God is in the cloud ; and always, if we only listen, we may hear words of love.

" Sorrow touched by love grows bright
　　With more than rapture's ray ;
And darkness shows us worlds of light
　　We never saw by day."

There was a voice out of the cloud testifying to the Divine sonship. The disciples had been staggered at what Jesus had said about His rejection and death. Now they are assured that He is the Messiah, and that they must hear Him. Even if they could not understand, and if the things He said seemed to destroy all their hopes, they were still to hear.

There are times when God's ways with us seem very hard, and we think disaster is coming to every fair prospect in our life. In all such hours we should remember that He who rules over all is the Son of God, our Friend and Saviour ; and our trust in Him should never fail. We should listen always to what He says ; and when everything seems strange and dark, we should never doubt or fear. What so staggered the disciples then we now see to have been the most glorious and loving wisdom. So in our strangest trials there are the truest wisdom and the richest love. Hereafter we shall know. It was out of the cloud that this voice came. Out of the clouds that hang over us come often the tenderest voices of Divine love, the most precious disclosures of Divine grace.

Failures

" *I brought him to Thy disciples, and they could not cure him.*"—MATT. xvii. 16

THERE are a great many teachers in our Sunday schools who have had similar experiences. Children have been brought to them possessed by evil spirits, and they have failed to cast out the demons. They have tried every device, gentle and severe ; they have prayed and laboured, they have talked and wept ; but the evil spirits in their scholars have defied all efforts to dislodge them. Teachers of such incorrigible scholars may learn some lessons here.

It may be a little encouragement, first of all, to know that even Christ's apostles met at least one case that they could not do anything with ; no wonder if common people like us fail now and then. It is failures like this in the apostles that bring them down to our level. When we see them victorious and successful at every point, we are discouraged. But when we find them baffled and defeated, we see that they were human, just like us, and could do nothing by themselves. We get far more real help from St. Paul's experience with his " thorn " than we get from his " third heaven " exaltation. (In this latter he is so far beyond us that we cannot follow him ; in the former we are on familiar ground.

It may be instructive also to study the reasons of the apostles' failure. For one, the Master was absent : the disciple cannot do anything without his Lord. This is a lesson we should deeply impress on our own minds. Unless we have Christ with us, all our Christian work will utterly fail. Of ourselves we can never change a heart. Another reason was want of faith in the disciples : unbelief makes any one weak. Though absent, Christ's power would have been theirs, had not their faith failed. Still another reason was the hardness of the case : all cases are not alike diffi-cult, some requiring more faith and spiritual power than others.

Aug. 19

The Unfailing Helper

" Bring him hither to Me."—MATT. xvii. 17

THE disciples had failed in their effort to cast out the demon, but there yet was hope. The Master Himself was now at hand, and He could not fail. There should be a great deal of encouragement in this for all who are trying to change people's lives into spiritual beauty. When parents have done all they can to make their children true and beautiful in their character, and have failed, they can take them to Jesus. He can cast out the evil that is in them. He can give them new hearts. He can put His own Holy Spirit within them, and thus transform them into Christlikeness.

When teachers have in their classes incorrigible scholars, on whom they can make no impression, their discouragement and failure should lead them to bring them to Jesus, for He is yet able to take them and change them into noble beauty. When troubled souls have sought in vain for comfort and help from the Church and from Christian ministers, they should go to Christ Himself, for He can comfort. No matter in what we have been defeated, Christ stands ready to take our humiliation and turn it into victory. The disciples had toiled all night in vain, but when they dropped their net at the Lord's bidding, great was their success. So always in the shadows of our human failure He stands to give blessing.

There is another thought here. It is to *Christ*, and not merely to the school or the Church or the minister, that we should try to lead our children and our friends. The teacher cannot regenerate the child. The Church cannot renew its nature. The minister cannot cast out the evil in the child's heart. Unless we bring our children truly to Christ they must remain unchanged. Baptism does not wash the heart. The Lord's Supper does not put grace into the life. We must bring our friends and ourselves direct to Christ.

Aug. 20

Desire for Place and Power

*" They held their peace : for by the way they had disputed
among themselves, who should be the greatest."*—MARK
ix. 34

SOMETHING is wrong when we have done that through
the day which we are ashamed to tell Christ about
when we come home in the evening and bow at His feet, or
when we have said that which we are not willing to repeat
to Him in our prayers when we come to talk face to face
with Him. Some day we shall be asked what we said and
did as we came along through life ; let us be careful to say
or do nothing which we shall be ashamed to confess before
our Lord and the angels and all the universe.

The disciples' ideas of position and rank were altogether
earthly. They wrangled for places in the kingdom Christ
was going to set up, very much as a company of modern
politicians wrangle over spoils of office. Peter thought he
ought to be prime minister, for he was the best speaker.
Judas thought he would certainly be secretary of the
treasury, which would give him a prominent place. John
was Christ's favourite, and felt sure he would be the greatest. Andrew had been first called, and claimed that this
fact ought to give him the precedence. So they bickered.

So Christians sometimes do to-day. They want official
places in the Church—want to be elders, deacons, or
trustees ; or want positions in the Sunday school, as super-
intendents, teachers, secretaries, or librarians ; or want to
be presidents or vice-presidents or something else of missionary societies, or mite societies, or Dorcas societies, or
of some other organizations ; or want to be pastors of
popular city churches. It is the same old spirit—the
idea that the way to be a great Christian is to be prominent
in some official position, to have honour and power among
men. It is a shame to see such scrambling in the Church
of Christ, but sometimes we see it ; perhaps we sometimes
scramble ourselves.

The Child in the Midst

" Jesus called a little child unto Him, and set him in the midst of them."—MATT. xviii. 2

THE child preached the sermon. It said to those ambitious disciples, " Shame on all your quarrelling about prominence and high places. Look at me. I am much higher up in the kingdom of heaven than you. You must get clear of all your proud thoughts and become lowly and simple-minded and childlike, or in the new kingdom you will have no place at all, much less a high place." Little children are all preaching sermons to us, if only we have ears to hear. Children, in their innocence, their simplicity, their naturalness, their sweetness of soul, wherever they go exert an influence upon other lives which no words can describe. They are at once the greatest preachers and themselves the most eloquent sermons.

This picture of Jesus with the little one in His arms is very beautiful. In all the Bible there is scarcely another which so well represents the attitude both of the soul and of the Saviour in salvation and in all Christian life. Jesus takes the child in His arms : there is love, tenderness, protection. The bosom is the place of warmth, of affection, of intimacy, of confidence. The encircling arms imply safety, support, shelter. He lifted up the child and held it in His arms ; so He carries His people through this world : He does not merely tell them how to go, but He takes them on His shoulders, carrying not their burdens only, but themselves. Thus He bears them on through life and through death.

Then look at the picture the other way—the child in the Saviour's arms. Its attitude speaks of trust, confidence, repose, peace, love, joy—just the feelings which belong to the true Christian. What a place the bosom of Christ is in danger, in storm, in sorrow, in death ! Shall we not learn just to nestle in our Saviour's arms in all our experiences ?

"For His Sake"

" Whosoever shall receive one of such children in My name, receiveth Me."—MARK ix. 37

THIS saying of Christ is rich enough to be studied long and deeply. To receive a child in a certain way is to receive Christ Himself. How must a child be received ? *In Christ's name*—that is, out of love to Him, for His sake, just as we would receive Christ Himself if He actually came in person. So it is not enough to love children, to care for orphans or those that are destitute. It must be for the sake of Christ that we do these things. Thus in every child do we see Christ stand before us, and we may have the honour of receiving Him.

The Christmas legends are full of illustrations of this truth. One of the most beautiful of these tells how on a Christmas eve a poor man, coming homeward through the forest, heard a cry, and found a little child, cold and hungry. The good man stopped and sought the little one, and took him with him to his house. His children gladly welcomed the stranger, and shared their evening meal with him. Then, while he sat there at the table, suddenly a change came over the child's appearance, and lo ! it was the Christ-child whom unconsciously the family had received in this needy, suffering little one. Christ is ever coming to our doors in the person of some poor or suffering one, and the reception we give the one He sends we give to Him. This ought to make us careful how we treat those who need sympathy or help, lest some time we slam the door in the face of Jesus.

These words of Christ have their precious suggestion for parents. The child that comes to them comes in Christ's name, comes in His stead. It brings blessings to them and to their home if they receive it in the right way— in Christ's name, with love, with thankfulness, with reverence. Suppose they do not receive it with welcome, as from God, it is as if they rejected Christ Himself.

Little Deeds of Love

" Whosoever shall give you a cup of water to drink in My name, because ye belong to Christ, verily I say unto you, he shall not lose his reward."—MARK ix. 41

IT seems wonderful indeed that God should keep note of such a little thing as the giving of a cup of water to a thirsty Christian. It shows how dear to Him are His people, since the smallest things done to one of them He accepts, remembers, and rewards. The mention here of the giving of a cup of water suggests that this promise is for little, commonplace acts, rather than for great deeds. We are too niggardly with our helpfulness. God has put His gifts of love into our hearts that they may be given out. We would call a man selfish who should refuse a cup of water to one who was thirsty. Yet many of us do this continually: it is the heart that thirsts, and the water we refuse to give is human kindness.

> " 'Tis a little thing
> To give a cup of water, yet its draught
> Of cool refreshment drained by fevered lips
> May give a shock of pleasure to the frame
> More exquisite than when nectarean juice
> Renews the life of joy in happiest hours.
> It is a little thing to speak a phrase
> Of common comfort, which by daily use
> Has almost lost its sense, yet on the ear
> Of Him who thought to die unmourned
> 'Twill fall like choicest music."

Kindness is just the word for these small acts. Kindness is love flowing out in little gentlenesses. We ought to carry our lives so that they will be perpetual benedictions wherever we go. All we need for such a ministry is a heart full of love for Christ; for if we truly love Christ we shall also love our fellow-men, and love will always find ways of helping. A heart filled with gentleness cannot be miserly of its benedictions.

Aug. 24

Wise Sacrifices

" *It is better for thee to enter into life halt or maimed, rather than having two hands or two feet to be cast into ever-lasting fire.*"—MATT. xviii. 8

THIS life is so full of peril that even its best things may become stumbling-blocks. Our very qualities of strength may become fatal forces driving us to ruin. Human beauty is a memento of unfallen life, and yet beauty has proved a snare to many a woman, drawing her away from God. Power to make money is a perilous gift, which has led many a man to spiritual ruin. The appetites, desires, and affections are part of the glory of humanity, and yet unbridled they have whirled many a noble life to destruction. These are illustrations of our Lord's meaning when He speaks of cutting off the hand or the foot which causes us to stumble.

It is better to throw away altogether the money-making power and go poor through life with the talent wasted and shrivelled, and reach heaven, than to exercise the gift and grow rich, and be lost for ever. A steam-vessel came into port which had long been out on the sea. An accident had happened which caused delay. The coal gave out ; then all that would burn—cargo, stores, furniture—had to be burned up to bring the vessel home. At last she gained the shore, but stripped of everything of value. Yet it was better to burn up all her cargo and stores than perish at sea.

Some men can get to heaven only by sacrificing every earthly pleasure and crucifying every desire ; but who will say the prize is not worth the sacrifice ? The hand had better be chopped off than steal or strike down another. The foot had better be cut off than carry one into crime or sin. The eye had better be put out than by its lustful gazing set the soul on fire. A man on a wrecked vessel had better throw his bags of gold into the sea and have his life saved, than hold on to the gold and sink into the waves.

"The Joy set before Him"

" *When the time was come that He should be received up.*"
LUKE ix. 51

THERE were a great many painful steps to take before our Lord could reach this blessed hour and be received up to glory. The immediate future was full of struggle, loss, and pain. On yonder heights His eye saw the radiancy of heaven, with its opening gates and its welcome home ; but before His feet could enter the shining portal there was a broad battle-plain to pass through, and it was full of enemies. There were days of toil and nights of loneliness. At last He must pass through Gethsemane's gloom, and all that *via dolorosa* which led to Calvary. He must die and go into the grave. All this before He could be received up.

But He did not think of any of these painful steps. He did not let His eye rest on the shadows that lay in the valley, but lifted it up to the mountain-top beyond, where the splendours of heaven blazed. Keeping His thoughts away forward on the glories that were to be His when He had ended the journey, He forgot the toils and the tears and fainted not.

This is a wonderful secret which all of us ought to learn —not to think so much about the toil and hardness of the way, but to look beyond to the brightness of the end. No matter how rough the road is if it only brings us home at last. Many of us go worrying all through this life, keeping our eyes always downcast on the path we are treading. We see all the troubles, the difficulties and discouragements, but we never raise our eyes to see the joys and the blessings that are waiting for us. We ought to learn this life-secret which made Christ forget the shame and sorrow of His cross and see only the glory beyond. Learn to look up toward heaven. Think of its joys, its blessedness, until earth's trials shall melt away in the brightness, and its griefs and losses be forgotten in the hopes of glory.

Aug. 26   "Go Forward"

"He stedfastly set His face to go to Jerusalem."

LUKE ix. 51

WE do not know what lies before us in life. Some great sorrow or anguish may be awaiting us on the morrow, but it casts no gloom over our spirits to-day, because we are ignorant of it. This is a merciful provision in our lives. If some of us knew all that we must pass through in the future, it would make our lives very bitter, even while our joys are unbroken. It is a great deal better that we should not know until God leads us to the edge of the experience.

But there was no such kindly veiling of the future from Christ's eyes. He saw every step of the sorrowful way to the close of His life. Yet this makes the scene before us all the more grand. Knowing all, see how eager He is to press on in His path. He could not be held back. He steadfastly set His face to go, and bent His steps with intense haste to His journey, which He knew would lead Him to Gethsemane, Gabbatha, and Golgotha. In this, as in all things, He left us an example, that we should follow His steps. It is thus that we should ever go forward in the path of duty, no matter what the dangers, the sufferings, the sacrifices, that lie in our path. We are too apt to hesitate and count the cost, when hard tasks are assigned to us, instead of eagerly pressing on in duty's path.

That walk to Jerusalem, every step a step toward the cross always in plain view, is one of the finest heroisms of history. Let us not forget why the walk was taken. That cross meant salvation and eternal blessedness for millions of lost souls. Love was the heart of that heroism. Jesus pressed on with intense earnestness, because the accomplishment of His mission would be life for the world and glory for the Father. We ought to bare our heads in reverence as we see Jesus thus hastening to His cross; it was for our sakes He set His face steadfastly to go to Jerusalem.

An Open Fountain

"If any man thirst, let Him come unto Me, and drink."
JOHN vii. 37

EVERY word here is full of meaning. "If" marks the one condition to which the Saviour's invitation is addressed. Of course if we do not thirst we will not care to come to the well and drink. Souls are dying all about us, not because there is no water near, but because they are not thirsty. Intense thirst is a pitiable condition; but the lack of soul-thirst is infinitely more pitiable: it is hopeless. The words "any man" show us how universal is our Lord's invitation. The cry was not to "any Jew," nor to "any man of good character," but to "*any* man." No one is left out.

The word "thirsty" describes the need which Christ is able to supply. It is not bodily thirst, but thirst of the soul, which He offers to quench. For the soul as well as the body has its thirsts, and there is no spring of earth at which they can be satisfied.

The words "let him come" show us the gate to the fountain flung wide open. There is no barrier in the way. "Let him come" reminds us, however, that if we would have our thirst quenched by Christ we must really come to Him. We must leave our dry wastes, where no water is, and come to Christ. We cannot find Christ while we stay in our sins.

The word "drink" tells us that we must receive Christ Himself into our hearts if we would have our thirst satisfied in Him. Merely going to a spring and looking at its sparkling waters will never quench any one's thirst; we must drink of the waters. So, looking at Christ is not enough to bless us; we must take Him into our life and let His Spirit fill our hearts. This new picture of Christ presents Him as a great well in the desert. The water gushes from a cleft in the rock. We understand the meaning of the cleft—Jesus died that there might be water for our soul's thirst.

Words of Life

"*Never man spake like this man.*"—John vii. 46

IN all literature there are no words like those which Christ spoke. We remember what wonderful power His words had. One of them dropped upon the wild sea and quieted it in a moment; another touched the blind man's eyes and opened them; another fell upon the sparkling water and changed it into wine; another fell into a dark grave and caused a dead man who lay there to arise and come forth.

Then we remember how His words comforted sorrow and gave peace to troubled ones; how they reached men's hearts and changed the whole purpose of their lives. Those who heard His words rose up from their business and from their sins, and left all to follow Him in His homelessness and loneliness. Demons listened trembling when He spoke, and instantly recognized His power, and cowered and obeyed.

These words of Christ still have the same power. They are yet calming tempests, and opening blind eyes, and expelling evil spirits, and raising the dead. They are yet giving comfort to sorrowing ones, and hope to despairing ones, and forgiveness to penitents. They are still changing hearts, sweetening bitter fountains, and making flowers bloom where thorns grew before. If you lean upon a word of Christ, you will find the everlasting arm underneath it. If you are sinking in the waves of trial and grasp one of these blessed words, you will find the Divine hand gloved in it, and will be upheld by it. If you are pursued by spiritual enemies and seize a word of Christ, you will find in your hand an all-conquering sword, before which all foes will fly. If you are weary, or in sorrow, and pillow your head on one of these precious words, you will find that you are lying on your Father's bosom, close to His warm, beating heart. The world's richest treasures to-day are the words of Christ. "Never man spake like this man."

Experience the best Evidence

" Doth our law judge any man before it hear him and know what he doeth ? "—JOHN vii. 51

NICODEMUS asked justice for Jesus, and pleaded that He should not be condemned without a fair hearing. The same principle of justice should appeal now to men who are uttering hostile opinions of Christ. His enemies are never really those who have by experience proved His promises unworthy of confidence. The world has never yet known of a true follower of Christ who has honestly made experiment of Christ's salvation and has been disappointed.

All who have trusted Him have found every word true on which He caused them to hope. No one that has tried Him as Saviour, Deliverer, Helper, and Friend has ever become His enemy. Those who oppose Christ are they who know nothing about Him by experience. They judge Him before they hear Him. But is this just ? Is it right to condemn any man if we really have no knowledge of the facts alleged against him ? Would it be right to condemn a book we had never read, or of which we had no actual knowledge ?

Surely no one has any right to be an enemy of Christ without having honestly and conscientiously examined Christ's claims and then proved them untrue and unworthy of confidence. No one should put away Christ until he find something better than Christ—something that will do more for him, that will bring him better help in trouble, a better salvation in his lost condition, that will make a better man of him, lifting him up to nobler heights of holiness and beauty.

The best evidence of Christianity always is experience. " Come and see," was all the eager disciple asked, when the man invited doubted. " Come and see " is better always than argument. If we can only get people to try Christ's religion for themselves, they will not condemn it.

No Longer Captives

" *Ye shall know the truth, and the truth shall make you free.*"—JOHN viii. 32

EVEN among the followers of Christ there is still much bondage because of ignorance of the truth. Superstitious people are in terror of certain imagined dangers, but their terror instantly vanishes when they learn the truth. They are slaves of ignorance until knowledge makes them free. So it is in spiritual things. There are Christians who are in perpetual distress about their sins, thinking that God's wrath still rests upon them, when in reality they passed long since from under wrath into blessed forgiveness. They do not know the truth about Divine forgiveness, and therefore miss all the joy. If they but knew the truth, the truth would make them free.

At the end of the last war between France and Great Britain there were a number of French ships that had been out for some years. They did not know that peace had been proclaimed in their absence, and they wanted to get back to their own country without meeting any British men-of-war. A gale scattered them, and one vessel was carried away from the others, and when the morning broke she found herself opposite the coast of England, with a British war-vessel lying close by. The French captain was greatly perplexed and in terror. His first thought was to sink his vessel rather than allow her to fall into the enemy's hands. At length his ship was hailed from the man-of-war, and he was told that peace had been proclaimed between Great Britain and his own country. When he had been assured of this fact his fear vanished.

So the truth of the gospel makes us free, by telling us of the peace which had been made for us by Christ's cross The moment we truly accept Christ we are free for ever from sin's curse and condemnation. We are no longer captives, but free.

Aug. 31

Christ's Yoke True Freedom

" We be Abraham's seed, and were never in bondage to any man."—JOHN viii. 33

SELF-CONFIDENCE is the peril even of the truest piety. We are in danger of forgetting that we are nothing, and that Jesus Christ is our all in all. This very day children of godly parents need to be on their guard against the sin of these ancient Jews. By what species of mental hoodwinking they fancied themselves " free," when at that very time Roman soldiers stood guard about their city, we cannot understand.

But both these errors are common enough. Many people boast more of their " blood " than of anything else. It truly is a great privilege to have good ancestry ; it is good capital with which to start in life ; but beyond a certain point it does not count. The first question may be, " Who is your father ? " but the next question will be, " Who are you ? " Parents may lead a child to Christ in infancy, but when the child is old enough for moral accountability it must accept Christ by a personal faith. Nothing else really avails for salvation. We must enter Christ's kingdom as individuals. Abraham had some descendants who were far enough away from his virtue, and whom he would scarcely wish to recognize as his children ; and many a godly father nowadays has worthless sons.

Then the illusion of freedom, while one is really in chains, is not altogether rare. A great many people living in sin imagine they are the only free people there are. They have thrown off the restraints of religion and of law, and they think they are free, while they regard those who follow Christ as slaves. Sin plays strange tricks with men. Insane people sometimes deck themselves out in tinsel, and imagine that they are some great personages. The devil often puts similar notions into the heads of his deluded followers. None are free but those who wear Christ's yoke.

Servants of Sin

" Whosoever committeth sin is the servant of sin."
JOHN viii. 34

SO the people who boast so of their freedom are really slaves after all. They look upon a Christian with a sort of pity, because he cannot do the wicked things they do. " Oh, I forgot ! You cannot go to the theatre ; you cannot play cards ; you cannot drink wine. You are a Christian. I would not be so bound up ; I want to be free." So these people talk while they enjoy their licence—which they call liberty ! They do not imagine that they are the slaves, and that the Christians whom they so pity are really the only free people there are in the world.

Every one is a servant of some master, the only difference being in the master. There is no dishonour in having a master, if the master be worthy of us, able to lead us up to glory. The Christian has Christ for his master, while he who lives in sin has sin for his master. Christ is a blessed master ; serving Him lifts one up to eternal glory. What sort of a master is sin ? We need but to look about us to see. What does sin do for its slaves ? What life did it ever ennoble or lift up ?

It is said that one of the great prisons of this country was built by the prisoners themselves. They dressed the stones and built the walls which afterwards shut them in. The legend is familiar, too, of the man to whom the devil came ordering a chain of a certain length. Coming at the appointed time, he ordered the chain made longer, and then went away. When at last it was finished he came again, and with it bound the poor man who had fastened its links at his command. So sinners are everywhere building their own prison walls, and with their own hands fashioning the chains to bind them for ever. We need to be on our guard perpetually against little sins of thought, of habit—mere gossamer threads at first, which will become cables at last if we allow them to be wrapped about our souls.

Passing By

" *By chance there came down a certain priest that way : and when he saw him, he passed by on the other side.*"— LUKE x. 31

WE must not suppose that all priests were thus cold and heartless. Ministers are generally warm-hearted men ; they ought all to be so ; they ought to set the people the example of kindness and sympathy ; they ought to be like Christ—and He was always ready to help anybody in trouble. No doubt many of the Jewish priests were kind and generous ; but here was one who was not. This shows us that one may occupy a very sacred place, and yet have a cold and hard heart. But it is very sad when it is so.

This priest did not even stop to look at the sufferer, or to ask him how he came to be injured, or to inquire what he could do for him He kept as far to the other side of the road as he could get ; perhaps he even pretended not to see the wounded man. No doubt he had excuses ready in his own mind. He was in a great hurry, or he was very tired, or he could not do anything for the poor man if he should stop, or he was very tender-hearted and could not bear to look on blood.

No matter about his motives ; it is more to our purpose to avoid repeating his fault. Do we never pass by human wants that we know well we ought to stop to relieve ? Do we never keep out of the way of those whose needs strongly appeal to us ? Do we never have trouble hunting up ex-cuses to satisfy our own clamorous consciences because we have passed by some one we ought to have helped ? Some people look the other way when they are passing a blind man on the wayside. Ministers have refused to go to see sick people because they were weary Persons have stayed away from church because there was to be an appeal for money for a needy cause. This verse is an ugly mirror, isn't it ? It shows us blemishes that we didn't know we had.

Sept. 3

My Neighbour

" *A certain Samaritan......had compassion on him, and went
to him, and bound up his wounds.*"—LUKE x. 33, 34

NOW we must not conclude that the half-heathen
Samaritans were better as a class than the highly-
favoured Jews. Our Lord uses a Samaritan in His parable
because He wants to impress the law of love. No matter
who the sufferer is that we come upon in any of life's paths,
he is our neighbour. He may be a very worthless sort of
man ; but no matter, he is our neighbour. As we look
closely at him, we may see that he is an enemy. Once he
did us a bitter, cruel wrong, and he has no claim whatever
on us for sympathy or for help ; but no matter, he is our
neighbour. The person of the human race that we find
suffering or in need of any kind becomes for the time our
neighbour—the one neighbour to whom for the present
we owe love.

There is more definition here : we learn what the word
" love " means. You say, " I can't love hateful people ; I
can't love criminals ; I can't love a poor tramp." Nobody
expects you to love such people as you love your wife, your
child, your friend. It is not likely that this Samaritan had
a tender affection for this wounded Jew while he was helping him. Samaritans were not in the habit of loving Jews
very deeply. But he did not look at the man and calculate
whether he loved him or not before he began to attend to
his wounds. Yet he loved him precisely as the commandment meant he should love him. His love was not a warm
emotion ; it was a very practical affection.

First it was pity : he had compassion on him. But pity
is sometimes a very useless emotion—merely a tear that
comes easily, and costs nothing. This good wayfarer had
more than a tear. His pity got into his hands and into
his pocket. He went to the man and bound up his wounds
and helped him to an inn, and gave attention to him until
he was restored.

Spiritual Blindness

" *As Jesus passed by, He saw a man which was blind from his birth.*"—JOHN ix. 1

THE blind man illustrates every one's natural condition. For one thing, he had never been able to see. So men are born in a state of sin. Whatever we may say about the sweetness, innocence, and purity of childhood, the Scriptures plainly teach that no one is born by natural birth *in* the kingdom of heaven, but that all must be born again to enter it.

Another point of analogy is, that this man's blindness shut off from him a whole world of beauty. There were lovely things all around him—green fields, sweet flowers, blue skies, bright sunshine, shining stars; but he never saw any of these things. So there is a whole world of spiritual beauty lying about the unregenerate and above him—the love of God, Divine promises, blessed hopes, the heavenly kingdom, all the joys of salvation; but he sees nothing of all this glorious world.

It is said that a lady looking at one of Turner's pictures, delineating some scene of nature, said to the artist, " Mr. Turner, I cannot see in nature what you put in your pictures." The artist's quiet answer was, " Don't you wish you could, madam ? " Men of the world observe the raptures of Christian faith and Christian hope, and read the joyous words of Christian experience, and say with a sneer, " We cannot see any such joys as these in religion." The only proper answer is, " Don't you wish you could ? " It takes the artist's eye to see the glory of nature; it takes the opened eye of Christian faith to see the glories of God's spiritual kingdom.

For another thing, this blind man's condition was incurable. In this, too, his case illustrated the condition of every sinner. The sinner is incurable, and none but Christ can remove his spiritual blindness. " Except a man be born again, he cannot *see* the kingdom of God."

"The Night Cometh"

" I must work the works of Him that sent Me, while it is
day : the night cometh, when no man can work "—
JOHN ix. 4

EVEN Jesus felt the pressure of time's brevity, and the necessity for doing promptly and quickly the work which had been given Him to do. How much more should we feel this pressure, and hasten to improve the moments as they fly. We have all some work given us by God Himself. We are in the world on Divine missions—sent from God to take some specific part in blessing the world.

To do this work we have just a " day " of time. Each one's day is his lifetime. A day is a brief time : it is not long from the rising to the setting of the sun. It is a fixed time : when the sun comes to his going down, no power in the universe can prolong his stay for one moment. When death comes he will not wait one instant. Unfinished then, unfinished for ever.

Yet the day is long enough for God's plan. The sun never sets too soon for His purpose. Each little life is long enough for the little part of the world's work allotted to it. This is true even of the infant that lives but an hour, merely coming into this world, smiling its benediction, and flying away. It is true of the child, of the young man or young woman, of him who dies in the maturity of his powers, with his hands yet full of unfinished tasks. No one can ever offer as an excuse for an unfulfilled life-work that the time given to him was too short. It is always long enough if only every moment of it be filled with simple faithfulness.

To have our work completed at the end, we must do it while the day lasts. Mr. M'Cheyne had on his watch-dial a picture of the setting sun, and over it the words, " The night cometh." Every time he looked at his watch, to see the hour, he was reminded of the shortness of life, and of the urgent necessity for earnestness in duty. We should all catch the lesson.

Sight to the Blind

" *When He had thus spoken......He anointed the eyes......and said......Go, wash.*"—JOHN ix. 6, 7

IT is related that one day the Empress of Austria was riding over the country in her carriage, and saw a woman a little distance from the road acting in a strange manner. She soon discovered that the woman was blind, and further, that she was close to a precipice —that another step might hurl her to death. The empress quickly left her carriage and hurried to the poor woman, just in time to save her life. The world admires the act ; but here is one still more beautiful. The King of Glory sees a poor blind beggar sitting in darkness, is moved with compassion for him, and stops to open his eyes.

We may trace here the course of Christ with this blind man. He saw him, and was touched by his condition. So the sight of a sinner always touches Christ. He came unasked to the blind man, and brought the healing unsought to him. He touched his eyes, bringing Himself as the light of the world into contact with the man's darkness. So Christ comes first to us, not waiting to be sought. In His incarnation He brought Himself in contact with our fallen nature to save it. By His spirit He touches each blind soul that believes, and brings light and salvation to it.

He used means, making clay with the spittle, anointing the man's eyes, then sending him to wash. Christ uses means in the opening of men's spiritual eyes. He sends His grace to us through His Word, through the sacraments, through the touch and love of human friends.

He gave this man something to do, something requiring obedience and action. So He gives the sinner something to do, asking him to believe, to rise up, to wash in the fountain, to confess his Saviour, and follow Him into lowly service. Thus the curing of this blind man illustrates the opening of the spiritual eyes.

The Blind Man's Obedience

" *He went his way therefore, and washed, and came seeing.*"
JOHN ix. 7

WE must mark the promptness of this blind man's obedience. See him rising from his place, and led by some attendant, walking along the street with the patches of mud upon his eyes. People probably laughed at him as he went along, but he did not mind it. Christ had told him to go to the pool of Siloam and wash, and he was going to do it. Was not the great blessing of sight boon enough to compensate for any trouble in going after it ? He would not be laughed out of the cure that was so near to his hand.

Perhaps some people told him it was all nonsense—that mud never cured any one's blindness, and that the Siloam water had no such wondrous power. Still he pressed on through the long streets, amid the hooting and laughing people, until he came to the pool. There he washed, and lo ! as he washed, his eyes, which never had seen before, now saw clearly. For the first time in all his life he saw the beautiful things about him—the skies, the hills, the buildings, the colours, the faces of the people. So his faith was rewarded.

In all this there is an analogy which is so obvious that it scarcely need be written out. This man's faith in taking that walk through the streets to the pool illustrates the kind of faith every sinner must exercise in obeying Christ. if he would have his spiritual eyes opened and be saved. People sneer at the Christian, and ask, " What good is it going to do you to trust in Christ and unite with the Church ? " Then the result—the opening of his eyes to see the world of natural beauty never seen before, though lying close all the years—illustrates the revelation which faith in Christ brings to the believing soul. God's face and heaven's invisible things burst upon the spiritual vision of him whose soul's eyes are opened. So faith has its reward.

The Good Shepherd

" *He calleth His own sheep by name.*"—JOHN x. 3

THERE is a great difference between the care which the owner gives and that which a servant or hireling gives. There is a difference between the way a true mother looks after her child and the way a hired nurse does it. This is seen especially when the child is sick or in danger. The nurse serves for pay; the mother serves for love. Christ the Good Shepherd is the owner of His sheep.

There is something very sweet in the thought that Christians are Christ's *own*. It suggests how dear they are to Him. " Having loved *His own* which were in the world, He loved them unto the end." The thought also brings with it the assurance of love and care. His will is that " His own " shall be with Him in heaven for ever. The thought suggests also much about our duty to Christ. If we are of " His own," He has the entire right to the disposal of our lives and our services.

There is something very wonderful in the thought that Christ calls His sheep by their individual names. There are some pastors who do not know their people by name when they have but a few hundred to know. Christ has millions scattered over all the world; it is hard for us to realize that every one of these He knows personally by name. The Bible tells us that He calleth the stars by their names, but then the stars are so big that it does not seem so strange. But here is a poor widow, one of His own, living in a desolate garret in the heart of a great city, amid thronging thousands. Does He know her name? Here is a little orphan child, one of His own, left with no human friend to protect him. Does He know this little one? Certainly He does. This ought to be a very precious truth to every one who loves Christ and belongs to Him. He knows if any of His own are suffering or in need, or if they are in danger; and He will never neglect even the least of them.

Following Jesus

*" He......leadeth them out......He goeth before them, and the
sheep follow Him."*—JOHN x. 3, 4

THE Oriental shepherd does not drive his sheep, but
leads them wherever he wants to take them. At
night he leads them into the fold for safety. In the
morning he leads them out to pasture. So Christ never
drives His people; He goes before them and leads them,
and they follow him.

Sheep need to be led. They have no such instinct for
finding their own way as most other animals have. Christ's
people are just like them. Sheep wander away, and a lost
sheep never finds its way back. " All we like sheep have
gone astray ; " and we could never find the way home again
if the Good Shepherd did not seek us and lead us back.
Christ leads His people *gently*. He goes before His sheep.
He is very thoughtful for the weak ones. " He gathers
the lambs in His arms, and carries them in His bosom."
He never leads His sheep too fast. He takes them sometimes over rough and dangerous ways, but He never loses
any of them. Not a sheep of Christ's was ever yet lost by the
way under His guidance, even in the most perilous paths.

An old guide said to a tourist in the Alps, who was
afraid to trust himself to the guide's hand to be helped
over some perilous ledge, " This hand never lost a man."
Christ never lost a man. He has led millions home over
this world's paths, but not one of them ever perished in the
way. " Those that thou gavest Me I have kept, and not
one of them is lost."

Christ leads His sheep to the pastures and by the still
waters. Sometimes He leads them over deserts, and along
thorny paths, and through dark gorges ; but He is always
just before them, and where He is they are safe. At the
last He leads them through the valley of the shadows into
the heavenly fold. There they shall be safe eternally, and
be blessed in His love.

Green Pastures

" By Me if any man enter in, he shall......find pasture."
JOHN x. 9

THE shepherd takes care that his sheep are well fed. Christ also feeds His people, and leads them out to find pasture. The Bible is His pasture-land, and the pasturage there is always good. Every chapter is a field of rich grass. Some of these fields seem at first to be bare and sterile ; but even in the barest there is enough pasture to feed a hungry soul.

Then there are the pasture-fields of prayer. These lie very close to the border of heaven. They are always up in the quiet valleys among the mountains. The Good Shepherd leads us to them through the gates of prayer. We bow down in lowly humility, and enter with Him into the green pastures, and feed our souls until their hunger is satisfied.

The Church is another of our Shepherd's pasture-fields. We enter the gates of the sanctuary, and at once we find spiritual food. We find it in the services, in the ordinances, and in the sacraments.

In our common life in this world, if we are faithfully following Christ, we are continually in fields of rich pasture. Christ never leads us into any places in which there is nothing to feed us. Even in the hot plains of trial and sorrow there is food. We sometimes think there is only barrenness in our toilsome life, filled with temptations, cares, and sacrifices ; but the Good Shepherd is ever with us, and there is always pasture.

Thus the whole world is a rich field when Jesus leads His flock. If any Christians are not well fed, it is because they will not feed. The trouble must be that they do not hunger for spiritual food. The saddest thing in this world is not a passionate cry for bread, but a soul that has no hunger. Many souls die in the midst of the provision made by the Good Shepherd, not for want of food, but for want of appetite.

Sept. 11

Christ Knows His Own

" *I......know My sheep.*"—JOHN x. 14

THE Oriental shepherds had certain marks by which they knew their own sheep. Even in this country the farmers put marks on their sheep—their own initial, or an " ear-mark," or some other particular sign by which they will know them anywhere. Christ knows His people by certain distinguishing marks.

He knows them by their faces. There is something in every true child of God which shows where he belongs— some family likeness, some feature of the Divine image shining out. The prodigal's father knew his son when he saw him a long way off. In his rags, his beggary, amid the traces of dissipation, the eye of love recognized the child. Christ knows His own, however dim the likeness, by their faces. The crowds do not recognize heaven's princes in the humble Christians they meet ; but every angel knows them. Not only does Christ know His own by their faces, but also by their voice. The mother knows her child's voice anywhere, even in the darkness, and can distinguish it among a thousand voices. Christ knows the voices of His own wherever He hears them speak or cry.

He knows them also by their character. Even if the outside is rough and uncouth, it does not hide from His eye the inner life, the spirit, the heart. He saw the future Peter with all his grandeur of character in the rude Simon who was brought to Him. He knows His friends by their obedience. He knows the white garments of righteousness which His redeemed ones wear. He knows His disciples by their following where He leads. He knows the penitent heart by the fragrance it puts forth. It is an altar of incense. It is a box of ointment broken open. As we find out the hiding-places of flowers by their odours, so God knows the home of the penitent heart by the sweetness that floats up from it. He knows His own.

The Home of Bethany.

" A certain man was sick,......Lazarus, of Bethany."

JOHN xi. 1

THIS home at Bethany was wondrously favoured. The family seems to have been wealthy. It was a loving home, the three members named being bound together by very close and tender ties. This we know from the fact that Jesus found it such a congenial home for Himself. He surely would not have chosen a quarrelsome household for His own abiding-place. He could not have found a refuge there if it had been anything but a home filled with love's sweetness.

We know that it was an affectionate household, also, from the sorrow of the sisters when their brother was dead. As we read the matchless story we are sure it was no ordinary tie that bound the family together. In too many homes brothers and sisters are not to each other what they might be. Ofttimes there is at least a lack in the showing of the love. Brothers and sisters should be kindly and affectionate in their intercourse together.

Then it was a favoured home, also, because it was the one which Jesus chose to be the resting-place for His heart in the still evenings after the fierce strifes with His enemies in the temple. It was His love for the members of this family, and the honour He put upon their home, by which the little town of Bethany was immortalized.

Yet, highly favoured as was this home in these ways, sickness came into it. We get some lessons. No home can be made which will shut sickness out of its chambers. Wealth cannot keep it away, love cannot. Yet we learn, also, that sickness in our home is no proof that Christ does not love us. Into the households that are dearest to Him pain and sorrow come ; but we shall see that in the end blessing to the family and glory to God come from the trial. These thoughts should comfort us when sickness comes into our households.

Sept. 13

The Sisters' Message

"*His sisters sent unto Him, saying, Lord, behold, he whom Thou lovest is sick.*"—JOHN xi. 3

IN their trouble the first thought of the sisters was of Jesus, and they sent at once to Him. This lesson we should not overlook. No doubt they sent for the physician; but they sent also for Christ. We should never fail to send word to Christ when anything is wrong in our home. We should want Him always in our sick-rooms when our loved ones are suffering.

We must notice also the message which the sisters sent to Christ. It was very short and simple. They did not beg and plead with Him to come—indeed they made no request whatever; they merely told Jesus that His friend was sick, and left to Himself to decide what He would do. They knew that He would do the right thing from the prompting of His own heart. Notice also the plea. They did not say, "He who *loves Thee* is sick," but, "He whom *Thou lovest* is sick." They made their appeal to Christ's own heart rather than to any personal claim. This is always our best plea with Christ—His love for us, not our love for Him.

There is something also in this message which speaks of a deep feeling of peace in the midst of danger. Many persons in such experiences lose all their courage and oft-times their faith; but these sisters, though in such deep distress, maintained their composure. They had learned lessons of peace from Christ in the bright, sunny days beforehand, and when the trouble came they were ready for it, and were not disturbed. If we would get Christ's sweet comfort when sorrow comes, we must welcome Him in the days of gladness. If this Bethany family had shut Christ out of their home when they were all well and happy, they could not have had His blessed comfort in their sore distress. We must take Christ in the bright days if we would have Him when it grows dark.

Martha Going to Jesus

" *Martha, as soon as she heard that Jesus was coming, went and met Him.*"—John xi. 20

THE coming of Jesus to this Bethany home was never so welcome as on that day. It is the same yet in people's homes, even in those where He is most loved : Christ is never so dear and precious to us as when we are in trouble. Need reveals His preciousness. Many persons who do not desire the minister's presence during their days of prosperity and gladness are quick to send for him when sorrow comes. This was not Martha's way, however ; she had welcomed Christ to her home in the happy days when there was no sorrow, and that was what made His coming such a blessing to her now.

We get this lesson—that the only true preparation for trial is personal friendship with Christ. If we never turn to the Bible for comfort until some great grief is upon us, it will not give us much light ; but if we have it in the bright days, and its words are hung up then like lamps in our heart's chambers, when it grows dark the beams will shine out and change night into day.

When visitors to the Mammoth Cave are preparing to enter that wonderful cavern, the guide puts into the hand of each tourist a lighted lamp. It is noonday, perhaps, and it seems very foolish to walk down the green bank carrying little lamps in the bright sunshine. But when the party enter the mouth of the cave and go a little distance, they understand the use of their lamps. In the darkness they would perish but for their pale light. Some people do not think, when they are moving along in joy and gladness, that they need Christ ; but by-and-by it grows dark in some path of sorrow, and then they learn the blessing of having Christ beforehand. If they have Him in their hearts, they find it light all about them ; if they have Him not, the gloom is turned to despair.

Unbelieving "Ifs"

" Lord, if Thou hadst been here, my brother had not died."
JOHN xi. 21

WOULD Lazarus not have died if Jesus had been there? Do we not read that *because* Jesus loved the Bethany family, and *because* He learned of the sickness of Lazarus, *therefore* He remained two days after the messenger came? Did He not also say that He was glad He had not been there before Lazarus died?

One thing at least we know: it was better that Lazarus should die, and that Christ's power should be shown in his resurrection. It was therefore an unbelieving "if," and a groundless one, which fell from Martha's lips. But we are all apt to let similar "ifs" drop from our lips when trouble comes to us. If we had only tried another physician, or taken the matter in hand a little sooner, our friend had not died. We feel sometimes that sorrow is an evidence that God did not hear our prayers; if He had only heard our cry the trial would have been averted. Yet we have but to read this story through to the end to see that Christ's way was the better way here, as it always is the better way.

> " We sadly watched the close of all,
>   Life balanced on a breath ;
> We saw upon his features fall
>   The awful shade of death.
> All dark and desolate we were ;
>   And murmuring nature cried—
> ' Oh, surely, Lord, hadst Thou been here,
>   Our brother had not died.'
>
> " But when its glance the mourner cast
>   On all that grace had done,
> And thought of life's long warfare passed,
>   And endless victory won,
> Then faith prevailing wiped the tears,
>   And looking upward cried—
> ' Oh, surely, Lord, Thou hast been here :
>   Our brother has not died.' "

Life in Christ

" I am the resurrection and the life : he that believeth in Me, though he were dead, yet shall he live ; and whosoever liveth and believeth in Me shall never die."—JOHN xi 25, 26

MARTHA believed in the resurrection at the last day ; but that seemed far away, while her heart craved a present comfort. It was to this feeling, which many another mourner besides Martha has experienced, that our Lord spoke these wonderful words. His answer shows that He Himself is the bridge of life that unites the shores of eternity and time, filling up the dark chasm, and bringing the resurrection and life eternal close to earth's death.

The resurrection is not far away, for it is all in Christ's hands. When His believing ones die they but sleep in Him. They are not really dead ; indeed, those believing on Him never die at all. What we call dying is only passing through the gate into the immediate presence of Christ. Christ has abolished death. To Him death was real and full of terrors. But because it was so terrible to Him, it is only an entrance of glory for His people. He absorbed the blackness and the gloom in His own soul, as He passed through the valley, and left it a vale of brightness for His followers.

If we could all get into our hearts the truth of the immortal life as revealed in the gospel, it would take away all the gloom from the graves of our dead. Those who live here are in Christ, and those who have passed over are with Christ ; thus in Him we are still united. There is but one family in Christ—part gone over, part crossing now, soon all to be together. This truth of the endless life is one of marvellous power when we have, even in the least measure, realized it. Death is not the end of anything but of mortality, imperfection, and sin. Life goes on fuller, richer, nobler, with enlarged capacities, beyond the incident which we call death. We shall never die.

The Seeking Saviour

*" What man......if he lose one......doth not......go after that
which is lost ? "*—LUKE xv. 4

DOES the shepherd care when one of his sheep has left
the fold ? He has a hundred in his flock ; does
he care that one of them has gone ? Does he miss one
among so many ? Christ has millions of holy beings about
Him—angels and redeemed saints—who never go astray.
Does He care when on earth, in the heart of a great city,
or out in some lonely country town, *one* soul wanders away
into the darkness ?

> " There were ninety and nine that safely lay
>   In the shelter of the fold ;
> But one was out on the hills away,
>   Far off from the gates of gold,
> Away on the mountains wild and bare,
> Away from the tender Shepherd's care.

> " ' Lord, thou hast here thy ninety and nine ;
>   Are they not enough for Thee ? '
> But the Shepherd made answer : ' This of Mine
>   Has wandered away from Me ;
> And although the road be rough and steep,
> I go to the desert to find My sheep.' "

Christ misses even one, no matter who, that strays away.
Did any mother ever have so many children that if one of
them wandered from home she would not miss it ? We
have strange thoughts of Christ's love if we think He loves
us only as a race, and not as individuals. The father of
a stolen child said, " So long as I live I will continue to go
up and down the country, looking into the face of every
boy I meet, trying to find my own lost child ! " Think of
that weary, broken-hearted father going from city to city
and giving up everything in this one sad search ! Then
think of Christ seeking the lost one that has wandered
away from *His* home of love. Behold Him, weary, with
bleeding feet, as He goes on and seeks until He finds !

Brought Home

" *When he hath found it, he layeth it on his shoulders.*"

LUKE xv. 5

HE does not drive the poor weary sheep home. This is not the way the gentle Eastern shepherd does. He stoops down and lifts it up, and lays it on his own shoulder and carries it back. There is a wonderful revelation in this little touch in the picture. Let us be sure that we understand just what the words say.

We all know that Christ carried our sin when He went to the cross. We know, too, that we may cast our burdens upon Him. But here we learn that Christ wants to carry, not our sins only, not our burdens and cares only, but ourselves. The shepherd took up the sheep itself and laid *it* upon his shoulder.

" I am the Burden-bearer ; I
Will never pass the o'erladen by.
My feet are on the mountain steep ;
They wind through valleys dark and deep ;
They print the hot dust of the plain,
And walk the billows of the main :
Wherever is a load to bear
My willing shoulder still is there."

He does this with " rejoicing." Can this be true ? Has Christ really interest enough in any human being on this earth to be made sad by his wandering, and glad by his recovery ? The thought overwhelms me. We can understand a shepherd's rejoicing when he bears home a sheep that has been lost. We can understand a mother's joy when her lost child is brought to her door. But that the heart of Jesus rejoiced when He found us, and bore us back toward home, seems too amazing to be true. Yet here the word stands. Then listen to Zephaniah : " The Lord thy God in the midst of thee is mighty ; He will save, *He will rejoice over thee* with joy ; He will rest in His love ; *He will joy over thee with singing.*" How dear we are to Christ !

The Far Country

*" The younger son gathered all together, and took his journey
into a far country."*—LUKE xv. 13

A MAN has not long shaken off his subjection to God
before he begins his departure from Him. He first
gets the reins into his own hands, and then the old paths
are too straight and limited for him. He has taken all his
" goods " into his own keeping—that is, he has assumed
charge and control of all his own powers, gifts, and energies ;
and now he will go out and try life in his own way—the
way of licence and self-gratification. Every one has departed from God into the far country who is not *at home*
with God, who is not living as a child in the Father's house.

The " far country " is a costly place to live in. When
the prodigal got there his property soon began to go ; and
it was not very long till it was all gone—wasted in riotous
living. This story is the literal history of a great many
young men. There are thousands of them who are wasting
large fortunes every year in this same riotous living—in
drinking and all kinds of debauchery.

But how must we interpret this in its spiritual application ? The " substance " of the sinner consists in his
gifts, talents, powers, opportunities, and possibilities. He
" wastes his substance " whenever he does not use it for
God and for the good of the world—the uses for which God
bestowed it. He wastes it also when he squanders it in
sin. Here then is the picture : a man endowed with powers
fitting him for nobleness and usefulness, rushing into evil
courses, spending his strength in sin, destroying his body,
mind, and spirit in revelry and dissipation. The man with
one talent, who only hid it away and did not use it at all,
keeping it as it was, to be returned in the end, was condemned to outer darkness. How much sorer will be the
doom of those who squander their talents in sin, and use
them to curse the world and drag down other souls !

The Prodigal's Return

" When he was yet a great way off, his father saw him."
LUKE xv. 20

THE boy had, in the far-away country, a vision of his old home. As he sat there and thought of his dishonour and his ruin, there flashed before him a picture which made him very home-sick. The vision brought back the old home in all its beauty and blessedness. There was plenty there, while here the once happy, favoured son was perishing with hunger.

It was a blessed moment for the prodigal. It was God's message to him, inviting him to return home. When a child is stolen away from a lovely and tender household, it may be kept among wandering gipsies or savage Indians even to old age, but there are always broken fragments of sweet memories that hang over the soul like trailing clouds in the sky—dim, shadowy memories of something very lovely, very pure, reminiscences of that long-lost, long-forgotten past, when the child lay on the mother's arms, and was surrounded by beauty and tenderness. So there is something in the heart of every one who has wandered from God that ever floats about him, even in sin's revels—a fair, ethereal vision, dim and far away mayhap, but splendid as the drapery of the sunset. It is the memory of lost innocence, of the Father's love, the vision of a heavenly beauty possible of restoration to the worst.

When the prodigal reached home he found his vision realized. His father was watching for him—had long been watching for him. It is a picture of the heavenly Father's loving welcome of every lost child of His that comes back home. Thus He receives the worst who comes penitently. Our sweetest dreams of God's love are a thousand times too poor and dim for the reality. A great way off God sees the returning prodigal, and runs to meet him. No matter how far we have wandered, there is a welcome waiting for us at home.

Ube Beggar's Escort

" *The beggar died, and was carried by the angels into Abraham's bosom.*"—LUKE xvi. 22

NOTHING is said about his funeral—of course it was only a pauper's. Earth had no honour for the beggar, no splendid coffin, no flowers ; but the angels came, and were his bearers and escort to glory. Notice also that nothing is said about what became of his body ; but little matter, for the man himself was no longer in that old, worn-out, battered frame. He was soon far away in a realm of brightness. While the body was dropped, the beggar, the real man, was carried away to heaven ; and we see him there, a beggar no longer, enjoying blessedness.

There is still another thought here. We dread death. It seems the end of existence. But really to the Christian it is only an incident in his life. It is just a moment's passage through an experience we never can understand ; and then—glory. One minute this poor beggar lies at the gate, despised, suffering, hungry ; the next, a strange sensation passes over him, and all is confusion ; then he awakes flying through the air with angel-escort, and in a little time is inside the gate of pearl, and lives on. There is no break in his life.

Death came also to the rich man. His riches could not save him from that. No doubt he had a splendid funeral. There would be a long procession, many mourners, great waste of perfumes, every show of honour. But who would not rather have the beggar's escort after death than the finest funeral earth ever gave to mortal ? There have been funerals of rich men at which there was genuine sorrow, where those who had been blessed by their benevolence came and wept by their coffins. But in this case there were no sincere mourners, for the man had allowed the needy to lie hungry at his gates. He had lived for himself only, and no one really missed him when he was gone.

"Continue in Prayer"

" Men ought always to pray, and not to faint "

LUKE xviii. 1

A GREAT many people get discouraged in praying because the answer does not come at once. It should be settled in the mind, first, that God *always* hears the true prayer, and that He will always send *an* answer, though it may not always be the answer we desire. He never despises nor disregards the cry of one of His children, but sometimes for wise reasons He delays His answer. Perhaps it cannot be prepared at once. God's plans reach out widely, and He works slowly. Look at Joseph in Egypt— a slave, then a prisoner. No doubt he was praying every day for release, and he may have thought at times that the answer was long in coming. But when it came, he could see that one reason for delay was that all things might be gotten ready. It took years to prepare the answer that came at last with such blessing.

Or the reason of God's delay may be to draw out our faith, to increase our earnestness. The story of the Syrophenician woman illustrates this. At first Jesus " answered her not a word ; " but it was for her sake that He kept her waiting. She received a far better answer at last than she could have received at first. Suppose she had " fainted " after her first apparent repulse, think what she would have lost.

No doubt thousands of prayers are never answered because men faint at God's delay. Perhaps you have lost many a joy and blessing because you lost heart and faith before the answer came. A little longer patient perseverance would have brought you a great reward. After spending thousands of dollars in drilling for oil, the operator became discouraged and sold out for a trifle. The purchaser started the drill, and in six hours found a flowing well. We see what " fainting " cost the first owner. Many Christians lose heart just when the answer is about to be granted.

Two Prayers

" *God, I thank Thee, that I am not as other men are......God be merciful to me a sinner.*"—LUKE xviii. 11, 13

HERE we have two kinds of prayer set side by side for our instruction. The first really is no prayer at all; it is only a bit of self-felicitation in the presence of God. Yet it was not much comfort, after all, that the Pharisee found. He was better than certain other men, he said. He never thought of comparing himself with God, the only true thing to do.

This Pharisee has many followers. A great many people's whole stock of piety consists in not being as bad as some other one. The dishonest man felicitates his conscience with the reflection that he is sober and temperate. The false-tongued man is thankful that he pays his debts. The gossiping woman finds great comfort in the fact that she is not a heathen like her neighbour, who never goes to church at all. But it is a poor kind of virtue which has nothing better to build on than such imperfect relative goodness. One may be clear of a great many ugly faults that his neighbours have, and yet not be a saint himself.

The other man's prayer was different altogether. There was in him no measuring of himself with other men to see whether he or they were the worse. Then there was no going over sins he had *not* committed. He said nothing about his neighbour's sins, but was very free in speaking of his own sins. He stood before God burdened with the consciousness of his own personal guilt, and cried to God for mercy—mercy wholly undeserved, to be granted only through grace. It is very obvious which was the true and acceptable prayer. It is the penitent's prayer that reaches heaven. God wants honesty in our supplication; He wants humility. It is not enough to be worried about other people's sins; the particular sinner with whose sins each man ought to be most concerned is himself.

The Children's Friend

" *Then were there brought unto Him little children, that He should put His hands on them, and pray.*"—MATT xix. 13

THOSE children must have been glad in after days to remember that Jesus had laid His hands upon their heads and blessed them. Sometimes the remembrance even of a human hand laid on the head in childhood stays all through life, and is a benediction.

A Christian man said late in his life that he could still feel the touch of his dying mother's hand on his head as she bade him farewell and asked him to promise to follow Christ. A boy was brought to his father's bedside, and was " kissed and blessed and given to God." All through his youth, when there came any temptation to do wrong, the thought would come, " No, I must not do this, for I am the boy who was kissed and blessed and given to God." When, later in life, burdens pressed and he was about to yield to despair, he would remember his father's acts and words, and the remembrance would support him : " No ; am I not the boy who was kissed and blessed and given to God ? "

In the stress of life his mind at last gave way, and he spent years in the gloomy apartments of an insane asylum. And thence in his brighter moments he would write to his daughter : " Here I am shut away and very lonely. I have no one to sing to me as you used to do,—

'Jesus, lover of my soul,'

or

'Rock of Ages, cleft for me.'

It seems very dark and hard ; but yet I am the boy that was kissed and blessed and given to God." Thus all through his life he was sustained and strengthened by the remembrance of his father's last blessing. If all who have been consecrated to Christ, and have had His hand laid on them, would ever remember that holy touch, how pure and true would it make their lives !

Sept. 25

"Forbid them Rot"

" Suffer little children, and forbid them not, to come unto Me."—MATT. xix. 14

THE love of Christ for children was one of the most beautiful qualities in His life. It revealed His true human-heartedness. But we must remember too that it revealed His Divine interest in the children.

Jesus was much displeased when His disciples rebuked those who brought the little ones, and would keep the children away. " Suffer them to come to Me, and forbid them not," he said. So we have the caution for ourselves. We must be very careful that we never keep any children from coming to Christ.

We may do this in many ways. We may do this, if we are parents or older Christians, by our own worldly example. Undevout parents are likely to keep their children away from the Saviour, even unintentionally, by the influence of their own life. We may do it also by telling them they are too young to come to him ; by simply doing nothing, allowing them to grow up uninfluenced toward the right ; by allowing their minds to become pre-occupied with other things, to the exclusion of Christ.

Christ stands yet and calls upon us to clear every hindrance out of the way, that the children may come to Him, and besides to do all we can to bring them to Him. It must be noticed that it is to Christ Himself the children are to come. Suppose they cannot understand " the plan of redemption," or cannot know the doctrines of the Church, or cannot answer the hard questions we sometimes put to inquirers, shall we therefore keep them back ? No ; Christ says, " Let them come to Me." No matter how little they know of the way, we are to put up no gates, we are to make no standards of knowledge or experience ; we are only to be sure we hinder them not, and that we let them come to Him. After that there will be time enough to teach them.

The Young Ruler

" There came one running, and kneeled to Him, and asked Him, Good Master, what shall I do that I may inherit eternal life ? "—MARK x. 17

THIS was a young man, with all his powers fresh and full. He was rich, with all the honour, ease, distinction, and influence that riches give. He was a man of good reputation among his fellows ; for he was a ruler of the synagogue. His character was above reproach ; for he had scrupulously kept all the commandments. He was a lovable man, with many fine qualities, attractive and winning ; for Jesus loved him when He saw him. Yet he was not satisfied. His heart-hunger was also very strong, driving him irresistibly in all haste to Christ.

There never was a more important question asked than he put to Jesus. Eternal life is the most glorious prize in the universe to be gained. It embraces all the blessings of salvation in this world, and then a place in the family of God for ever. It is no wonder this young man *ran* to ask Christ this question. The wonder is that so few people ever do run to make the same inquiry. Men run to seek earth's poor prizes, but they are slow in their pace when they are seeking eternal life.

It is a prize too which can be gained. It lies within the reach of every one. There is no one who may not obtain it. It is a prize, however, that cannot be gotten merely by *doing* anything. There is plenty of room for doing in the Christian life, but this is not the place for it. Eternal life cannot be gained by saying so many prayers, or fasting so many hours, or being baptized in a certain way, or joining a particular Church, or by giving so much money to charity, or by any other kind of religious act or service. Eternal life is the gift of God ; it is obtained through Jesus Christ. It is bestowed upon all who will accept it. The way to get it is to take Christ as Saviour and Lord.

Sept. 27

"Not Far from the Kingdom"

" Jesus beholding him loved him, and said unto him, One thing thou lackest: go thy way, sell......give.......and follow Me."—MARK x. 21

JESUS loves every one, but there was something in this young man that specially drew out His affection. He saw in him many amiable qualities, many elements of beauty of character, many things that by Divine grace could be made into great loveliness and power. Here are a few thoughts suggested by this statement:—Christ loves those who are not His disciples; some people think He only loves those who have begun to love Him. Christ is deeply interested in every young man; He beholds the possibilities in every young life. He sees lovable things even in the unsaved; but amiable qualities are not enough to save one.

Our Lord's answer to the young man's question is very instructive. What is the one thing which, besides all we can do for ourselves by obedience and cultivation of character, makes one a Christian? It is important to be able to answer this question, for it is often asked. A man says: " I live as well as Christians do. I attend church; I keep the commandments; I am kind to my family and generous to the needy and poor; I live conscientiously in all things. What do I lack ? "

What shall we answer him? Shall we tell him to sell his farm or his property and give all he has to the poor? Was that the one essential thing in the Master's counsel to this young man? No: the essential thing was following Christ; the selling and giving away were but parts of this. The young man's heart was attached to his wealth, and the " one thing " was to take Christ instead of his wealth. So we should answer our inquirer by telling him that he must accept Christ as his Saviour and Lord, that he must lay his money and all that he has at Christ's feet, to be used only for Him and as He directs, and must take Christ as his sole portion for ever.

Serving Others

" Not to be ministered unto, but to minister."—MATT. xx. 28

THE art of photography is now so perfect that the whole side of a great newspaper can be taken in miniature so small as to be carried in a little pin or button, and yet every letter and point be perfect. So the whole life of Christ is photographed in this one little phrase. He came not to be served ; if this had been His aim He would never have left heaven's glory, where He wanted nothing, where angels praised Him and ministered unto Him. He came to serve. He altogether forgot himself. He served all He met who would receive His service. At last He gave His life in serving—gave it to save others, to redeem lost souls.

You say you want to be like Christ. You pray Him to print His own image on your heart. Here, then, is the image. It is no vague dream of perfection that we are to think of when we ask to be like Christ. The old monks thought that they were in the way to become like Christ when they went into the wilderness, away from men, to live in cold cells or on tall columns. But surely that is not the thought which this picture suggests. " To minister "—that is the Christ-like thing. Instead of fleeing away from men, we are to live among men, to serve them, to live for them, to seek to bless them, to do good, to give our lives.

Christ tells us also that this is the stairway to the highest reaches of Christian life. " Whosoever of you will be the chiefest shall be servant of all." To worldly men this seems indeed a strange way of rising. According to this, all man's scrambling for place and power is really scrambling downward rather than upward. The real heights in human life are the heights of self-forgetfulness and service. We are to use all our redeemed powers in doing good to others in Christ's name. That is what Christ did with His blessed life, and we are to follow in His steps.

Jesus Passing By

" When he heard that it was Jesus......he began to cry out."

MARK x. 47

NO doubt the blind man had been wishing that Jesus would come to Jericho. He had grown to believe that if He would only come He could open his blind eyes. What a burst of joy filled the poor man when he learned that Jesus was passing by ! Now was his opportunity. Instantly he began to cry out. The lesson here is, that when Jesus is passing by all who need help should at once call upon Him.

But when may it now be said that Jesus is passing by ? Of course He is always present everywhere. We cannot get out of His sight for a moment. Yet there are times when He seems specially to visit certain places. The day of Israel's visitation was when Jesus was going through the land teaching and healing. So times of revival in a church are times of peculiar visitation. When the Spirit is working mightily, when many hearts are bowing down in penitence, then Jesus of Nazareth is passing by, and then is the time to call upon Him. When conscience is tender, when the Spirit is silently striving, when some peculiar providence has awakened the soul, again is Jesus passing by.

He passes by in youth. There is no other time when He is really so near. Then the heart is tender, the affections are unengaged, the life is plastic, and He comes specially close. There will never be a time in after life when it will be so easy to call upon Him and be saved as in youth. This blind man wisely seized the opportunity. Jesus was passing now, was close to him, could readily hear his call. Now was his time ; if not now, perhaps never. Surely we ought to act as wisely in seeking Christ while He is near. It must not be forgotten that Jesus really never passed through Jericho again. If Bartimeus had said, " I will wait till He comes again," what would have been the result ?

Faithfulness

" Because thou hast been faithful in a very little, have thou authority over ten cities."—LUKE xix. 17

IT is remarkable how much the Word of God makes of faithfulness—simple faithfulness. It is not great things that God requires of us unless our mission is to do great things ; He asks only that we be faithful in the duties that come to our hand in our commonplace days. That means that we do all our work as well as we can ; that we serve well in the varied relationships of life in which from time to time we find ourselves ; that we stand heroically in our lot, resisting temptation and continuing true and loyal to God ; and that we fulfil our mission in all ways according to the grace given unto us, using every gift and talent for the glory of God and the good of the world. The world crowns " success ; " God crowns " faithfulness."

Jesus tells us that faithfulness in this life lifts us to places of authority hereafter. So, then, life here is only a trial to see what we are capable of doing. It is after all a real probation to find out who may be set over large trusts. And the real life is to be begun in the other world. Those who prove faithful here will have places of responsibility in the kingdom of glory.

This ought to give a new and mighty motive to our living in this world. Our eternal honour and employment will depend upon the degree of our faithfulness here. Good men and women often say at the close of their lives, " If I could only begin now, with all my experience, I could live my life much better." Well, if they have been faithful, that is the very thing they will be permitted to do in the next world. A mother who had brought up a large family said : " I have just learned now *how* to train children. I could do it well if I could begin it again." If she has learned this, that is just what Christ wanted her to learn. Now she is ready for full service in His kingdom.

Household Duties

" They made Him a supper ; and Martha served."

JOHN xii. 2

THERE are certain Bible people that we never fail to recognize. We know Martha by her busy serving. Each time we meet her we find her engaged in active duties. She represents those whose love for Christ takes the practical form. Some people like to criticise Martha ; but, after all, her type of piety is important in this world where there is so much need for service. Beautiful as the Mary-spirit is, it would not do if all were Marys ; for who would then do the work that needs so much to be done ? A wife and mother, for instance, who should spend all her time in Bible-reading and prayer, giving no thought to her household duties, would not make a very happy home.

" Yea, Lord !—Yet some must serve ;
    Not all, with tranquil heart,
Even at Thy dear feet,
Wrapped in devotion sweet,
    May sit apart.

" Yea, Lord !—Yet some must bear
    The burden of the day,
Its labour and its heat,
While others at Thy feet
    May muse and pray.

" Yea, Lord !—Yet some must do
    Life's daily task-work ; some
Who fain would sing must toil
Amid earth's dust and moil,
    While lips are dumb.

" Yea, Lord !—Yet man must earn,
    And woman bake the bread ;
And some must watch and wake
Early for others' sake,
    Who pray instead.

" Yea, Lord !—Yet even Thou
    Hast need of daily care.
I bring the bread and wine
To Thee, O Guest Divine !
    Be this my prayer."

At His Feet

" Then took Mary a pound of ointment of spikenard, very costly, and anointed the feet of Jesus."—JOHN xii. 3

WE see Mary three times in the gospel, and each time she is in the same posture—at Jesus' feet. When we have our first glimpse within the Bethany home, we find Martha in her characteristic attitude—serving ; and Mary we see sitting at the Master's feet, eagerly listening to His words. Our next view of Mary is when Jesus came back to Bethany after the death of Lazarus, and the sisters went out to meet Him. Again she is at the feet of Christ, this time in deep sorrow, seeking comfort. Here a third time we find her at Christ's feet, and now it is in honouring her Lord.

We think of Mary, therefore, as a woman who was always at Christ's feet. In the bright, common days she sat there as a learner, looking up into His face, drinking in His words, and absorbing His spirit into her soul. When grief came she went to His feet for comfort, pouring out her sorrow there, looking up into His face for consolation. Then, when the trouble was over, and there were joy and victory instead, we find her again in her wonted place, honouring Jesus with her heart's richest gifts. There is no fitter place for the redeemed life than at the Saviour's feet.

In Mary's gift she brought the best she had, the richest gift in all her possession. We should always bring our best to Christ. No ointment in the world is half so precious to Him as the love of human hearts ; we should bring Him our best love, giving Him the first place in our affections. We should give Him the best of our lives, our youth in all its freshness and purity, our body and mind when they are at their best. We should give Him the best of our time, not the weary moments of languor only, but the hours when we are most alert. We should give Him the best of our services, doing our finest work of all kinds for Him.

fleeting Opportunities

" *Me ye have not always.*"—MARK xiv. 7

WE ought to learn well the value of opportunities. They do not bide our convenience ; but while we linger indecisive they are gone. Then, when they are gone they come not again. Whatever was done for Jesus He said must be done at once, for they would not have Him always. To put off the act of love would be to miss doing it altogether ; for when He was once away, however much they might want to do the kindness for Him, it would be too late. The poor they would always have—they might care for them at any time ; but whatever act of love they would render to Jesus they must render at once.

There ought to be a deep lesson for us in our Lord's word in this place. There are certain things that we shall never have the opportunity to do but once. Here is a mother in a home : for years she has given her life in loving, self-denying service, poured it out like rich ointment for the good of her children. Now she is growing old, and as her children look upon her it is as if she said to them, " Whatever kindness you would do to me you must do now, for you will not have me always."

We hear of a neighbour who is sick. Just now is the time to perform whatever act of love we desire to render, for we may not long have the friend. To-morrow he may be gone. There have been tears shed over coffins and graves by those who would have given worlds to get their dead back again, to do for them the things that they neglected to do while they had them. The best time to do a kindness is now.

Some one has beautifully said : " I expect to pass through this world but once. If, therefore, there be any kindness I can do for any fellow-being, let me do it now. Let me not defer or neglect it, for I shall not pass this way again."

𝔄cceptable 𝔒fferings

" She hath done what she could."—MARK xiv. 8

THIS was wonderful commendation to come from the lips of the Christ. Mary could not have done better than this if she had been a thousand times as gifted. We get two lessons. One is that all Christ wants is what we have ability and opportunity to do. He asks no impossibilities. The poorest things, the smallest offerings, are acceptable if they are really our best in the circumstances.

A child in a mission-school offered her teacher a handful of weeds and grasses, wilted and soiled at that, which she called a bouquet. Did the teacher refuse the gift, and criticise the poor, withered weeds? No; she accepted them with as sincere gratitude and as many thanks as if some wealthy friend had offered her an elegant bouquet of flowers. The child did what she could; and the teacher looking behind the gift saw the love in the little heart, and that transfigured her poor gift. So it is that Christ accepts our poorest work or our homeliest offering if it is our best.

But the lesson has another side. " She did *what she could.*" It is this, then, that pleases Christ. Are we doing what we *could* do? Do we always bring to Him our very best gifts? Do we never put Him off with the faded flowers, keeping the fresh and fragrant ones for ourselves? Do we do for Him our very best work? Are we faithful? If we are only doing half what we might, we cannot take the comfort of this commendation. The widow's mites were very acceptable coming from her, because they were all she had; but they would not have elicited any such commendation if one of the rich men had given them. A little child's ministry is very beautiful for a child, but it would not be as fitting in the father or mother. We must really do the very best we can if we would have this commendation.

Oct. 5

"Not Your Own"

"The Lord hath need of him."—MARK xi. 3

THERE seems to have been no formal request of the owner for the use of the colt. Jesus sent His disciples to take it by Divine authority. So then the Lord has a right to anything we have. No property right that we can get takes the title out of His hands. We talk about our possessions as if they were ours indeed. Nothing is really ours save as lent to us by the Lord to be used for Him.

There are practical inferences here which we must not overlook. Christ has a right to call for anything we have whenever He wants to use it. He has a right to ask for our money, for it is His far more than ours. When our property is swept away by some providential act, we should not murmur, but should remember that the Lord has a right to do as He will with His own. The same principle applies to the loss of friends by death. The Lord has a right to take them, for He only lends them to us; and when He wants them with Himself He has a right to call them home.

Another thought here is that Christ may sometimes have special use for even the humblest of our possessions. The Lord had need of the good Samaritan's beast to carry the wounded man to the inn. He had need of the lad's five loaves to feed the multitude. A lady was trying to teach her child that she ought to give everything to Christ to be used in any way He might choose. "Why, mamma," she replied, "Jesus can never use my doll." Yet in an hour the child was letting a poor child that came to the door play with her doll. Was not the Lord using it then ? The Lord may need our horses to carry burdens for others, or to carry those who cannot walk. He often has need of our money, our hands, our feet, our lips, our influence ; and we do well when we hold all our possessions ready at any call of His to be used as He desires.

Nothing but Leaves

" Seeing a fig-tree afar off having leaves, He came, if haply He might find anything thereon."—MARK xi. 13

THERE were many other fig-trees in that region, but Jesus did not turn to any of them to look for food, because they gave no promise, made no show or pretence of having fruit. He went to this tree because by its early leaves it declared to all who saw it that it had also early fruit. Christ does not expect to find spiritual fruit on the life of the godless man or the worldly woman, but he *does* expect it on the life of the man or woman who professes to be a Christian.

As Jesus turned to that fig-tree, drawn thereto by the tree's profession of fruitfulness, so hungry souls turn to the Church and to God's professed people to find spiritual food. What that tree with leaves and no fruit was to Jesus, the Jewish Church was to the people in their soul-hunger. With their burden of sin, with their deep heart-questionings, with their sorrows, with their unsatisfied longings, with their yearnings for help and sympathy, they turned to the priests, the professed spiritual guides, if haply they might get from them what they wanted. So the mission of every Christian Church is to feed hungry souls. In the hour of penitence, when the soul is conscious of guilt ; in the day of trouble, when the world has no more to give ; in the shadow of death, in all the great crises of life, even the most worldly turn to the Church for what they need.

A church is like a great tree in the desert which holds out the promise of fruit, and toward which all the spiritually hungry turn. There can be few sadder things in this world than a church, promising by its very name, by its spire pointing to heaven, by its open doors, by its songs and services, by its bells of invitation, to give food to the hungry, refreshment to the weary, comfort to the sorrowing, and then failing to keep its promises to the souls that come expecting.

Believing Prayer

" *And all things, whatsoever ye shall ask in prayer, believing,
ye shall receive.*"—MATT. xxi. 22

THERE are other scriptures qualifying this. In the first place, it is not all asking that is really praying, and therefore not all asking that receives. St. James says, " Ye ask, and receive not, because ye ask amiss, that ye may spend it in your pleasures." A man asks for money, not to use it for the glory of God and the good of others, but for his own glory and pleasure. Again, the Psalmist says, " If I regard iniquity in my heart, the Lord will not hear me." That is, if one is cherishing a secret sin in his heart while he is trying to serve God, no prayers that he offers will be heard or answered. So here are at least two kinds of asking that will not bring an answer.

Then there are conditions. One is that we must ask in Christ's name. That implies that we believe in Christ as our Saviour, and are His faithful friends, and therefore have a right to use His name. This condition narrows down the promise to the true followers of Christ. Another condition is that we are abiding in Christ, and His words are abiding in us. So there is a double " if." Even a Christian who is following afar off does not come within the circle of this promise.

Then there is another qualification which belongs to all promises to prayer. God Himself must be the judge as to the things we ask, whether they would really be blessings to us or not. There may be things we desire very earnestly that it would be the greatest unkindness to grant us. Is God then bound by this promise to give us what we crave ? By no means. " What is *good* the Lord will give." " No *good thing* will He withhold from them that walk uprightly." But He will withhold even from the most upright the things which in His Divine wisdom He sees would not be good things. This is implied in every such promise as this.

A Forgiving Spirit

" *When ye stand praying, forgive, if ye have aught against any ; that your Father also which is in heaven may forgive you your trespasses.*"—MARK xi. 25

IT is told of a Christian woman that a friend entered her room and found her with bowed head, as if in prayer. At length her friend spoke to her tenderly, knowing that a great sorrow was on her heart. " I have been trying to say the Lord's Prayer," she answered, " but I cannot get through it." She had said the words thousands of times in sunny childhood, in joyous youth, on her wedding-day, and then along the gladsome years that followed, amid songs and flowers and prattling child-voices, and in the sweetness of an unbroken home-circle ; and they had flowed from her lips like rippling music all the while. But now a great sorrow had come, and since that she had begun a hundred times, " Our Father who art in heaven, Hallowed be Thy name. Thy kingdom come. Thy will—" But she could not get any farther. She could not yet say, " Thy will be done."

A story is told of a nobleman in Alexandria, in olden days, who complained bitterly to the bishop of his enemies. While in the midst of the recital of his wrongs the bell rang for prayers, and bishop and nobleman dropped to their knees, the former leading in the Lord's Prayer, and the latter leaving his story unfinished for the time and joining in the prayer. When the bishop came to the words, " Forgive us our trespasses, as we forgive," he suddenly stopped and left the nobleman to go on alone. The nobleman attempted to say the words, but startled by the sound of his own voice unaccompanied, and recalled by the bishop's silence to the meaning of the prayer, he stammered, ceased to pray, and rose in great despair ; and it was only when he had learned to cherish a forgiving spirit toward others that he could say from his heart, " Forgive us our trespasses, as we forgive those that trespass against us."

Oct. 9

The Corner=Stone

" The stone which the builders rejected, the same is become the head of the corner."—MATT. xxi. 42

THOSE to whom Christ first came did not think Him suitable to be their Messiah. So they refused to accept Him, and nailed Him on a cross instead. But now what do we behold ? That same Jesus whom they thought unfit to be their king God has made King of glory, Lord of heaven and earth. All things are in His hands, all power, all mercy, all judgment. The very rulers who rejected Him and demanded His crucifixion, when they awake on the judgment-morning shall see as their Judge the same Jesus whom they thus despised and condemned to die.

A great many people now think Christ unsuitable to be their Master. They do not consider it an honour to be called a Christian. They blush to own His name or to enroll themselves among His followers. They do not care to model their life on His holy and perfect life. All such should remember that Christ has highest honour in heaven. No angel is ashamed to speak His name. Redeemed spirits praise Him day and night. God the Father has exalted Him to the throne of eternal power and glory. Why, then, should sinful men be ashamed to own Him as Lord ?

They should remember, further, that God has made Him the corner-stone of the whole building not made with hands. No life that is not builded on Him can stand. There is no other rock on which to rest a hope. If they ever are saved, it must be by this same Jesus whom they are now rejecting.

" How can they live who, sinning, never seek
  To have their sins forgiven ;
Who, knowing that the strongest yet are weak,
Ask not Thy grace and never know Thy peace—
  The gift unspeakable of Thy release,
    The pardon sealed in heaven ? "

"Let Him Take All"

" Thou shalt love the Lord thy God with all thy heart, and with all thy soul."—MATT. xxii. 37

WE are to notice, first, that it is love God wants. We may give Him our life's highest honour, but He is not satisfied with honour. We ought to obey Him. He is our God and our King, and we owe Him the fullest obedience. But obedience is not enough. We owe Him service also, for we belong to Him, and we ought to pour out our lives for Him. But it is neither honour, obedience, nor service that this command requires. We are to *love* God. If it were possible for us to render such honour, obedience, and service as the angels give, and yet not love Him, He would not be satisfied. Nothing but love will satisfy Him.

We are told here also the *measure* of the love that we are to give to God. It must be an all-absorbing love. God wants no half-hearts. He must be loved supremely— more than all tender friends, more than all worldly things. Then this love must draw the whole life after it—the mind, the soul, the strength ; it must lead to true and entire consecration.

Suppose a mother gives her child a beautiful flower-plant in bloom, and tells her to carry it to a sick friend. The child takes the plant away, and when she reaches the friend's door she plucks off one leaf and gives it to her, keeping the plant herself. Then afterward, once a week, she plucks off another leaf, or a bud, or a flower, and takes it to the friend, still retaining the plant. Has she obeyed ? Nothing but the giving of the whole plant would be obedience. Yet God asks for all our life—heart, soul, mind, and strength ; and we pluck off a little leaf of love now and then, a bud, a flower of affection, or one cluster of fruit, and give these little things to Him, keeping the life itself. Shall we not say, " Let Him take all " ? This commandment requires the complete consecration of the whole life to God.

The Widow's Mite

" This poor widow hath cast more in than all."

MARK xii. 43

IT is good to have here our Lord's estimate of earth's gifts. We know that as He saw the offerings that day, and spoke of their worth, so He always beholds how we give, and always weighs our gifts in the same balances. It is most cheering to us to note that it is not the earthly size of our offerings that makes them either great or acceptable in Heaven's sight. The widow's mite outweighed the rich man's heavy coins.

No doubt this poor woman felt that her gift was so small that it was scarcely worth while to give it ; but in the eyes of the Divine Lord its value was very great. There are two scales weighing all human acts, and all human gifts and offerings. There are the earthly scales, which weigh in ounces and pounds; and there are the "balances of the sanctuary," which weigh spiritual values. In the latter scales this widow's mites weighed more than the great glittering coins of the rich which were given with so much ostentation.

This was not only because her gift was proportionally larger—the rich still having much left after giving, and she having nothing left—but also because of her motive and spirit in giving. She gave because she loved God's house, and wished to do her part in maintaining its ordinances. She gave humbly, not to be seen of men, but to honour God and win His approval. She gave also largely according to her ability, putting to shame the rich men who gave so much and yet had riches left. Christ sees into the heart while we make our offerings ; and if our heart is right, and we give as we are able, and give out of love for God and desire for His glory, even the smallest offering that we can bring will be acceptable in God's sight, and will bring down Heaven's commendation. Gifts are not estimated in heaven by dollars and cents. Many a million gift is exceedingly small when the angels weigh it.

Oct. 12

"Behold the Lamb of God"

" *We would see Jesus.*"—JOHN xii. 21

THESE men had heard of Jesus, but they wanted to see Him for themselves. It does not do for us to see Jesus only through other people's eyes. No matter how vividly they may portray His beauty before us, this is not the seeing that blesses us and prints His image on our souls. We must behold Him for ourselves. In those terrible days in the ancient camp when the people were bitten and the brazen image of a serpent was set up, a mother could not look for her child, nor a friend for a friend. It is so in beholding Christ. No one can behold Him for another.

It is through seeing Christ that all spiritual blessings come to us. When we are burdened with sin, we are pointed to the Lamb of God that taketh away sin. When we seek to grow better, we are exhorted to behold as in a mirror the glory of the Lord, and thus be transformed into His image. When we ask for a model for our life, we are told to look unto Jesus. Many a fleeing slave, by simply keeping his eye fixed on a star, was led away from bondage to liberty. Keeping our eye on Christ will lead us from chains to glory.

These Greeks came to a disciple and asked him to introduce them to Jesus. What nobler service can we render in this world than that of introducing people to Jesus ? To do this we must know Him well ourselves. But let no one think that he really needs any one to introduce him to Jesus. A little child was dying, and she said she was not afraid to die, but she wished her mamma could go with her to introduce her to Jesus. " For you know, mamma," said the little one, " I was always afraid of strangers." But no one will find Jesus a stranger ; He loves to be sought, and to have people want to see Him, and He is always glad to reveal Himself to every seeker. He is not hard to find ; He is near all the while, and we really need no one to take us to Him.

Oct. 13

Two Ways of Living

" He that loveth his life shall lose it ; and he that hateth his life in this world shall keep it unto life eternal."—JOHN xii. 25

WE have our choice. We may live for self, take good care of our lives, not exposing them to danger, not making sacrifices, looking out for our own interests, and we may prosper in the world ; people will commend our prudence and congratulate us on our success. We may reach old age hale and well preserved, and greatly enjoy our accumulated honours and possessions. This is one way of living. There seems to be something pleasant about such a life, but really it is only the grain of wheat preserved in the garner and kept from falling into the ground. The life abides alone, well enough kept, perhaps, but with no increase. It has been no blessing in the world. It has done nothing for the glory of God. It has fed no hunger ; it has won no reward. That is the whole outcome of selfishness. " He that loveth his life shall lose it."

The other way is to forget self ; not to think of nor care for one's own life, but to throw it away in obedience to God and in unselfish service. People will say you are foolish thus to waste your golden life, thus to sacrifice yourself for the sake of others or in Christ's cause. But was Christ Himself foolish when He went to His cross ? Let the redeemed Church be the answer. Were the martyrs foolish when they threw their lives away for Christ's sake ? Ignatius said, when facing the fierce lions in the arena, " I am grain of God. Let me be ground between the teeth of lions if I may thus become bread to feed God's people." Were such martyred lives wasted, thrown away ? Is any life wasted that becomes seed-corn to produce bread by-and-by for the world ? The way to make nothing of our lives is to be very careful of them. The way to make our lives eternal successes is to do with them just what Christ did with His.

A Saviour for All

" I, if I be lifted up from earth, will draw all men unto Me."
JOHN xii. 32

AS we read the gospel story we are surprised to see how few persons were really drawn to Christ during His life. Crowds followed Him—many from curiosity—but very few were drawn to Him in heart and life. We see at the last how few ; there was but a little handful of clinging friends about His cross.

It was not until He had made His great sacrifice, had been " lifted up " on the cross, that all men began to be drawn to Him. Why was the influence of a crucified Jesus so much greater than that of a living, miracle-working Jesus ? For one reason, the death of Christ revealed the wonderful love of God. All His sweet, gentle, helpful life told of love, too ; but it was when He went to His cross that the full, rich glory of the Divine love was manifested. And love always draws. It is love that men need, and wherever they find it they want to come and rest in its warmth and tenderness.

Another reason why Jesus drew most powerfully after He had been lifted up, was because then the Divine Spirit was present to work on human hearts and lives. Without the drawing of the Spirit none would ever come to Christ. There was an old legend that when Jesus was dying a dove came and settled on His cross. It is only a legend ; yet it suggests the truth that even after the precious blood had been poured out men would not have come to Christ had they not been drawn by the Holy Ghost. Keble writes :—

" Should'st thou not need some mighty charm
　　To win thee to thy Saviour's side,
　　Though He had deigned with thee to bide ?
The Spirit must stir the darkling deep,
　　The dove must settle on the cross,
Else we should all sin on or sleep
　　With Christ in sight, turning our gain to loss."

Oct. 15

Watching and Praying

" Take ye heed, watch and pray : for ye know not when the time is."—MARK xiii. 33

IT is the time of our Lord's coming again to which these words refer. He is coming; but when, no one can know. He will come suddenly, without warning. Since, then, we cannot know what moment the Lord may appear, we must take heed, watch and pray, lest He come and surprise us unprepared. This does not mean that we are always to be talking and thinking of the event and waiting for it in dreamy idleness and useless gazing. What Christ wants us to do is so to live at all times that His coming at any moment of the day or night will not find us unready.

For one thing, we should be sure of our personal salvation. If we are not saved now we should instantly see to the matter ; for He may come the next hour, and there will be no time then to seek salvation. We should keep our work faithfully done, day by day, leaving nothing unfinished any evening ; for before morning He may come. We should live at peace with all men, never allowing the sun to go down on our wrath or on any enmity or bitterness ; for before another day dawns He may come, and we would not want Him to come and find us in strife and bitterness. We should be careful what we do any hour ; for He may come suddenly and find us in sin. We should watch where we go, lest His coming may surprise us in some place where we would not want Him to find us.

This truth, kept ever as a living force in our consciousness, would be the weightiest motive to faithfulness in every duty, and watchfulness against every sin. His coming will be so sudden and so unexpected that there will be no time then to set wrong things right, to finish uncompleted tasks, to get sin-stains washed out, to undo evil deeds. The only safe way to live is to make each task complete—a fit ending for all of life.

Mysterious Providences

" What I do thou knowest not now ; but thou shalt know hereafter."—JOHN xiii. 7

LIKE many other words of Christ, this saying of His has a much wider application than its primary reference to Peter's perplexity. It furnishes the key to very many of the providences of all our lives. We do not understand them at the time. We do not see how they can have any blessing in them for us. They seem altogether dark. But we have no right to judge of our Master's work in us or with us until it is finished. " What I do thou knowest not now." How could we be expected to understand all the Master's great thoughts ?

Yet this is not the end. " Thou shalt know hereafter." This mystery is to be explained. This perplexity is to be resolved into the clearness of noonday. You do not understand now because you cannot yet see the end. The Master Himself knows just what He is going to bring out of each strange work of His, and therefore He is not perplexed. Then He says that we also shall know hereafter. We shall see the cloud as it departs, glorified by the rainbow arching its dark folds. We shall see the tangles resolving into lovely grace and beauty.

" Some time, when all life's lessons have been learned,
    And sun and stars for evermore have set,
The things which our weak judgments here have spurned,
    The things o'er which we grieved with lashes wet,
Will flash before us, out of life's dark night,
    As stars shine most in deeper tints of blue ;
And we shall see how all God's plans were right,
    And how what seemed reproof was love most true."

What is the lesson ? That we should trust God when we cannot understand His ways with us. No doubt love has planned them all. No doubt there is blessing in the outcome as it lies now in God's mind. No doubt we shall see the blessing, too, hereafter.

Lowly Service

*" If I then, your Lord and Master, have washed your feet, ye
also ought to wash one another's feet."*—JOHN xiii. 14

ARE we to take this literally ? Some have understood
it in this way. No, say others ; He would teach us
to do lowly service for one another. Yes ; but what kind
of service ? What did Christ's washing of the feet of His
disciples mean ? It was more than a little lowly act of
service ; He taught them that He would thus cleanse their
souls of remaining faults and blemishes of character, and of
the stains gotten in the world as they pass through.

Our service to one another is to be of the same kind.
We are to come to each other with basin and towel. We
are to help each other to be clean Christians. We are to
seek the sanctification, purification, and upbuilding in character of all our fellow-disciples. Of course we cannot wash
away sins—Christ alone can do that ; but we can do something toward making others purer and holier. We can try
to bring to Christ for salvation those who are not yet
saved ; then we can admonish others in love, and tell them
of their faults, seeking the removal of the faults and
blemishes.

This requires much grace and great wisdom ; we need
lowliness of heart and tenderness of affection to discharge
a duty so delicate. Especially must we be cleansed ourselves if we would seek the cleansing of others. What if
our own hands, with which we would wash the feet of
other disciples, are not clean, but are themselves covered
with sin ? Instead of cleansing the lives we touch, we
shall then leave stains upon them. So we must see that
our own hands have been washed in the blood of Christ
before we undertake to wash the feet of others. Then we
must be willing to yield over our own feet to the water.
The washing is to go all around ; we are to wash one
another's feet. The secret of all must be genuine love for
others.

Resting on Jesus

*" There was leaning on Jesus' bosom one of His disciples,
whom Jesus loved."*—JOHN xiii. 23

WE are not told the name of this disciple, but we
know him by his place and posture. What were
the traits in John's character which made him the beloved
disciple ? One was his humility ; another was his love.
Artists always paint his face in features of gentleness and
affectionateness. Another of his winning traits was his
trust. He never seems to have doubted.

When was it that he reclined on Jesus' bosom ? It was
in a time of great darkness. The Master was about to go
away, and all the hopes of the disciples were being destroyed.
But where was John in that darkness ? Sorrow, instead
of driving us into despair, should drive us nearer to Christ
—to His bosom.

> " He's better to us than many mothers are,
>   And children cannot wander beyond reach
>   Of the sweep of His white garment.
>   Touch and hold,
>   And if you weep still, weep
>   Where John was laid
>   While Jesus loved him."

Where was it that John leaned ? On Jesus breast.
Not merely on His arm, the place of strength ; nor upon
His shoulder, the place of upholding ; but on His bosom,
the place of love and tenderness. It is good to know that
the Divine omnipotence is underneath us in all our weakness ; but mere omnipotence is cold. How much better
is it when omnipotence has the heart of love within it.

But *what* did John do ? He *leaned.* He rested his
weight on the omnipotent love of his Lord. Christ wants
all His friends to lean upon Him. He wants to carry our
burdens for us—He wants us to lay upon Him our sins and
all our cares ; but more than this—*ourselves.* He wants
to bear us as well as our loads.

The Last Supper

" Jesus took bread, and blessed it, and brake it, and gave it to the disciples, and said, Take, eat."—MATT. xxvi. 26

THERE was a meaning in every act. The bread itself is an appropriate emblem of Christ's body. Bread is food ; Christ is food for our spirits. Something may be learned from the manner in which bread is prepared. The wheat is crushed and broken, and then the bread is baked in the fire before it is ready for use. So Christ died, His body was bruised and broken, and He was exposed to the fire of great sufferings before He could become the food and life of our souls.

The breaking of the bread is also significant, denoting the breaking of the body of Christ on the cross. We ought never to forget, in our sweet enjoyment of the blessings of grace, what it cost our Lord to provide them for us. Whenever we sit at our Lord's table and see the bread broken, we should remember the anguish and suffering endured by our Redeemer in saving us.

The giving of the bread to the disciples had also a deep meaning. It signified the freeness of Christ's offer of Himself to men. He is ever standing, reaching out His hands with the bread of life, imploring men to take freely all the blessings of salvation.

The taking of the bread by the communicant is significant of the act of faith by which Christ Himself is received. He offers ; we receive. It is not enough that Christ gave Himself on the cross for sinners, and now holds out in pierced hands the blessings of redemption. These stupendous acts of love and grace alone will not save us. There is a needed link which we must supply : we must reach out our hands and accept and take what Christ so graciously and lovingly offers to us. Then, since bread to nourish us must be eaten, we must receive Christ into our life as our soul's sustenance, feeding upon Him.

Remembering Jesus

" This do in remembrance of Me."—LUKE xxii. 19

THERE is something very tender in the thought of the Lord's Supper as a memorial. We all know the value of mementoes in keeping in mind one whose face we cannot see. A young man sat one morning in his pastor's study, and drew a letter from his pocket, saying that he had just heard from his sister away in the English home. Opening the letter, he showed his pastor some little pressed flowers and some dried grass-blades. The young man's voice was choked with emotion as he said, " These flowers and grasses are from my mother's grave in England." The little memorials brought back the whole life of the mother, and the son sat there and spoke most affectionately of her love, her fidelity, her beauty of spirit, her sacrifices, then of her death. So it is that memorials of the Last Supper recall to our forgetful hearts the sacred scenes and events of our Lord's passion, and the love that led Him to such sacrifice.

But mere remembering is not enough ; the remembering ought to kindle love and keep us faithful. A young man was about to go abroad for a long journey. Just before he set out his father took his watch from his pocket. On the dial were the pictures of both his parents. " Take this watch," said the father, " and carry it with you in all your journeyings. Every time you look to see the hour the eyes of your father and mother will look up into yours. When you see these home faces, remember that we are thinking of you and praying for you. Go to no place where you would not want us to see you. Do nothing you would not want us to witness." In the Last Supper, Jesus has given us His own picture—His broken body, His blood shed ; He wants us to remember Him and be faithful. Remembering Jesus should always keep us from doubting and sinning, and inspire us to nobleness and beauty.

Oct. 21

The Remission of Sins

*" This is my blood of the new testament, which is shed for
many for the remission of sins."*—MATT. xxvi. 28

SO right in the heart of the Lord's Supper we are reminded of two things—of the price paid for our
redemption, and of the deliverance that this redemption
brings to us. The price paid was the precious blood of
Christ ; the deliverance is the remission of sins.

There is a singular Oriental custom which may help us
better to understand the way Christ made atonement for
our sins. " When a debt had to be settled," says Dr. A. J.
Gordon, " either by full payment or forgiveness, it was the
usage for the creditor to take the cancelled bond and nail
it over the door of him who had owed it, that all passers-
by might see that it was paid. Oh, blessed story of our
remission ! There is the cross, the door of grace, behind
which a bankrupt world lies in hopeless debt to the law.
See Jesus, our bondsman and brother, coming forth with
the long list of our indebtedness in His hand. He lifts it
up where God and angels and men may see it, and then, as
the nail goes through His hand, it goes through the bond of
our transgressions, to cancel it for ever, blotting out the
handwriting of ordinances that was against us. He took
it out of the way, nailing it to the cross.".

This is the wonderful act of remission that is portrayed
for us with such vividness in the cup of the Lord's Supper.
The nail that went through those bonds and fastened them
there on the cross went also through the body of the Lord
Jesus. Blood flowed at the remitting of our sins—the blood
of the Son of God. The cup that is so sweet to us was
emptied of terrible bitterness by the Lord Himself, then
filled with heaven's choicest blessings and brought to us.
While we rejoice at the remission, let us not forget what
it cost our Redeemer ; nor let us forget the wonderful
grace that puts all our sins away as far as the east is from
the west.

The Heavenly Feast

" *I will not drink henceforth of this fruit of the vine, until that day when I drink it new with you in my Father's kingdom.*"—MATT. xxvi. 29

THE Lord's Supper points forward as well as back. It keeps the past in remembrance ; we are to think of what happened nineteen hundred years ago. The Supper is a memorial. But it is also a prophecy. Christ wrote the white lines of a blessed hope amid the mementoes of sorrow. He lifted the veil and gave a glimpse of a fulfilment very glorious beyond earth's shadows. Even the Holy Supper, precious as it is, is but a faint picture of something far better.

The disciples would not have Jesus with them at the table any more. This was their " last supper " together. Henceforth on earth His place would be vacant. But in telling them this He gave them sweet comfort in the assurance that He would sit down with them again, by-and-by, not here, but in another kingdom. These words are full of luminous brightness. They tell us of a supper in glory, of which the Lord's Supper on earth is but the shadow. In the Revelation it is called " the marriage supper of the Lamb." So it will be a memorial, too, of Christ's death and love.

That night when the Master and His disciples sat down together in the upper room, a great sorrow hung over their hearts and His : for Him it was the shadow of His cross, with all its mystery of woe ; for them it was the shadow of sore loss and separation. But the other side of the cloud was very bright. Out of Christ's death came blessed and glorious salvation ; now in heaven Jesus sees of the travail of His soul, and is satisfied. Out of the brief separation there came to the disciples an abiding presence of Christ which filled their hearts full. Jesus went away from them for a little time that He might be with them for ever. So out of these sad memories came great joys.

Comfort in Sorrow

" Let not your heart be troubled "—JOHN xiv. 1

JESUS always loves to comfort. He loves to put little candles in the darkened chambers of sorrow. He loves to dry tears and change grief into joy. Then He is *able* to give comfort, because He has the comfort in Himself. We cannot give what we have not to give. We often say to one another in trial, " Do not worry ! do not be troubled ! " when we have no comfort to give, nothing to cure the worry or brighten the darkness. Standing on the ship in the midst of a wild sea, Jesus said, " Peace ! " and the winds and waves instantly became a calm. He had the peace in Himself, and could give peace to the sea. It is the same with His comfort : His words of consolation are not like so many of ours ; they have power to quiet the troubled heart.

It was a time of the deepest grief and the sorest sorrow for the disciples when Jesus said this. Not only were they to lose their best Friend, but they were to lose Him in the saddest way—by death in the shame of the cross. Nor was that all of their sorrow. They had hoped He was the Messiah ; now that hope was gone. They were in utter desolation—in a starless midnight. Surely there *could* be no comfort for such grief as theirs, they thought that night, as with breaking hearts they sat there in the darkness.

Yet right into the midst of this despairing grief came the words, " Let not your heart be troubled." Let us never say, therefore, that there is any, even the bitterest, grief for which there is no possible comfort. No matter how dark the night is, Christ can put stars into our sky, and bring a glorious morning after the darkness. There *is* comfort for Christ's disciples in the most hopeless grief. We have but to look forward a few days to see the sorrow of these men turned to blessed joy. So it always is. However we may grieve, there is never any reason why we should lose our peace.

𝔓eace in 𝔅elieving

" Ye believe in God, believe also in Me."—JOHN xiv. 1

WE should all learn how to comfort others. No duty of Christian love requires more delicacy. We may study our Lord's way of comforting to learn to give comfort ourselves to those who are in trouble. We see that He did not go over the cold platitudes we are so accustomed to use when we try to console our friends in their grief.

" One writes that ' Other friends remain,'
    That ' Loss is common to the race,'—
        And common is the commonplace,
And vacant chaff well meant for grain.

" That loss is common would not make
    My own less bitter, rather more :
        Too common ! Never morning wore
To evening but some heart did break."

But not in this empty way does Christ comfort His people. Here He offered no explanations, answered no questions, gave no reasons ; He told His disciples simply to believe. They could not understand this terrible grief. They could see no star in the sky. But they did not need to understand, did not need to see any light. They were to do nothing but believe—just cling to Christ in the darkness and believe.

In all deep grief this is the truest way to find comfort. There is no use to ask questions, for no one can answer them. There is no use to strain our eyes trying to see the light, for as yet there is no light to see. All we can do is just to throw ourselves on our Saviour's bosom and lie there till the light breaks. We may always be sure of the love and the faithfulness of Christ. We may nestle down, as John did that same night, upon the Saviour's bosom, and be quiet and confident in the time of our sorest calamities. " In the world ye shall have tribulations "—" In Me ye shall have peace."

Oct. 25

Ʒbe Way to Ibeaven

" I am the way......no man cometh unto the Father, but by Me."—JOHN xiv. 6

A WAY always leads somewhere: Jesus is the way from earth to heaven, and also from heaven to earth. Through Him we get to God, and through Him God comes to us. He is the true and only ladder whose foot rests on the earth, and whose top reaches up to the very glory of God. In His humanity Jesus comes down to the lowest depths of human need and sorrow. Had He been God only, and not man, He could not have done this. The incarnation was the letting of the ladder down until it rested in the deepest valleys. There is now no spot of shame or guilt in this world from which there is not a ladder of light, with its celestial steps leading upward to God and heaven.

For while Christ's humanity brings the ladder down to earth's places of sorest need, His divinity carries the ladder up past the shining stars, into the very midst of the glory of God. On one page of the New Testament we find Jesus on a cross, dying in darkness and shame, between criminals. We open another page, and we see that same Jesus in the midst of the heavenly brightness, wearing still the woundmarks, but crowned in glory. Behold the ladder from earth to heaven !

A ladder is a way for feet to climb : Christ is the way, therefore, by which sinners can go up out of their sins to the purity and blessedness of heaven. One thing to mark specially is that there is but one way. Christ is the only Mediator. We can enter the Father's family only through Him. Grace can come to us only through Him. There is, then, no choice of ways : if we do not go by this one way we can never reach home. Nor must we forget that a way is meant to be walked in. We must put our feet on this ladder and go up rung by rung until we reach the topmost step, which will be heaven.

Knowledge of Christ

" Have I been so long time with you, and yet hast thou not known Me ? "—JOHN xiv. 9

THERE seems to be pain in the Master's question. This disciple had been with Him for three years. He had seen His beautiful and gentle life. He had witnessed His works of power. Surely by this time, after such long and close intimacy, the disciple ought to have known Jesus. Yet Jesus tells him here that he did not really know Him.

We get this lesson—that it is possible to be with Christ a long time, and to know very much about Him, without *knowing* Him in the true sense of the word. Philip knew Jesus as a man, as a worker of miracles, as having a very beautiful character ; but he seems never to have gone below the surface in understanding Him. He did not know Him as the revealer of the Father. He never saw Divine glory in the radiance that streamed from that blessed life. And not to know Christ in this aspect, to know Him only as a man, is not to know Him at all. To leave out the Divine in our thought of Christ is not to have any Christ at all.

We may be quite familiar with the facts of our Lord's life, from His birth in Bethlehem to His ascension from Olivet, and yet may not know anything of Him as a personal Saviour, saving us from our sins, or as a Helper in our times of need. Such knowledge will do us no good unless it lead us to the true knowledge of Christ as Saviour, Lord, and Friend.

There is something very touching in the thought that for so long the Son of God walked with His disciples, all the glory of divinity dwelling in His humanity, and that they did not recognize Him. But is it any better with us ? The Divine love is close to us perpetually, flowing all about us, with all its infinite tenderness, but how unconscious we are of it ! May our prayer be, " Lord, make Thyself known to us ! "

Immanuel

" *He that hath seen Me hath seen the Father.*"—JOHN xiv. 9

THAT was surely a very strange thing for a man to say. Can we imagine John, the beloved disciple, saying of himself that those who had seen him had seen the Father ? The fact that Christ said it shows that He was conscious of divinity, that He really claimed to be the Son of God. So it is in all Christ's words : He speaks always as God. Wherever we turn in the gospel we find the outflashings of Christ's divinity ; it were easier to pluck the stars from the sky than to tear the truth of Christ's deity from the pages of inspiration. Everywhere it shines—its light the brightest beam in all the radiant splendour that blazes there.

What did Jesus mean when He said this ? Evidently that although He was a man, He was also the incarnation of God ; that He was living out in a human life, which men could see, the invisible life of His father. Men on earth could never see God. Then God sent His Son that He might veil His Divine splendour in flesh, and show people how the unseen God feels and acts.

Thus, when we see Him taking little children in His arms, laying His hand on their heads and blessing them, we see how God feels toward children. When we see the compassion of Jesus stirred by human suffering, we learn how our heavenly Father is touched by the sight of earthly woe. When we see Jesus receiving sinners and eating with them, speaking forgiveness to penitents who crept to His feet, and making soiled, stained lives white and clean, we learn the mercy of God. When we follow Christ to His cross and see Him giving His life a willing sacrifice to make redemption for lost men, we see how God loves. So the meekness and patience and gentleness of Christ were mirrorings of the same traits in His Father. If we would see the likeness of God, we have but to turn to the story of the gospel. To know Christ is to know the Father.

The True Vine

" I am the true vine, and My Father is the husbandman "
JOHN xv. 1

THIS is a wonderful Vine. It grew up like a root out of a dry ground, with no form nor comeliness. The soil in which it was planted seemed too poor to produce anything good. But its origin was heavenly, and it grew into luxuriant beauty. By-and-by it seemed that men in their rage had altogether destroyed this Vine, which had in it so much blessing for the earth ; however, it was not destroyed, but was only lifted away from earth and transplanted to heaven. There in the garden of God its roots were fixed, and the Vine itself dropped down to earth again, and began to send out branches in all directions. Every poor little human life which attaches itself to this Vine is grafted on it and becomes a branch in it, drawing life from the Vine's fullness, and sharing its fruitfulness.

These branches are not left to grow wild and untended, but have wise and skilful care. It ought to be a great comfort to us to know that as branches we are under the culture of a husbandman who is none other than our heavenly Father : " Your Father is the husbandman." We are very sure that His care will be both wise and tender. If an ignorant, inexperienced, unskilful man were to enter a beautiful vineyard and begin cutting away at the vines, he would soon destroy them. He does not know what he ought to prune off, or what he ought to leave on the vines. But if the man who comes to tend the vineyard understands vines, and has had long experience and is skilful, there is no danger that he will do harm in his pruning. Sometimes, indeed, he may seem to be cutting the vine to death ; but we know that he understands what he is doing, and that all his prunings are for the good of the branches. By-and-by we shall see increased fruitfulness as the result of his unsparing work.

The Pruning-Knife

" Every branch in Me that beareth not fruit He taketh away; and every branch that beareth fruit He purgeth it, that it may bring forth more fruit."—JOHN xv. 2

CHRIST taught many lessons on the sin and doom of uselessness. One of His parables told of a tree that bore no fruit. The soil was good, and the tree was carefully planted and well tended; still, when the master came at the proper season, expecting to find fruit, He found none. Fruitlessness is cursed. The tree with nothing but leaves is made to wither. There is no place in the Lord's kingdom for uselessness.

We must notice here that it is the fruitful branch that is pruned. The husbandman does not prune the unfruitful branch; it would do it no good. It is the true Christian that the Father chastens and causes sometimes to suffer under sore discipline. The wicked are let alone; but in their luxuriance there is no spiritual fruit.

Another thing to be noticed here is, that the object of the Father's pruning is that the branch may be made to bear more fruit. It seems sometimes as if the pruning were destructive; but He who holds the knife knows that what He is doing will make the vine far more luxuriant in the end, and its fruit sweeter and more luscious. The aim of God in all His pruning is greater fruitfulness.

> " Now the pruning, sharp, unsparing,
> Scattered blossom, bleeding shoot;
> Afterward the plenteous bearing
> Of the Master's pleasant fruit."

If we would but remember this when we find ourselves suffering under God's chastening hand, it would help us to bear the pain with patience, and also to co-operate with God in His design of blessing for us. Earthly prosperity often is to the Christian like the luxuriance which the vine-dresser must cut away to save the vine's life.

"Abide in Me"

" *As the branch cannot bear fruit of itself, except it abide in the vine ; no more can ye, except ye abide in Me.*"— JOHN xv. 4

AS a truth in nature the meaning of this is very plain. A branch torn off a vine or a tree, and lying on the ground, will not bear fruit. Indeed, it cannot even live, but soon withers. The analogy holds in spiritual life. It would be just as unnatural to expect the professing Christian who has given up praying and has ceased to read his Bible, and withdrawn from loving and trusting Christ, to be really a fruitful Christian. The branch has no life but what flows into it from the vine or the tree ; the Christian has no spiritual life but what comes from Christ's life, through faith and prayer and the Holy Word. We live as Christians only when Christ lives in us. Said St. Paul : " I live ; yet not I, but Christ liveth in me : and the life which I now live in the flesh I live by the faith of the Son of God, who loved me, and gave Himself for me." All spiritual beauty in us must be the life of Christ reproduced in us, just as the foliage and the fruit on a tree are produced by the tree's life flowing into the branches.

A mere Christian profession will not therefore yield the fruits of a true Christian life. One might take a branch that had been torn off and with cords tie it on a green tree, but that would not make it a fruitful branch. It would draw no life from the tree, and would soon be withered and utterly dead. One may be tied to Christ by the cords of profession, but if there is no real vital attachment of the life to Christ by faith and love, Christ's life cannot flow into it, and it is only a dead, withered branch. We must be truly in Christ and have Christ in us, or there can be no life in us and no fruitfulness. We must also abide in Christ, maintaining our communion and fellowship with Him year after year, or we cannot be fruit-bearing Christians.

Oct. 31

Fruit=Bearing

" Herein is My Father glorified, that ye bear much fruit ; so shall ye be My disciples."—JOHN xv. 8

WHAT is fruit in a Christian ? We know what it is in the natural world, and know its uses ; what is it in the spiritual world ? It is not merely Christian activities. True, well-directed activities are fruits ; but there is danger in these days, when work is so lauded, that we overlook another kind of fruit which certainly is as essential as the forth-putting of consecrated energy. In nature, fruit is part of the branch itself, not something apart from it. There are spiritual fruits that are part of the life, growths into holiness and Christlikeness. Thus St. Paul says, " The fruit of the Spirit is love, joy, peace, long-suffering, gentleness, goodness, faith, meekness, temperance." Very evidently these fruits are such as appear in the character itself. The aim of Christ's religion is not merely to make workers of us, to send us out to do good in the world, to fight against evil, to help the weak, and to minister to the sorrowing and the suffering. Its first aim is to make us good, to transform our character, to produce in us the likeness of Christ. Then we shall be ready to minister. · While, therefore, we are to be fruitful in every good work, we are to seek also to be fruitful in the qualities of Christlike character.

In nature the tree's fruits feed the hunger of men. No tree consumes its own fruits ; it drops them for those who come to gather them. This suggests that we should not be selfish in our fruit-bearing. We should not seek the culture of our characters merely for our own sake. Our aim should be to provide something in our lives that will feed others and bless the world. All about us are hungry hearts. There are those who crave sympathy and love, those who yearn for comfort, those who desire to be saved. We are so to live that our lives shall yield bread for these.

Light Behind the Cloud

" It is expedient for you that I go away."—JOHN xvi. 7

THE disciples thought that Christ's going away would be an irretrievable loss for them. It was the crushing of all their hopes. They thought they would be left in darkness and loneliness; for they had built up all their Messianic hopes on the idea of His remaining and ruling as a king over His people. Not only were they about to lose the dearest friend they had ever known, but they were to lose also the one in whom they had trusted as the promised Deliverer and Saviour. They saw no silver lining whatever in the dark cloud that was gathering.

But now Jesus says to them, " It is expedient *for you* that I go away." There *was* a silver lining, after all, in that black cloud. What seemed an irreparable loss would in the end prove a gain. The disciples did not understand it now, but there were the Master's words for it.

The same is true now in the case of all the Master's disciples when He calls away their human friends. We can readily see how it is well for our Christian friends when Christ takes them. They exchange earth for heaven, sin and sorrow for holiness and eternal joy. There is no doubt that death is gain for those who depart; but how about those who remain? How about the friends who are left with bleeding hearts to walk on lonely and sad over earth's ways? This word of Christ applies: " It is expedient *for you* that I go away." We cannot understand this; but neither could the disciples understand at the time how Christ's departure could be better for them than His staying with them would have been. Afterward they knew; and afterward we shall know how even for us the going away of our friends will become a blessing if we in faith submit ourselves to God. " We know that all things work together *for good* to them that love God."

The Comforter

*" If I go not away, the Comforter will not come unto you ;
but if I depart, I will send Him unto you."*—JOHN
xvi. 7

WHY did the coming of the Comforter depend on
Christ's going away ? We may say, for one thing,
that the Comforter could not come until the great offering
for sin had been made. The Father sent the Son to be
the propitiation for the sins of the world. Without shed-
ding of blood there could be no remission of sins. There
was, therefore, no redemption to be offered and applied
until Jesus had made His great sacrifice. It was necessary,
therefore, that He should go away and should die before
the Comforter could come. The precious alabaster box of
Christ's humanity must be broken open in order that the
sacred ointment of His most blessed life might be poured
out on the dead world.

It was necessary, also, that Christ should return to the
Father as the Son of man, the representative of humanity,
and be received into the Father's bosom as such. " Humanity was to ascend to heaven before the Spirit could be
sent to humanity on earth." Christ also says that He will
send the Comforter. He could not do this until He had
returned to His glory and been exalted, in His humanity,
to His throne of power.

These are hints of the reasons why Jesus had to go
away before the Comforter could come. We live now
under the blessed reign of the Holy Spirit. Sometimes we
wish we had lived in the time of Christ's human presence
in this world, and look back on the period of the incarnation as earth's brightest and most glorious days ; but really
we have far richer privileges than had those who knew
Christ in the flesh. We have the same blessed Presence
that they had, only without the limitations of flesh. Christ
is now to millions everywhere even far more than He was
then to a few favoured ones.

Life=Giving Knowledge

*" And this is life eternal, that they might know Thee the only
true God, and Jesus Christ, whom Thou hast sent."—*
JOHN xvii. 3

ANY one, therefore, who truly knows God has eternal
life. Knowing God, however, is more than knowing *about* Him. One may have all the doctrinal knowledge
of God's character, attributes, and works which the Bible
reveals, and yet not know God at all in the way that gives
life. We may know all about some great man biographically, and yet not know the man at all personally. But
suppose we then meet him, and become intimately associated with him, and he becomes our dear friend, and we
learn to love him and trust him, then we really know him.
It is this personal knowledge of God that is meant in these
words. We first learn about Him, and then we seek Him
and find Him; and He receives us into His family, and
sheds abroad His love in our hearts, and gives us His
Spirit. Then we learn to trust Him and to love Him.
This is the knowing God which gives eternal life.

But how can we meet God, and get personally acquainted
with Him, and form this intimate friendship with Him ?
There is another word in this verse which helps us to the
answer. "That they might know Thee......and *Jesus
Christ.*" We are clearly taught elsewhere that we can
know God only through Jesus Christ. "Neither knoweth
any man the Father, save the Son, and he to whomsoever
the Son will reveal Him." Jesus Christ is the revelation
of the Father to men : "He that hath seen Me hath seen
the Father." We can get aquainted with Christ in His
humanity, and thus know God, and have Him for our
nearest Friend. M'Cheyne said : "I seem to know more
of the Lord Jesus Christ than of the most intimate friend
I have on earth." Should we not all seek after Christ's
personal friendship ? The more we trust Him the more
shall we know of Him, and the better shall we love Him.

Divine Protection

" *Holy Father, keep through Thine own name those whom Thou hast given Me, that they may be one, as We are.*"
JOHN xvii. 11

THERE is matchless tenderness in the picture which these words in our Lord's intercessory prayer suggest. We think of a dying mother about to leave her children behind her in this world, exposed to all the world's dangers. During her own life she has cared for them with all tenderness and fidelity. Now, however, she is going away, and can guard them no more. But she cannot leave them without securing for them shelter and protection. Looking up to God, therefore, she commends them to His care. She knows that He never goes away, that He is present everywhere, and that He will look after her motherless children.

In like manner Jesus, about to go away and leave His disciples, commends them in their peril and need to His Father's care. The prayer suggests two things. It gives us a glimpse of the heart of our Saviour, and of His deep, tender, yearning love for His disciples. It ought to be a great comfort to us to know that He has just the same love for us if we are His. When we are going into any danger He looks down upon us with deep, affectionate longing, and intercedes for us as He did here for His disciples.

The other suggestion here is that if we belong to Christ we are divinely sheltered and kept. We cannot keep ourselves, but we have the Lord for our keeper ; the wings of the Almighty cover us wherever we go. I have slept in camps in war times, when hostile forces pressed close upon the lines ; but we all lay down at night in quiet confidence and peace, without fear, because all around the camps sentinels waked and watched. So God's angels encamp around His children, and so always the Lord keeps those who trust in Him. To have Christ for Saviour is to have the Divine protection and guardianship.

Life Worth Living

" *I pray not that Thou shouldest take them out of the world.*"
JOHN xvii. 15

IT would be a great deal safer, in one sense, for believers to be taken at once to heaven as soon as they begin to follow Christ. They would then have no temptations, no enemies to fight, no conflicts and struggles to pass through. But who would then do Christ's work in the world ? There would be none to tell sinners about the Saviour, none to show to men the beauty of Christ in a holy life, none to witness for God and to fight His battles.

There is another reason why Christians are left here. They are not the most majestic trees that grow in the sheltered valleys, where no storms break, but those rather which are found upon the hill-tops and on the mountains, where they must encounter the fierce gales. It is so with men : the noblest are grown amid difficulties and hardships, not in pampered ease. Even Jesus Himself was trained in the school of conflict and struggle. It may be the easiest thing to have no battles in life, to grow in some sheltered plain where the storms never blow, to meet no hardships, to have no burdens to carry ; but what sort of life comes in the end from such a career ? If we would reach the heights of blessedness we must be content to pass through the fields of struggle.

When armies return from victorious war, the loudest cheers are not for those who have fought the fewest battles, nor for the flags which are cleanest, but for the regiments which are cut down to a few men, and for the colours that are shot to pieces. So it will be in heaven when the redeemed are welcomed home : those who have fought the most battles, and bear the most " marks of the Lord Jesus," will receive the highest honours. It is better, then, even for Christians themselves to stay in this world, and to grow to strength through duty and conflict.

Nov. 6

Our Great Intercessor

" *Neither pray I for these alone, but for them also which shall believe on Me through their word.*"—JOHN xvii. 20

THUS in this wonderful intercessory prayer our Lord reached out beyond the little circle of imperilled disciples that stood around Him that night, and gathered in His arms all those who to the end should believe on Him. It embraced us, therefore, who in these days believe on Christ. He looked down along the ages and saw us and our dangers, and amid the deepening shadows of His cross prayed for us. How sweet to be prayed for by Christ !

Even that is not all, precious as it is ; for we are told elsewhere that Jesus ever lives to make intercession for His people. We are not to think of Him as losing interest in this earth when He went away. This intercessory prayer, whose sentences we catch as we read this chapter, is but a momentary revealing to us of Christ's continual pleading for us within the veil. We are to think of Him as in heaven watching us perpetually and praying for us in every time of danger. He sees each stealthy temptation as it approaches, and asks, " Father, keep Thy imperilled child."

It is a very precious comfort even to know that a dear human friend is praying for us. Many a time in my youth was I kept from doing wrong things by the thought that in my quiet home far away my father and my mother, every morning and every evening, stretched out holy hands in earnest, loving prayer that God would keep their boy. I could not do the wrong thing with this vision in my mind. Still more powerful in its restraining influence upon us should be the assurance that day and night Jesus in heaven is thinking of us, watching us from His holy height in glory, and at every appearance of evil prays for us. How could we do the evil thing if we but stopped long enough to think of this Divine intercession for us ?

"Songs in the Night."

"*And when they had sung an hymn, they went out into the mount of Olives.*"—MATT. xxvi. 30.

THIS is the only record of our Lord's singing when He was on the earth. It is worthy of special notice that it was just as He was starting out to Gethsemane that He sung a hymn with His disciples. It would not have seemed so strange to us if He had sung that night on the Transfiguration Mount, or the day He entered Jerusalem amid the people's hosannas, or on some other occasion of great gladness and triumph; but that the only time we hear Him singing should be in the darkest night of His life is very suggestive.

It tells us of the deep gladness that was in the heart of Christ under all His griefs and sorrows. He knew the agony into whose black shadows He was about to enter. He saw the cross, too, that stood beyond Gethsemane. Yet He went out toward the darkness with songs of praise on His lips. There is a Scripture word which tells us that "for the joy set before Him He endured the cross, despising the shame." This was the joy that broke forth here in a hymn of praise. It was the joy of doing the Father's will and of saving lost souls. We get thus here another glimpse of Christ's great heart of love.

We learn a lesson, too, for ourselves. We should go forward with joy to meet sorrow and sacrifice when we are doing our Father's will. We should learn to sing as we enter life's valleys of shadow. It is a great thing to be able to sing as we work, and sing as we suffer. The secret of Christ's song here was His looking beyond the garden and the cross; He saw the reward, the glory, the redemption accomplished. If we look only at the sorrow before us, we cannot sing; but if we look on to the joy of victory, and the blessedness of the reward, and the ripened fruits that will come from the suffering, we can sing too as we enter the sorest trial.

Nov. 8

The Baffled Tempter

" Satan hath desired to have you, that he may sift you as wheat."—LUKE xxii. 31

PETER was put through Satan's winnowing; but the chaff only in him was blown out. He was a smaller man after the winnowing, just as the bulk of the wheat pile is reduced when the chaff is blown out; but he was a better man. He lost his rashness, his self-confidence, his pride, and became again a humble man, but stronger, majestic—a power to bless the world.

Thus through the grace of Christ even the falls of believers are made to work for their good. Much of the grandeur and power of Peter's after life came out of that costly lesson. "The oyster mends its shell with a pearl." Where the ugly wound was there comes a gem, hiding the scar, and making it a spot of lustrous beauty. So true repentance of sins changes the weakness of our lives into strength. If we are Christ's true followers, even our defeats become blessings. Longfellow says of Peter's sifting,—

" One look of that pale, suffering face
    Will make us feel the deep disgrace
            Of weakness ;
    We shall be sifted till the strength
    Of self-conceit be changed at length
            To meekness.

" Wounds of the soul, though healed, will ache,
    The reddening scars remain and make
            Confession ;
    Lost innocence returns no more ;
    We are not what we were before
            Transgression.

" But noble souls through dust and heat
    Rise from disaster and defeat
            The stronger ;
    And conscious still of the Divine
    Within them, lie on earth supine
            No longer."

Nov. 9

Strength out of Weakness

" When thou art converted, strengthen thy brethren."
LUKE xxii. 32

PETER was not to be lost in the terrible experience through which he was to pass. Christ had made intercession for him, and he would come again from the trial humbled, bruised, defeated, but saved, and a better man. Our Lord tells him here that after his restoration he should turn his experience to account in helping other souls. " Do thou, when once thou hast turned again, stablish thy brethren." He would be able then to warn others of the dangers in which he had suffered so terribly. We can imagine Peter in after days counselling Christians against self-confidence and the other false steps which led to his own fall, and thus strengthening or stablishing them in safe ways. Then there is no doubt that his experience of penitence, and of the grace and love of Christ in that experience, enabled him to be a wise and safe guide to many another disciple who had fallen into sin and was seeking to be restored.

The lesson is important. All the lessons that God teaches us we should teach others. When we are helped it is that we may then help others. When God comforts us in any sorrow, He thereby ordains us to go forth to comfort others with the comfort wherewith we have been comforted of God. When we fall in temptation, and God lifts us up and restores us, He wants us to use our experience in helping other weak ones in their temptations

" O lead me, Lord, that I may lead
    The wandering and the wavering feet ;
O feed me, Lord, that I may feed
    Thy hungering ones with manna sweet.

" O strengthen me, that while I stand
    Firm on the rock, and strong in Thee,
I may stretch out a loving hand
    To wrestlers with the troubled sea."

The Man of Sorrows

" My soul is exceeding sorrowful, even unto death."
MATT. xxvi. 38

WE ought often to sit down with our Lord in Gethsemane, and look upon Him while He suffers. We never can understand more than a very little of the anguish of that hour in the garden, yet we should often study it. Some hints of its meaning may be reverently mentioned.

Before our Lord there lay the betrayal, the arrest, the trial with all its mockery and humiliation, then death amid the ignominy of the cross. These physical sufferings alone made an anguish that was terrible to endure. Another element of our Lord's suffering was the falseness of the human hearts about Him. There were the traitorous kiss of Judas, the sad denial of Peter, the flight and desertion of the other disciples, the rejection and crucifixion by the people He had come to save. All this He foresaw from Gethsemane.

But that which made the very essence of the anguish of Gethsemane was the fact that Jesus was bearing our sins. What that meant to Him we never can know. We know only what is most dimly shadowed for us in the deep words of Holy Scripture, which speak of His vicarious sacrifice. They are such words as these : " Behold the Lamb of God, which taketh away the sin of the world ! "—" The Lord hath laid on Him the iniquity of us all "—" He bare our sins in His own body on the tree "—" He hath redeemed us from the curse of the law, being made a curse for us." We are sure, at least, that the death of Jesus was not like the death of any other man, even though the other could endure all the physical sufferings that attended our Lord's agony. In some way, though innocent and holy Himself, and without sin, He died for sin. The mystery we never can fathom, but the fact we must remember as we watch with our Lord in Gethsemane.

"Watch with Me"

" Tarry ye here, and watch with Me."—MATT. xxvi. 38

THIS request shows the humanness of our Lord. As He entered the darkness He craved sympathy. He wanted His dearest friends near to Him. It was not because of anything they could really do to help Him. They could not lighten the awful load by so much as a feather's weight. They could not in any way share the burden. But their presence would make Him stronger to endure. The consciousness of tender love close beside Him would sustain Him in the fearful anguish.

We all understand this from personal experience. A little child's terror in the darkness is instantly soothed by a word from the mother or by her touch. A sufferer can endure his pain better if a friend sits beside him and holds his hand. We all crave companionship in life's great trials. These are hints of our Lord's feeling and desire that night when He asked His three best beloved disciples to accompany Him, and begged them to watch with Him while He entered into His agony.

Jesus no more suffers in any Gethsemane, yet He still calls us to watch with Him. Many of His people suffer, and He would have us come up close beside them and by loving sympathy and tenderness sustain and strengthen them. He who thus watches with one of the least of Christ's brethren in time of pain or sorrow watches with Christ Himself.

We can also watch with Christ by being loyal and devoted to Him in every dark hour when His cause languishes, and when many are proving recreant and untrue. The time to be faithful to one's friend is when the popular clamour is against him. Our loyalty to Christ, in like manner, should be most emphatic when His enemies are most active and when His friends are fewest. He wants us then to be true. He wants us to keep near Him. Surely we should never pain Him by coldness or want of interest.

Nov. 12.

"Thy Will be Done"

"O My Father, if it be possible, let this cup pass from Me: nevertheless not as I will, but as Thou wilt."—MATT xxvi. 39

AMONG other lessons which we learn from our Lord's prayer in Gethsemane is this, that all our crying to God should close in acquiescence to the Divine will. It is right to plead earnestly for what we want—earnestly, but never unsubmissively. We should recognize the fact that our Father has a plan for our lives, and that what we crave may not be in accordance with His plan. We should never want, therefore, to press our will against God's will.

There was an ignorant man who wished to pray, but did not know what he needed. Taking the letters of the alphabet, he laid them down and said: "Lord, I do not know what I need, or ought to ask for. Do Thou take these letters and arrange them into the prayer I ought to make, and give me that."

The best thing possible for us is always what God wills for us. Sometimes it may be pain or worldly loss or sore bereavement; yet His will is always love, and in simple acquiescence to this will we shall always find our highest good. No prayer, therefore, is pleasing to God which does not end with this refrain of Gethsemane. This is the way also to peace: as we merge our own will in our Father's, the peace of God flows like a river into our souls.

> " 'Not as I will!'—the sound grows sweet
> Each time my lips the words repeat.
> 'Not as I will!'—the darkness feels
> More safe than light when this thought steals
> Like whispered voice to calm and bless
> All unrest and all loneliness.
> 'Not as I will,' because the One
> Who loved us first and best has gone
> Before us on the road, and still
> For us must all His love fulfil—
> 'Not as we will.' "

"Watch unto Prayer."

" *Watch and pray, that ye enter not into temptation : the spirit indeed is willing, but the flesh is weak.*"—MATT. xxvi. 41

WE must learn both to watch and pray. It is good to watch. There is danger everywhere. An army in an enemy's country never rests a moment without its encircling line of pickets, keeping watch against danger at every point, and reporting instantly any hostile movement. We are living in the enemy's country, and cannot safely pass an hour without watching. But watching is not enough ; for we are not able to keep ourselves when the danger comes. Hence we need also to pray, asking God to keep us. But as watching without praying is not enough, neither is praying without watching. God means us to use our eyes and to keep our wits about us, as well as to cry to Him for help.

We must not say that every one who makes a good profession, and then fails, is insincere or a hypocrite. Peter was neither when he made his bold avowal that he would never deny Christ, and that he could die with Him. He loved Christ, and meant to be true to Him. His spirit was eager and earnest, but he was weak in himself ; and because he relied only on himself, he was not able to hold out against the sore temptations which came upon him.

We are all just like Peter. If we are true Christians we mean to be faithful to our Lord. But sincerity is not enough. "The flesh is weak," and we need to rest continually upon God for help to be true and faithful. If young Christians would learn this lesson they would not fall so easily. If the drunkard who resolves to reform learned it, he would be safer and stronger. No matter how good his intentions are, he is not able of himself to fulfil them. None of us are as good as we want to be and strive to be, and only through the mighty help of Christ can any of us live a true and noble life.

Nov. 14.

Lost Opportunities.

" He cometh the third time, and saith unto them, Sleep on now, and take your rest: it is enough, the hour is come."—MARK xiv. 41.

THE time for watching was past. Jesus had now passed through His agony, and on His face was the radiance of peace. He did not need any longer the help of the sympathy which in vain He had craved in the darkness. He looked toward the city gate, and there was the traitor coming. There was neither need nor use now for the disciples' waking and watching, and they might as well sleep on.

The lesson is plain. Whatever we do for our friends we must do when they are in need of our help. If one is sick, the time to show our sympathy is while the sickness continues. If we allow him to pass through his illness without showing him any attention, there is little use when he is out again for us to offer kindness.

If one of our friends is passing through some sore struggle with temptation, then is the time for us to come up close alongside of him and put the strength of our love under his weakness. If we fail him then we may almost as well let him go on alone after that. Of what use is our help when the battle has been fought through to the end and won without us ? Or suppose the friend was not victorious ; that he failed—failed because no one came to help him—is there any use in our hurrying up to him then to offer assistance ? Thus on all sides the lesson presses.

> " We might have lent
> Such strength, such comfort and content
> To you out of our ample store ;
> We might have hastened on before
> To lift the shadows from your way,
> Darkened, ere noon, to twilight's gray ;
> With earth's chilled air love's warm heart-scent
> We might have blent."

Never Despair

" Rise up, let us go."—MARK xiv. 42.

THERE seems to be a voice of hope in this call. The disciples had sadly failed in one great duty: they had slept when the Master wanted them to watch with Him. He had just told them that they might as well sleep on, so far as that service was concerned, for the time to render it was gone for ever. Yet there were other duties before them, and Jesus calls them to arise to meet these. Because they had failed in one hour's responsibility they must not sink down in despair. They must arouse themselves to meet the responsibility just before them.

Again the lesson is plain. Because we have failed in one duty we must not give up in despair. Because a young man has wasted his youth he must not therefore lose heart and think all is lost. There are other opportunities waiting for him. The loss of youth is irreparable. The golden years can never be gotten back. The innocence, the beauty, the power, are gone for ever. Yet why should a man squander all because he has squandered the best ? Because the morning has been thrown away, why should all the day be lost ?

The lesson is for all who have failed in any way. Christ ever calls to hope. He bids us rise again from the worst defeat. In the kingdom of grace there is always margin enough to start again, and to build up a noble life. Even down to life's latest hour this remains true. The door of opportunity opened to the penitent even on the cross in his dying hour : there was no time to make anything good or beautiful of his life on the earth, save in his dying confession and testimony ; but the eternity into which he passed is very long, with time enough for a glorious career. So it is always. In this world, blessed by Divine love and grace, there is never any need for despair. The call after any defeat or failure still is, " Rise up, let us go."

Nov. 16

"Pray without Ceasing"

"Jesus ofttimes resorted thither with His disciples."

JOHN xviii. 2

THESE words give us a glimpse of our Lord's devotional habits. The deep quiet of the Olive garden was His closet. Here He had been wont to go for seasons of prayer. There were other places, too, which were sacred resorts to Him. There were mountain-tops, where He often spent whole nights in communion with His Father

Our Lord's example teaches us that we should spend much time in devotion. Some people manage to get along without much praying, but it is always at the expense of their spiritual life. Not feeding their souls, they grow very lean. There really can be no beautiful, strong, helpful Christian life without much closet work. Every tree has a root, which people do not see, which has no beauty, but which in secret, in the darkness, performs service for the tree, without which the tree could not live. What the root is to the tree, that is the Christian's secret devotional life to the external and visible life which the world sees. We shall flourish and be fruitful in spiritual life just in proportion to the earnestness, the reality, and the intensity of our devotional life. A great deal of praying needs to go with a very little working.

Our Lord's example teaches us also the importance of regular habits of praying. Some people say that praying should be spontaneous, and that stated times and places make it formal, and take the life out of it. But we are such creatures of habit that if we do not pray at regular times each day we shall very soon not pray at all. But if we always go to our closet at the same time, our devotions will become part of our daily life, and we shall never live a day without its moments of prayer. If our Lord's holy life required regular habits of prayer and communion, much more do our broken, imperfect lives require the same.

The Traitor.

" *Judas also......knew the place......Judas then, having received a band of men......cometh thither.*"—JOHN xviii. 2, 3.

EVERY new line in the story of the betrayal shows new blackness in the heart of Judas. Going out from the supper-table he hastened to the priests, and was quickly under way with his band of soldiers. He probably first hurried back to the upper room, where he had left Jesus; not finding Him there, he knew well where the Master had gone, and hastened to the sacred place of prayer. Then the manner in which he let the officers know which of the company was Jesus shows the deepest blackness of all: he went up to Him as to a dear friend and kissed Him—kissed Him over and over, and with feigned warmth and affection.

Let us remember how the treason grew in the heart of Judas, beginning in greed for money, growing into theft and falseness of life, ending at last in the blackest crime the world ever saw. The lesson is, that we should watch the beginnings of evil in our hearts.

" A picture in the royal gallery of Brussels represents Judas wandering about on the night after the betrayal. He comes by chance upon the workmen who have been making the cross on which Christ shall be crucified to-morrow. A fire near by throws its light full on the faces of the workmen, who are sleeping peacefully while resting from their labour. Judas's face is somewhat in the shade; but it is wonderfully expressive of awful remorse and agony as he catches sight of the cross and the tools used in making it —the cross which his treachery had made possible. But still, though in the very torments of hell, as it appears, he clutches his money-bag, and seems to hurry on into the night. The picture tells the story of the fruit of Judas's victory—the money-bag with the thirty pieces of silver in it (and even that he could not long keep), carried off into the night of fiendish despair: that was all."

Nov. 13

The Traitor's Kiss

"*Hail, Master ! and kissed Him.*"—MATT. xxvi. 49

THE very reading of the words makes us shudder. A kiss has always been the token of affection and the seal and pledge of fidelity. Judas's going up to Christ and kissing Him was a solemn protestation of sincere friendship. Yet the kiss was not only false, but was the sign of betrayal. No words are strong enough to characterize this crime. We remember the fable of the poisonous reptile taken into the bosom of a kindly man to be warmed, rewarding the benefactor by striking its deadly fangs into his flesh. But even this does not illustrate the baseness of Judas's act. It is no wonder that he is the execration of the world. A poet represents him as placed in the lowest circles of the lost, as the sole sharer with Satan himself of the very uttermost punishment, and shunned even there and even by the guiltiest.

In studying the character and the sin of Judas the following lessons may be brought out :—1. We must not be surprised if some bad men enter the Church, for even among the twelve was one Judas. 2. It is no proof that Christianity is untrue when some of its professors prove hypocrites. The defection of Judas did not leave a stain on the name of Christ, nor did it disprove the loyalty and fidelity of the other disciples. 3. One may be very near to Christ and not be made holy in character. Judas was three years with Christ, heard His words, lived in the atmosphere of His love, and remained unchanged. An empty bottle, hermetically sealed, may lie long in the ocean and continue perfectly dry within. A heart sealed to Christ's love may lie in His bosom for years and not be blessed. Only when the heart is opened to receive His grace does closeness to Him sanctify. 4. Sin grows, and we never can know to what terrible extent a wicked thought or desire may reach.

God's Will is Best.

" The cup which My Father hath given Me, shall I not drink it ? "—JOHN xviii. 11

THE "cup" is our portion, embracing all the experiences of our earthly lives. Our Father gives us the cup, therefore it must be the very best that the wisest love can provide. When death enters a Christian home there is sweetest comfort in the thought that God has really done the best possible for the friend whom He has taken away. We prayed Him to crown our loved one with His richest blessings, and is not that just what He has done? Here is a little poem which in a beautiful way illustrates this :—

" ' Give her, I pray, all good:
    Bid all the buds of pleasure grow
To perfect flowers of happiness
    Where'er her feet may go ;
Bid Truth's bright shield and Love's strong arm
Protect her from all earthly harm.

" ' Lest there should be some other thing,
    Better than all the rest,
That I have failed to ask,' I said,
    ' Give Thou the very best
Of every gift that Thou dost deem
Better than aught I hope or dream.'......

" She lies before me still and pale ;
    The roses that I prayed
Might bloom along her path of life
    Are on her bosom laid.
Crowned with a strange, rapt calm, she lies,
Like one made dumb with sweet surprise.

" ' Better than I can ask or dream !'
    This was my prayer, and now
That she is lying still and pale,
    With God's peace on her brow,
I wonder, sobbing, sore dismayed,
If this be that for which I prayed."

Peter's Fall

"*Peter stood and warmed himself. They said therefore unto
him, Art not thou also one of His disciples?*"—JOHN
xviii. 25

FOR our own sakes we should mark the steps which
led to Peter's fall. One was his self-confidence.
When forewarned, he resented the Master's foretelling, and
declared that though others might deny Christ he never
would. When we grow boastful we are in great peril.
Safety lies in a consciousness of our own weakness, and in
implicit trust in God.

The next step toward Peter's fall was his sleeping in
the garden when he should have been watching and praying. That hour was given for preparation for temptation,
but was not improved.

Another step was his rashness in drawing his sword in
the garden. This act made him liable to arrest, and this
fact made him nervous and afraid of recognition. He tried
to hide his connection with Jesus, lest he should be arrested
for his assault in the garden. Rash acts are sure to make
trouble for us afterward.

Another step toward denial was Peter's following Christ
afar off. This showed timidity and failing faith. His
courage was leaving him. Following Christ at a distance
is always perilous. It shows a weakening attachment and
a trembling loyalty. It is in itself partial denial. The
only worthy and the only safe discipleship is thorough,
unwavering devotion and whole-hearted consecration.

This apostle took another step toward his fall when he
sat down among the servants of the high priest. He went
among them to hide his relation to Jesus. The only safe
thing for a Christian is unequivocally to declare his discipleship wherever he goes.

When Peter had taken these steps he could scarcely do
otherwise than openly deny his Lord. The time for us to
guard ourselves is at the beginnings of defection.

The Great Denial

" *He denied before them all.*"—MATT. xxvi. 70

ONE thing that made Peter's denial so peculiarly sad was that he had received so many marks of special favour from Christ. He was one of three disciples who had been taken into the inner circle of friendship. The more Jesus has done for us, the worse is it for us to prove unfaithful to Him.

Another thing was that Peter had so boldly confessed Christ. It was he who said, when Jesus asked the disciples whom they believed Him to be, " Thou art the Christ, the Son of the living God." It was he who, just a few hours before his denial, so vehemently avowed his loyalty and his readiness to die with his Lord. These repeated protestations of fidelity made the evil of denial more grievous. It is a greater sin for one who has publicly declared his love for Christ to prove disloyal to Him than for one who has never made such confession.

Another thing that made the sin worse was the fact that Jesus had forewarned Peter. We say " forewarned is forearmed ; " but it did not prove so in this instance, because the disciple utterly disregarded the Master's warnings. We are all warned of danger ; do we heed the signals ?

Still another aggravation was that it was in our Lord's hour of sorest need that the disciple denied Him. Had it been in some time of popular favour, the denial would not have been so base ; but it was when Jesus was deserted, and was in the hands of His enemies. Was that a time for the bravest disciple, the most honoured friend, the noblest confessor, to turn his back on his Master ? When the shadow falls on your friend, when the tide has turned against him, when others fall away from him, is that the time for you, his long-time bosom companion, the recipient of his favours, to turn craven and desert and deny him ?

The Holy One

" What accusation bring ye against this man ? "
John xviii. 29

THAT was a fair question. The Jews wanted Pilate to put Jesus to death ; but Pilate had a right to ask why such sentence should be pronounced. No man should ever be condemned without a trial.

We have a right to ask the same now of those who condemn and reject Christ. What wrong thing has He done ? What flaws are there in His character ? Whom has He injured ? The Jews attempted no answer to Pilate's question ; indeed there was no answer possible, for no accusation could be brought against Jesus. He had never injured any one. A little girl kissed her young brother's hand as he lay in the coffin, and said, " Mamma, this little hand never struck me." It could well have been said of Christ when He lay in death, " This hand never struck any one. These lips never spoke a word that gave pain. This heart never cherished an unkind thought or feeling."

On the other hand, the life of Christ was a perpetual blessing to all who knew Him. His hands were ever stretched out in healing—until finally they were stretched out on the cross and fastened back there, but outstretched still in blessing. His lips were ever speaking words of comfort, of love. His heart was ever full of love and grace. Who could ever bring any accusation against Him ? In truth no one ever did ; He was hurried to death by men's hate, without reason or charge of any kind.

This same Jesus stands now before men, asking for their love and their faith. What reason is there that He should not be received ? What has he ever done to discredit His own claims ? What charge of evil can any one, the worst enemy, bring against Him ? Has He ever led a confiding soul into wrong paths ? Has He ever disappointed the hopes of any heart that has trusted in Him ? Why, then, should any reject Him ?

Pilate's Indecision.

" Then said Pilate unto them, Take ye Him, and judge Him according to your law."—JOHN xviii. 31.

PILATE wanted to evade the responsibility of trying and sentencing Jesus. But instead of honestly refusing to have anything to do with His condemnation, Pilate sought by evasion simply to get clear of the case. He could not do it, however; for each time Jesus came back and stood before him waiting for his decision.

One of Pilate's questions a little later than this was, " What shall I do with Jesus ? "—a question he was compelled to answer in the end. Jesus stands before every human soul, as He stood before Pilate, demanding reception or rejection, and every one of us must answer this same question. The question may be postponed, but we cannot get it off our hands. We may send Jesus away, but presently we find Him back, standing again at our door. Every soul must sit in judgment on Christ, and give a decision.

Look on a little. Here we see Pilate on the judgment-seat, and Jesus standing before him to be judged. " Knowest Thou not that I have power to crucify Thee, and power to release Thee ? " Awful power for any man to hold ! The scene closed, and Jesus went to His cross. Pilate soon fell into disgrace, and in a few years committed suicide. When he stood before the throne of the Divine Judge, into whose eyes did the poor, guilty Roman look ? Ah, what a reversal there was ! Once Pilate was judge, and Jesus stood at the bar ; now Jesus is judge, and Pilate is before Him.

Jesus stands now before sinners, meek and lowly, asking to be received ; but the scene will soon be changed for those who reject Him—they will be hurried away into eternity, and the Judge before whose bar they shall find themselves will be the same One who stood so long, patient and loving, waiting to save them.

Nov. 24.

Christ our King.

" *The governor asked Him, saying, Art Thou the King of the Jews ?* "—MATT. xxvii. 11.

JESUS did not look much like a king as He stood there, His hands bound, a cord about His neck. Pilate's question sounds like ridicule. Yet Jesus answered, " Yes, I am a king." Strange answer ! Where, then, was His power ? Where were His throne, His crown, His sceptre, His royal robes ? Who recognized His sway ? Pilate probably looked at Him with mingled contempt and pity.

But to us to-day how different does it all appear ! He is throned now " far above all principality, and power, and might, and dominion, and every name that is named, not only in this world, but also in that which is to come." In heaven He is honoured as King of kings and Lord of lords. On His head are many crowns. All over the earth, too, His sway is felt. Wherever His gospel has gone, with its revelation of Divine love and grace, the influence of His kingdom has reached.

And Jesus was as really a king when He stood before Pilate that day, to human eyes bound and powerless, as He is now, exalted on heaven's throne. His kingdom was spiritual ; it was a kingdom of truth, of righteousness, of holiness, of grace, and of love. He seemed the weakest of all men that morning, but in reality He was the mightiest, the grandest, the kingliest. What, then, is greatness ? What is power ? What is kingliness ? Not anything external, not anything that men's eyes can see. The world bows down before thrones that glitter, and crowns whose jewels flash in sunlight, and worships power whose majesty is expressed in material splendour. But the real power of the world is Christ's power—the kingdom whose sway is over human hearts and lives. It is spiritual. It makes men better, and lifts them up into noble life, into purity, holiness, and Divine beauty.

"Behold the Man!"

" Pilate saith unto them, Behold the man ! "—JOHN xix. 5

WE cannot do better than obey Pilate's word, "Behold the man ! " and fix our eyes in loving gaze upon Jesus as He is led out from the palace and stands before the multitude. On His head He wears a crown of thorns ; around His bleeding body is thrown a purple robe, mock emblem of royalty. He had been called King of the Jews, and the rude soldiers tried to carry out the farce, as it appeared to them.

Behold the man ! Behold the man enduring shame and contempt, set forth before the people as a spectacle of mockery, in order that at last we may be presented in glory, and honoured before angels and the Father. Behold the man wearing a crown of thorns, that we may wear a crown of glory and of life ; robed in mocking purple, that we may wear the white garments of righteousness. Behold the man in the majesty of meekness—reviled, yet reviling not again ; hated, yet still loving on ; wronged, yet speaking no resentful word. We should study the character of our Lord as manifested amid the terrible scenes of that morning. How His sublime patience shames our miserable impatience ! We fret and vex ourselves with our sickly discontents over the smallest discomforts ; let us behold the blessed peace of Jesus in the midst of the sorest trials. We fly into anger and cherish bitter resentments when others slight us or wrong us in merest trifles ; let us behold the sweet spirit of Jesus—loving, gentle, meek, under the greatest cruelties and wrongs ever inflicted on any life.

Behold the man, the God-man, divinity manifested in humanity, humbling Himself and becoming obedient unto shame and death that He might save our souls. Behold the man, holy, undefiled, separate from sinners, yet bearing upon His own head, as the Lamb of God, the sin of the world. Let us look and weep, and love and trust, and rejoice.

Power Belongs to God

" *Knowest Thou not that I have power to crucify Thee, and have power to release Thee?......Thou couldest have no power at all against Me, except it were given thee from above.*"—JOHN xix. 10, 11

AUTHORITY is one of the entrusted talents. Men talk very boastfully of their power, forgetting that it is delegated power which they hold, and that they must wield it for God, and must give account to Him for their use of it. No man's power belongs to himself to do with as he pleases; it is given him from God, the source of all power. This is true of the authority of parents and teachers, of the power possessed by civil magistrates, and of all power whatsoever.

Men are eager to obtain offices in the city or nation; and they do not always realize the responsibility which attaches to such positions. Power belongs to God, and must be used for God, or its misuse will bring sore penalty. It is a talent which is given to us to be accounted for, and no treason is worse than malfeasance in the employing of power. This is true all the way from the power of the child on the playground to the power of the president of the nation or the king on his throne. " Thou couldest have no power ......except it were given thee from above."

There is a comforting thought suggested by the words in this sentence, " Thou couldest have no power against Me." Christ in this world was under the protection of His Father, and no one on earth could lift a finger against Him but by the Divine permission. What was true of Him, the Son of God, is true of each one of the sons of God in all their earthly life. Each believer, the humblest, the weakest, is kept in this world as the apple of God's eye. No one can touch one of God's little ones save by Divine permission. This shows how safe we are, amid all the world's dangers and enmities, while we trust ourselves in our Father's keeping.

Fatal Decision

" Then delivered he Him therefore unto them to be crucified."
JOHN xix. 16

SO we see the sad and terrible end of Pilate's weak struggles with his conscience and his sense of right. He first tried every way to avoid the issue ; then he temporized, hoping in some manner to get free from responsibility. At last he yielded ; and his name goes through history pilloried for ever as the man who delivered Jesus to be crucified. He is known by no other act. It had been a thousand times better for him if he had remained for ever in obscurity, instead of going to that high place of power where he had to meet and deal with this momentous question of history.

We read that Pilate took water in the presence of the Jews and washed his hands—thus by symbol declaring that he was not responsible for the sentencing of Jesus to die. But the water did not wash away one particle of the stain of the guilt of that terrible sin. Pilate had the misfortune to be the only man in all the province who could send Jesus to the cross. Upon him, therefore, the final responsibility rested, no matter the pressure that was brought to bear upon him by the enemies of Jesus. The fact that others urge us to sin does not take away our guilt for that sin. No being in the universe can compel us to do wrong ; if, then, we do wrong, the sin is our own.

We remember that the Jews responded to Pilate's act of washing his hands, " His blood be on us, and on our children." No one who has read the story of the next forty years can doubt that their self-imprecation was fulfilled. Thirty years later thousands of the best people of the Jews were crucified. The crime of the Jews was successful ; but what came of the success in the end ? Let us learn the lesson that sin brings always terrible woe, and that the worst of all sins is sin against the Lord Jesus Christ.

Nov. 28

"Take up Thy Cross"

" And He bearing His cross went forth."—JOHN xix. 17

AT first there was no one to help Jesus to bear His cross; though fainting from loss of rest and from the gashing and laceration of His body by the scourge, and still more from the untold anguish through which He had been passing, He yet had to carry His cross for Himself until nature gave way. Yet we must remember that while Jesus had to bear the cross unaided, it really was not for Himself that He bore it, but for us. He endured the shame and pain, and staggered beneath the awful burden, that He might set us free from the burden of sin's curse. The Baptist said, when Jesus passed by him at the beginning of His ministry, " Behold the Lamb of God, which taketh away the sin of the world ! " We may say the same words as we see Jesus bearing His cross. That is what He is doing. It was not the mere wood that was so heavy; the real load which Jesus bore that day was the mountain of our sins. It was this that made Him faint and sink down by the way, and that wrung from Him such cries and tears in Gethsemane and on Calvary.

A little later He sank down under the burden, and then the officers compelled a passer-by to help him. After that the scene was this—Jesus and Simon of Cyrene together carrying the cross, Jesus in advance carrying the heavy end, and Simon coming behind bearing the lighter end. Here again the picture is very suggestive in two ways:— We must share the cross with Christ before we can be saved; that is, we must accept our place with Him under the cross and follow Him. Then we can turn the picture another way, and we see Jesus helping His people to bear their crosses. Every cross we have to bear, His shoulder is also beneath it, and He always bears the heavy end of it. No believer ought to be unable to bear any cross *with Jesus*. No load that He shares should crush us.

The Perfect Sufferer.

" They gave Him vinegar to drink mingled with gall : and when He had tasted thereof, He would not drink."—MATT. xxvii. 34

THE offer was kindly meant. There was an association of women at Jerusalem, a compassionate sisterhood, whose work was to provide such stupefying draughts for those who were crucified. The object was to produce partial unconsciousness, so that the terrible agonies might not be so keenly felt. It is pleasant to find that such an association existed at that early day among the Jewish people. True religion always yields such fruits. Christianity has filled the world with just such gentle ministries. Wherever there is pain Christian women go to alleviate it.

But it must be noticed that Christ did not accept this potion. He tasted it, showing His recognition and appreciation of the kindness that offered it, but He did not drink it. One reason probably was that He would not seek to lessen in any way the bitterness of the cup which His Father had given Him to drink. He would drink it to its last drop, and not dull the sense of suffering in Himself to make the draught any less bitter.

Another reason doubtless was that He would not cloud His mind in the least degree as He entered the last experiences of life. He would not dim the clearness of His communion with His Father by any potion that should impair His full consciousness. The example of Christ does not teach that it is wrong in ordinary cases to use anæsthetics to deaden the sense of pain. There were peculiar reasons why our Lord would abate nothing of the bitterness of His suffering. Chloroform and ether have been wonderful agents of mercy and blessing in the world. But it does seem proper that a person should not when dying be given any potion which would cloud the mind, or send the soul in a state of stupefaction through the experiences of death and into the presence of God.

Nov. 30.

The Crucifixion.

" *They crucified Him.*"—MARK xv. 25.

HERE we come to the mount of our Redeemer's sorrows, and we should bare our heads in holy reverence as we stand in the silence of wondering love and gaze upon Him on His cross. Many thoughts will come to us as we contemplate this scene.

What a terrible thing sin is, that its expiation required such a sacrifice ! Shall we go on carelessly sinning when we see what our Saviour suffered to save us from our sins ? What wonderful love there must be in the heart of God to cause Him to give His Son to endure such a death to save sinners !

What worth there must be in human souls, under all the ruin of sin, that Jesus was willing to make such a sacrifice of His own precious and glorious life to redeem the lost !

What a pattern for all life have we here ! The cross is Jesus giving Himself to bless and save others. The more completely we forget ourselves and live for others, the nearer do we get to the example of Christ. How can we ever complain again of our little privations and sacrifices for the sake of others ? The cross, where Christ is giving all, should make us ashamed even to mention again any little thing that we have done or suffered for another.

Crucifixion was such a blot at that time, wrapped a name in such ignominy, that one who died thus was buried for ever in shame. He never could be mentioned but with thought and memory of dishonour. But Jesus, instead of being covered and borne down for ever by the cross, in the black waters of reproach, lifted the cross itself to glory, until to-day it is the emblem of hope, of victory, of blessedness, and of joy wherever the gospel has gone. Let no one be afraid to endure for Christ's sake. for when the cross is taken up in His name it becomes a " weight of glory."

The Sacred Garments

"They parted His garments, casting lots upon them, what every man should take."—MARK xv. 24

WE love to think of those sacred garments which our Saviour had worn. Perhaps they had been made by His mother's hands, or maybe by the hands of some of the other women who followed Him from Galilee, ministering unto Him. They were the garments, too, that the sick had touched in reverent faith, receiving instant healing. We treasure the garments of those we love when they are gone from us. How sacred they are! How it would pain us to see them divided among rude enemies and worn by them about the streets! A peculiar sacredness clings to everything that Jesus ever touched; and what desecration it appears to our hearts to see these scoffing, heathen soldiers take His garments and divide them among themselves as booty! Then what terrible sacrilege it seems to see them throwing dice and gambling under the very cross while the Saviour hangs there in agony.

Why was Jesus stripped of His garments? Was there no meaning in it apart from the mere custom? Was it not that He might prepare garments of righteousness for us in our spiritual nakedness? One night of bitter cold and pitiless storm a mother was out in the wilds with her child in her arms. Unable to carry her precious burden and find a shelter, she took off her own outer clothing, and wrapping it about her little one, she laid him in a cleft of the rock, and hastened on, hoping to find help. Next morning some shepherds heard the cry of a child, and found the babe safe and warm in the rock's cleft. Then, not far away in the snow, they discovered the mother—dead. She had stripped off her own garments and died in the cold to save her child. Did not Jesus do the same? He took off His raiment and hung naked on His cross, that we may stand in the final judgment arrayed in robes of beauty.

Dec. 2

The King of the Jews

" *And set up over His head His accusation written, This is Jesus the King of the Jews.*"—MATT. xxvii. 37

THERE was no other crime charged. He had done nothing amiss. Pilate had satisfied himself of that. He had examined Him, and could find no fault in Him, hence he would not write any charge on His cross but this, that He was the King of the Jews. The rulers objected to this, and wanted him to write that He *said* He was King of the Jews; but Pilate would not change a word, and there it stood above His head during all the agony and all the darkness—*the King of the Jews.*

So He was. The tablet told the truth, though erected to mock the people. He was the Messiah who had been promised all through the centuries. He was the King of whom David was but the type. He was the Christ who had been foretold by prophets, and waited for age after age by the nation. At last He came. Angels sang at His birth. His life had been one of great blessing and power. He had wrought miracles of mercy all over the land. He had taught, speaking as never man spoke. He had fulfilled all the Messianic conditions. Yet His enemies had rejected Him; and at last they led Him out to Calvary and nailed Him on the cross. Still He was their King—their King rejected, their King crucified. His throne was His cross; His crown was the circlet of thorns that the soldiers had twisted and wound around His head.

It does not seem to us a kingly hour in our Lord's life when He hangs on His cross dying, yet really it was the time of His highest earthly exaltation. He spoke of going to His cross as going to be glorified. He was indeed King of the Jews. They crucified their King. He is *our* King too. How are we treating Him? Are we obeying Him? Are any of us rejecting Him? Are any of us crucifying Him afresh? We had better answer these questions.

Divine Forgiveness

" Father, forgive them ; for they know not what they do."
LUKE xxiii. 34

THIS was the first word spoken by our Lord on His cross. It was uttered just when the soldiers were in the act of crucifying Him—driving the terrible nails through His hands and feet. It was a moment of excruciating, inconceivable anguish. Yet He uttered no cry of pain, no word of execration upon those who were causing Him such suffering, but calmly prayed for His brutal, pitiless murderers—" Father, forgive them ; for they know not what they do."

The moment the sacred blood began to flow the intercession for sinners began. The pleading was first for the ignorant heathen soldiers who were acting as executioners ; but it was not for these alone. It certainly widened out, and took in all who had been concerned in the condemnation and crucifixion of Jesus. It was for the Jewish rulers and people who had rejected their Messiah. May we not believe that many of those who on the day of Pentecost and afterward were brought to repentance were forgiven and saved because on His cross Jesus made intercession for them ? Then the prayer went out beyond the people who had a direct part in the crucifixion. From His cross Jesus saw the lost world down to the end, and prayed for all men. We know, too, that the word of prayer was but the beginning of an intercession that is going on yet inside heaven, where Jesus pleads the merits of His own sacrifice for the salvation of sinners.

This word of Jesus teaches us a great lesson on Christian forgiveness. He prayed for His murderers. We should pray for those who injure us. There are some fragrant trees which bathe in perfume the axe that gashes them. So should it be with Christ's people. Instead of resentment and injury for injury, we should show only sweet, tender love to those who harm us.

Dec. 4

Self=Sacrifice

" *The rulers......derided Him, saying, He saved others ; let Him save Himself, if He be Christ.*"—LUKE xxiii. 35

IT was because He would save others that He could not save Himself. The soldier in the battle cannot save himself and save his country. The mother cannot spare herself and save her child. Jesus could have saved Himself, but what would have been the fate of sinners ?

Three little children wandered from home one afternoon. Evening found them playing by the sea-shore. It grew suddenly dark and cold, and they could not return. In the morning they were found, the two youngest sleeping warm and safe under coverings of garments and sea-weeds, and little Mary, the elder, lying cold and dead, with her arms yet full of sea-weeds. She had taken off nearly all her own warm clothing to cover the younger children, and then carried grass and sea-weeds to pile upon them, until she died in her loving devotion. She did not save herself, because she would save the little ones entrusted to her care.

During a plague in Marseilles, the physicians decided that nothing could be done to save the people unless a victim could be dissected, and the nature of the disease thus learned. But who would do such a perilous work ? One physician arose and said he would do it. Saying farewell to his family he entered the hospital, made the dissection, wrote out the results, and in a few hours was dead. But now the physicians could treat the disease, and the plague was stayed.

These incidents illustrate Christ's devotion to death for sinners. Men could not be saved unless some one could suffer and die in their room, and Jesus became the propitiation for sins. In one sense He could have saved Himself, but then the world would have been lost. His death was voluntary. He gave His life for the sheep. We are saved because He saved not Himself.

" At home with the Lord "

" To-day shalt thou be with Me in paradise."

LUKE xxiii. 43

THIS was the second word on the cross. Something touched the heart of one of the robbers—may it not have been the Saviour's prayer for His murderers ?—and he became penitent in his dying hour, and cried to Jesus for mercy: " Lord, remember me when Thou comest into Thy kingdom." Quickly from the lips of the dying Redeemer came the gracious response, " To-day shalt thou be with Me in paradise." The words are full of meaning, of which broken hints only can here be given.

Though in the agony of death, Jesus could yet give life to a dead soul. Though draining the dregs of the cup of woe, He could give a cup of blessedness to a penitent. Though His hand was nailed to the cross, it yet carried the key of paradise, and opened the gate to allow a repentant soul to enter. Surely there was no more royal moment in all Christ's life than this.

The promise itself tells us what death is for the believer. " To-day shalt thou be with Me." There is no long, dark passage, therefore, through which the freed soul must go to reach blessedness. There is no purgatory in which it must wait to be prepared for glory. At once the spirit goes into the presence of Christ. St. Paul teaches us the same truth when he describes death as departing to be with Christ, and says that to be absent from the body is to be at home with the Lord. That same day, said Jesus, this penitent should be in paradise. We ought not then to be afraid to die if we are of Christ's redeemed ones.

The words tell us also in what heaven's blessedness really consists. " Thou shalt be with Me." Being with Christ is glory. No sweeter, more blessed heaven can be conceived of. We know but little about heaven as a place—where it is, what it is like ; but this much we know—there we shall be with Christ. Is not that enough to know ?

Dec. 6

The Divine Legacy

" *When Jesus therefore saw His mother, and the disciple standing by whom He loved, He saith unto His mother, Woman, behold thy son!* "—JOHN xix. 26

THIS was the third word spoken by our Lord from the cross. Not far away, in some quiet spot amid the multitude, stood a little group of His dearest friends. Most of them were women. As His eye looked down upon them He saw among them His own mother. Verily, the sword was piercing through her heart as she beheld her Divine Son on His cross.

As Jesus saw His mother in her deep grief, though suffering untold anguish Himself, His heart went out in compassion and love for her. He thought of her unsheltered, as she would be, when He was gone. He remembered what she had been to Him in His tender infancy and defenceless childhood as she had blessed Him with her rich, self-forgetful love.

" Stripped of everything," says Godet, " Jesus seemed to have nothing more to give. Nevertheless, from the midst of this deep poverty He had already made precious gifts : to His executioners He had bequeathed the pardon of God ; to His companion in punishment, paradise. Could He find nothing to leave to His mother and His friend ? These two beloved persons, who had been His most precious treasures on earth, He bequeathed to one another, giving thus at once a son to His mother and a mother to His friend."

In this beautiful act of our Lord we have a wondrous commentary on the fifth commandment. Every young person, or older one, with parents yet living, who reads this fragment of the story of the cross should remember the lesson, and pay love's highest honour to the father or the mother to whom he owes so much. No suffering or pain of our own should ever make us forgetful of our parents, and we should honour them to the last moment of their life.

The Dark Valley

"It was about the sixth hour, and there was a darkness over all the earth until the ninth hour."—LUKE xxiii. 44

IT was a mysterious and supernatural darkness. We may say, and we can say no more, that it was nature sympathizing with the crucifixion of its Lord. How dense it was we cannot tell; but it must have filled the hearts of the multitude about the cross with awe.

There was also a still deeper darkness around the soul of Him who hung on that central cross. It was so dark that He even seemed forsaken of God. We can never understand it, although we know that it was the sin of the world that made the darkness. Jesus wrapped the glooms of death about Himself that we might be clothed in garments of light. He died thus in darkness that we might walk into the valley amid the splendours of heavenly light. He had agony in His last hour that we might have joy. His head wore the crown of thorns, and had no place to rest in dying, that under our heads might be the pillow of peace.

It is profitable for us to contrast the death of Christ with that of His disciples in all ages since. He shrank from the "cup;" they are eager to drink it. He seemed forsaken of God; they look with ecstasy and unclouded vision into the Father's face. Why did death mean so much to Him, and why is it such a peaceful experience to them? It is easy to answer this question. Death has no bitterness for the Christian, because it was so bitter to the Redeemer. He drew the curse from it, and now it has in it only the sweetness of blessing. Indeed, there is no death any more for the Christian. Jesus abolished death. What we now call death is death no longer, since He passed through it. It is now only the shadow of death, and even the shadow is lighted up with the beams of Divine glory bursting from heaven. Let us never forget that we have light in our dying because Jesus had darkness.

Dec. 8

Christ's Cry on the Cross

" My God, My God, why hast Thou forsaken Me?"

MATT. xxvii. 46

THIS was the fourth word on the cross. It is too mysterious for explanation, and we may only ponder it with hushed hearts for a little.

"Why hast Thou *forsaken* Me?" It was not the nails in His flesh, nor the insults of scoffing enemies, nor the ignominy of the cross, but the fact that Jesus for the time had lost the sense of the Father's presence, that made the grief of the hour.

"Why hast Thou forsaken *Me?*" What had He, the beloved Son, done that the Father should forsake Him? It would not have seemed so strange if He had forsaken the angels or the saints living in glory; but why should He forsake His own Son?

"My God!" Why does He not say "My Father"? He said "Father" in the first word on the cross, and in the very last; why is it "My God" here? Has He in the darkness lost the consciousness of Sonship? Does He seem pushed far away from home, from the Father's heart, from the bosom where from all eternity He had reposed? So it seems. Yet mark how His faith clings in the darkness: it is still "*My* God!" He has not lost faith even in the darkness. His faith holds, though He cannot see God's face. No matter how dark the night about us, how heavy the cross that weighs us down, how lonely and deserted we may feel, we should never lose faith in God. Behind the blackest clouds His face ever beams with love. He is still our God, though for the time He may have left us alone.

"*Why* hast Thou forsaken Me?" Can we answer this " why "? We know only that Jesus was bearing our sins, and that it was for our sake He had to endure this hiding. He was forsaken then for a small moment that for all eternity we might enjoy the favour of God and dwell in communion with Him.

Divine Thirst.

" After this, Jesus knowing that all things were now accomplished......saith, I thirst."—JOHN xix. 28.

HERE we have our Lord's fifth word on the cross. It was just before the end. All things belonging to His work as Redeemer were now finished. He had suffered from thirst all the terrible six hours that He hung on the cross, but He restrained His anguish until His task was done. Now He gave expression to His desire for drink, the only word on the cross that referred to His physical sufferings.

Some one reached up to Him on a stem of hyssop a sponge which had been moistened in the sour vinegar that stood there. It was an act of kindness and pity, and was the only mark of human tenderness shown to Jesus in those hours. We cannot but be thankful for this slight ministry which must have given momentary relief to the holy Sufferer.

Earlier in the day, at the moment of crucifixion, He was offered drink which He refused. That was a stupefying potion, a deadening wine mingled with myrrh or wormwood. It was offered with the intention of dulling His senses, that He might not be conscious of His sore suffering. He refused it because He wished to preserve the clearness of His mind in the hours when He was making atonement for the world. This potion, offered now by the soldier, was not medicated wine, and was not stupefying in its effects. He needed refreshment to strengthen Him for the great final act—the giving of His soul up to God.

All the experiences of Jesus Christ which reveal human need and suffering bring Him very near to us. Since He suffered hunger and thirst, and pain and weariness and sorrow, He is able to sympathize with us in all our human experiences. He knows what we feel, for He has not forgotten even in heaven what He Himself endured in His incarnation.

Dec. 10

"It is Finished."

" He said, It is finished."—JOHN xix. 30

THIS was our Lord's sixth word on the cross. His allotted life-work was done; all His task was ended, all things set for Him to do were done, and nothing more remained for Him but to die. Many men come to the end even of long lives and find their work far from finished when the call comes to leave this world; but though the life of Jesus had been so short, He was ready to go. He had done each day the work given Him that day to do, and when the last hour of the last day came there was nothing that He had left undone. We ought to learn the lesson for ourselves and live as Jesus lived, so as to have every part of our work finished when the end comes. We can do this only by taking our allotment of duty each day from God's hand and doing it faithfully. Then when the last day comes we shall leave nothing unfinished.

But what was it that was finished when Christ bowed His head on the cross? The work of redemption was done. The atonement for sin was made. As Jesus died, the veil of the temple was rent in twain from top to bottom, and access made into the holiest for all who would enter. A famous picture represents Christ lifted up, and beneath Him an innumerable procession of the saints advancing out of the darkness and coming into the light of His cross. There can be no doubt that He had such a vision of redemption while He hung there; for we are told that He "endured the cross, despising the shame, because of the *joy set before Him*"—that is, the joy of receiving home the souls He had redeemed.

"It is finished" was, therefore, a shout of victory as He completed His work of suffering and sacrifice. Death seemed like defeat, but it was not defeat. He went down into the grave, but not to stay there. He came again, like a glorious conqueror, and because He lives all His people shall live also.

Last Words

" Father, into Thy hands I commend My spirit."
LUKE xxiii. 46

THIS was the seventh and last of the words spoken on the cross. Christ's work as Redeemer was now altogether done; His last word, "finished," marked its completion. Now He is ready to go back to His Father. Before Him now lies the mystery of death. He is about to lose consciousness; His spirit is about to escape from His body. Here we see His calm, trustful faith. The terrible struggle is over, and He is at perfect peace. The word "Father" which He here uses shows that His soul has recovered its serenity. A little while ago He was in the darkness, and felt Himself forsaken; now the darkness is gone and the full light shines in again, and the Father's face beams upon Him in loving approval. It is the first experience of the glorious joy of redemption, breaking over the Redeemer's soul, as He emerges from the shadows of His cross.

The words are peculiarly instructive to us as a picture of Christian dying. It is but a breathing of the spirit into the hands of the heavenly Father. It is natural to regard death as a strange and mysterious experience, and to think of it with shrinking, if not with fear. We are leaving behind everything with which we are familiar—the friends, the scenes, the paths, the life—and are going out into an untried way, into what seems to us darkness, a valley of shadows. What is death? Where shall we be when we escape from the body? Will it be dark or light? Shall we be alone or accompanied?

Here comes this word of our Lord, and we learn that the believing soul when it leaves the body passes at once into the Father's hands. Surely that is enough for us to know. We shall be perfectly safe eternally if we are in our Father's hands. If we think thus of death it will have no terrors for us. No child is ever afraid to go into its father's hands, and that is all of dying for a believer.

Dec. 12

The Rent Veil

' *The veil of the temple was rent in twain from the top to the bottom.*"—MATT. xxvii. 51

THE veil was the symbol of separation from God. In the Holy of holies behind it was the place where God's presence dwelt. Men could not pass the veil. The teaching was that God could not be approached by sinners; the way was not yet opened. Once in a year the high priest went behind the veil, implying that there *was* access to God, but only through a priest. He went with blood—never without it—signifying that only by blood, by sacrifice, could God be approached. The priest was a type of Christ, and his yearly entrance with blood into the Holy of holies was a constant prefiguration of Christ's once entering with His own blood to make atonement.

The rending of this veil at the time of Christ's death was not an accident caused by the earthquake. It was part of the symbolism—the end, the completion of it. Men were no longer to be excluded from God's presence, since the great sacrifice had now been made. The separating wall had been broken down by Christ's death. Hence the symbol of this separation was also removed. This rending of the veil was therefore a supernatural act, teaching that the way of access to God was now and for ever open to all.

The fact that the veil was rent from top to bottom (that is, torn in two pieces) signifies that the way is entirely opened—the veil is clean gone; the Holiest of all stands wide open, with its mercy-seat accessible to every sinner, without the intervention of any earthly priest. The *time* at which this rending took place is important. It was just after Christ had died—after He had cried, " It is finished." It was because the great atonement was now made that the way was opened; as soon as the sacrifice had been made, the way to God was thrown open to all.

Ministering Women

" And many women were there, beholding afar off."

MATT. xxvii. 55

THESE were the earliest of a great and noble army of holy women, attached to Christ by deep, personal love, following and ministering to Him. In all the ages since, Christian women have shown like devotion and constancy to Christ, and like heroic love in serving Him. The record of woman's ministry to Christ is one of the brightest in all the world's history. Woman owes an incalculable debt to Christ. He has lifted her from base thraldom and from degradation.

Woman has always been grateful too, and has served Christ with great devotion. Women are found in every sick-room, bending over the sufferer with unwearying solicitude, with matchless tenderness ministering to bodily comfort, and pouring the warmth of affection upon feverish spirits. They are found in the wards of hospitals and upon battle-fields, moving like God's angels in blessed, loving ministry. Christian mothers are following the Master and doing work which will shine for ever in glorious lustre. Christian teachers are doing in lowly paths quiet service which in God's sight is nobler than that of many of earth's famous ones.

Everywhere, too, there is field for woman's ministry. Christ is no longer here in person to be served as He was served by these women of Galilee; but in His needy and suffering followers He is ever present, and whosoever will may minister unto Him; for He said that in doing acts of kindness to the least of His we do them unto Him.

The practical teaching is in the picture which is here held up before every woman, inspiring her to follow Christ. Why will so many young girls choose a life of idle display, of aimless, purposeless existence, of mere dressing, promenading, and trifling, when such a life of glorious service is open to them?

Dec. 14

Joseph of Arimathea

" Joseph of Arimathea......went in boldly unto Pilate, and craved the body of Jesus."—MARK xv. 43

JOSEPH had been a disciple of Christ for some time before, but had lacked the courage to come out boldly.

He was rich and influential, and had feared the consequences of a public identification with Jesus. But now he throws away his timidity, and comes out boldly as a friend of Jesus. He did it at a time when all the other disciples, even the apostles, were paralyzed with fear and afraid to speak. He did it, too, at a time of greatest peril, when shame covered the name of Jesus, and the bitterness against Him was intensest. He did it also at a time when faith had died in the hearts of all Christ's friends, and when there could be no hope of personal preference or gain as a reward for his act.

There were several reasons why Joseph made this bold confession at this time. One was because he was a true disciple ; and true love for Christ cannot always hide itself. Then, when he saw Christ suffering so at the hands of His enemies, the loyalty of his own heart was strengthened, and he felt that he must avow it. When he saw Jesus dead, all the warm and long pent-up affection in his soul awoke. Then he saw how unworthy his conduct had been in hiding his friendship for Christ at a time when confession would have done Him good. It looks as if his act were an effort to atone for the imperfectness of his former discipleship.

We must ever be grateful that Joseph gave Jesus such noble burial. Yet we cannot but remember that his love blossomed out too late. It is evident that his discipleship was incomplete, that it missed much of the blessing of open discipleship, and that even to himself it was far from satisfactory when the great crisis came. Secret discipleship cannot always remain secret ; it must at some time and in some way confess itself, regardless of what it may cost.

Dec. 15

The Descent from the Cross.

" When Joseph had taken the body, he wrapped it in a clean linen cloth, and laid it in his own new tomb."—MATT. xxvii. 59, 60

ACCORDING to the Roman custom, the bodies of those who were crucified were left hanging until they were eaten by birds and wild beasts. This barbarous custom being revolting to the Jews, an exception was made in their favour, and burial was permitted. If relatives or friends made application, the body of a crucified man would be given to them to be interred as they saw fit ; but if none came it was thrown into a pit. Had it not then been for Joseph and Nicodemus, the body of Jesus would have been cast, with the bodies of the robbers by His side, into the common receptacle for criminals. Thanks to the love of these hitherto secret disciples, though dying on a cross, our blessed Lord was buried like a king.

We may dwell with loving thought upon the scenes of this hour. First, the body was taken down, not by the rude, unfeeling soldiers, but by Joseph himself, aided by Nicodemus, and probably by some other friends. How tenderly this would be done we can imagine when we think of the love that was in the hearts of these friends. Then the blood was washed from the face, hands, feet, and side. Next, the body was wrapped in the linen, with the spices and the ointments. Then, with farewell kisses impressed on the silent lips by the loving, sorrowing friends who stood by, the face was covered with the napkin, and the cold form was tenderly borne to the sepulchre near at hand, amid garden plants and flowers, and was laid away to rest.

We cannot study this scene of the burial of our blessed Lord without rich spiritual profit. Shall we not, for one thing, seek to carry away a spirit of loving gentleness which will make our love deeper and our touch softer as we go out among sorrowing ones ?

Dec. 16.

The Sepulchre.

*" In the place where He was crucified there was a garden ;
and in the garden a new sepulchre......There laid they
Jesus."*—JOHN xix. 41, 42.

AS we stand by this garden-tomb many thoughts are
suggested. Christ touched life at every point. Beginning at infancy, He went through every phase, at last
lying down in a grave. There is no path on which His
footprints are not seen. There is no place any of us shall
have to stand in of which we may not say, " Jesus was
here. He passed through this experience ; therefore He
knows all about it." We dread the grave ; we think of
its darkness ; but since Jesus has lain there, why should
we fear its gloom ?

Another suggestion comes from the fact that this tomb
was provided for Jesus by His friends. Writers have noted
this as another mark of His humiliation. When He was
born His cradle was a borrowed manger. During His ministry He had not where to lay His head. When He died
He was buried in a borrowed grave.

Another thought, as we look at the sepulchre, is how
hopeless everything seemed for the time. He on whom the
disciples had leaned as the Messiah is now silent in death,
His work apparently finished. All the expectations based
on Him depended on His living to ascend a throne. It certainly seemed now to His friends that all was over. Yet
the grave was simply the low gateway to glory. As we
see it now, in the light that streams from the gospel, it
interrupted no plan, quenched no light, destroyed no hope.
When shall we learn to bring the truth of immortality into
our own faiths and hopes ? We stand by the graves of
our Christian friends almost as disconsolate as were these
friends of Jesus about His grave. Why shall we not learn
faith ? Death ends nothing for those who die in the Lord
—nothing but struggle, sorrow, and sin. No hopes perish
when a Christian is buried. Just beyond is glory.

Love and Sorrow

" *Mary Magdalene and Mary the mother of Joses beheld where He was laid.*"—MARK xv. 47

IT was a loving watch, but a hopeless one, which those devoted women kept. No stars shone through their cypress trees that afternoon. To their faith their Christ was lost, because their faith had taken in only an earthly idea of Messiahship. Death was the end of all the hope they had yet learned to cherish.

It surely was a dark hour for the disciples when that Friday's sun sank in the west. Satan seemed to have conquered and utterly to have destroyed the good seed of life which God had sent down from heaven. A Persian fable says that earth was created a great barren plain, without tree or plant. An angel was sent to scatter broadcast the choicest seeds on every spot. Satan, seeing the seeds on the ground, supposed that the sowing of the seeds was God's work, and determined to destroy it. So he buried all the seeds in the soil, and summoned sun and rain to make them rot away. But while with malignant feeling of triumph he smiled on the ruin he had wrought, the seeds which had been buried away to rot germinated and sprang up, clothing all the earth with plants and flowers, and in beauty undreamed of before. And a voice said from heaven, " Thou fool, that which thou sowest is not quickened except it die."

The application is obvious. The burial of Christ was thought by His enemies to be the end ; but in truth this was the very way to the glory of Christ. He Himself had said, " Except a corn of wheat fall into the ground and die, it abideth alone ; but if it die, it bringeth forth much fruit." Christ's burial in the grave was but the necessary way to His final and glorious victory. So now when we lay our beloved Christian dead in the tomb it is in the assured hope of blessed resurrection. The grave is but the shaded way to glory.

Dec. 18

The First at the Sepulchre

" Mary Magdalene, and Mary.. ....and Salome......very early in the morning......came unto the sepulchre."—MARK xvi. 1, 2

NOTHING shines more brightly in the story of our Lord's cross and tomb than the loving fidelity of His women friends. They were last at His cross and first at His tomb when the Sabbath was past. They came very early in the morning, while it was still dark and the day was but dawning. They must have been up much of the night preparing their spices and ointments. Hope had died in their hearts when they saw Jesus dead and laid away in the tomb ; but love had not died. They had not forgotten the blessings they had received from His hand ; and though they had been disappointed in their Messianic expectations, they were eager to do all that could be done to honour His memory.

There are lessons in this picture that are so obvious that they need scarcely be written out. One is, that no matter how dark the hour, our love for Christ should never fail. Though our expectations fail of realization, though our blossoms of hope fade and fall and yield no fruit, still let us cling to Christ. Our disappointments often prove the richest blessings in the end. It was so with these faithful women. Their Messianic hopes were buried and never rose, but the true Messianic hopes came in full glory from the grave's gloom. So it is always with faith's hopes that seem to perish : they come again in immortal beauty.

Another lesson is that in the expression of our love for Christ we should bring to Him the very richest and best that our hearts can find or our hands can prepare. Still another lesson is that we ought always to come early in our service of love for Christ. We ought to come to Him in life's morning, while youth's purity and freshness are unsullied. We ought also to seek Him in the morning of each day, so that not one golden moment may be lost.

Dec. 19

The Stone Rolled Away

" *Who shall roll us away the stone?......They looked......the stone was rolled away.*"—MARK xvi. 3, 4

WE are all alike. Even these holy women on this most sacred errand went forward to borrow trouble. There was a stone in the way that must be rolled aside, and they had not strength to do it. Naturally enough, they began to be anxious as to the removal of this obstacle. When they came near they saw that the obstacle had been already removed. The Divine love had been beforehand in preparing the way for them. Angels had rolled the stone aside. The lesson is very simple and beautiful. We go forward worrying about the difficulties that lie before us, wondering how we can ever get through them, or who will remove them out of our way. Then when we come up to them we find that they are gone. Some one has been there before us and has taken them away. God always opens the way of duty for us if we quietly move on.

This applies to one beginning a Christian life. Many persons shrink from it. They say : " I never can be faithful. I never can do the duties. I never can bear the burdens." But as they enter and go on they find that an unseen and mighty Helper goes on before and prepares the way. The hard tasks become easy, and the heavy burdens grow light. It is so all through the Christian life. God's commandment seems impossible of obedience. Walls of stone seem built across the path we are required to walk over. But as we go on the commandment is easy, and a gateway is opened in the wall. Love and faith always have an advance of angels to roll away stones. The practical lesson is, that we are never to hesitate or shrink back because obstacles seem to lie before us ; we are to go right on, and God will take them away for us. When He wants us to go anywhere He will open the path for our feet. Knowing this, we may go on feeling confident of our own safety.

Dec. 20

The Empty Tomb

" *Fear not ye ; for I know that ye seek Jesus.*"
MATT. xxviii. 5

IT must have been a glad errand to the angels who were
sent to minister at the grave of the Redeemer, to roll
the stone away, to keep watch at the empty sepulchre, and
to tell the good tidings to the disciples who came with such
heavy hearts. Their message was one of great joy. Jesus,
whom His friends sought dead, was alive again for evermore.
He had been in the grave, but He was not there now.

The empty tomb has many glorious voices. It tells us
first that Jesus actually died. He was buried here, just in
this place. His head lay there, His feet here. Here are
the grave-clothes, the piece of fine linen which gentle hands
wound around Him. Here is the napkin that covered His
face. He lay just here. Look at the place and mark it
well, and never forget that He actually was dead. This is
important, for upon His death your acceptance with God
depends.

But look again. The grave is empty now. He *was* here,
but He is not here now, for He is risen. The grave is
empty. Here are the grave-clothes, but there is no body.
He is gone. The empty tomb tells, then, of resurrection.
Death could not hold the Christ. He burst its bands and
conquered the grave's power. This is important, for a
dead Christ could not have saved us. Had He never risen,
how could He have stood for us before God ? How could
He be our help in weakness, our support in trial, our Comforter,
our Friend, if His dust lay yet in the grave ? Therefore
He is alive to intercede for us, to help us, to save us.

Still another truth which the empty tomb teaches us is
that all who sleep in Jesus shall rise too. One precious
word of Scripture says : " For if we believe that Jesus died
and rose again, even so them also which sleep in Jesus will
God bring with Him." So let us learn to see through the
grave to the life beyond.

Go and tell Peter

" *Go your way, tell His disciples and Peter.*"—MARK xvi. 7

WHY "and Peter"? Why was Peter named, and none of the other disciples? Had Peter been the most loyal and faithful of all the Master's friends, that he deserved such a mark of distinction as this? Oh no ; we remember how Peter had fallen. The last word that had dropped upon the ear of Jesus from his lips was a bitter word of denial. Peter had acted worse than any other of the disciples.

Why, then, did Jesus send this special word to Peter? It was just because he had sinned. That last look of the Saviour broke his heart, and he went out into the night a penitent man, weeping bitterly. Those had been dark days for him since Jesus died. Not only was he overwhelmed with sorrow at the death of his Lord, whom he truly and most dearly loved, but his grief was made bitter beyond endurance by the remembrance of his own base denial at the very last. Deep must his sorrow have been, and all the deeper because he would never be able to ask forgiveness. How he must have longed to have Jesus back, if but for one moment, to confess his sin and crave pardon !

Jesus left this special word for Peter with the angel at the tomb, because He knew of the bitterness of His disciple's sorrow. Peter might have been saying, when he heard Jesus had risen, " Perhaps He will not own me any more," and so Jesus sent this message with Peter's name in it specially, just to let him know that he was forgiven and would not be cast off. What a world of comfort there is in this " and Peter " for any who have sinned and are penitent ! Those who have fallen are the very ones who receive the deepest, tenderest compassion from Jesus, because they need it most, and because He would help them to rise again. The gospel has always its special word for the penitent ; Christ still comes to call the sinner.

Dec. 22

Mary Magdalene

*" She turned herself back, and saw Jesus standing, and knew
not that it was Jesus."*—JOHN xx. 14

THE story of Mary of Magdala is one of very tender
interest. Jesus had wrought for her a very wonderful
deliverance, casting out the seven demons that possessed
her. From that time her devotion to Him was such that
she followed Him wherever He went, ministering to Him.
She was one of those who watched by His cross and tomb
and came early to do honour to His body In return for
her loving devotion Jesus appeared first to her the
morning He arose.

But when she saw Him she did not know Him, though
her heart was crying out for Him with intense yearning.
As she stood talking with the angel she heard a step behind
her, and turned, and there Jesus stood. Yet she did not
recognize Him, though she loved Him so much, and though
her heart was hungering for Him. She was thinking of
Him as dead, and she did not know Him when He stood
before her alive. Another reason she did not know Him
was, that her eyes were so full of tears she could not see
Him. Many a time it is the same with us : we need Christ,
and our hearts are crying out for Him ; yet when He comes
to us we do not know Him, and therefore fail to receive
comfort from His presence.

There is a picture which represents a mother in deep
distress ; yet close by her is an angel bending over her
to comfort her, his fingers touching at the same time the
strings of the harp in his hands. But she is so absorbed
in her own grief that she neither sees the angel nor hears
his celestial music. So her heart goes uncomforted and
still breaking while the comfort is so close at hand. We
should look up when we are in sorrow ; if we look down
only we shall never see the beauties and glories of the face
of Jesus, and our hearts shall be uncomforted though He
is close beside us.

Dec. 23

"Why Weepest Thou?"

"Jesus saith unto her, Woman, why weepest thou?"
JOHN xx. 15

THERE really was no cause for tears; for Jesus, whom she mourned as dead, was living. Does not Jesus ask the same question now of many a mourner, "Why weepest thou?" We cannot restrain our tears when a dear friend is taken from us; and there is nothing wrong in such tears. Jesus Himself wept beside the grave of His friend whom He was about to raise to life.

But with too many the grief at loss of dear ones is unsubmissive, unbelieving, even rebellious. When a Christian dies he but departs to be with his Lord; can we therefore weep for him? Surely not; death to him is glorious gain. Shall we weep because he is with Christ, in eternal blessedness; because he is past all pain and trial; because he has been exalted to a place in the King's palace? Shall we blame God, and weep bitter, rebellious tears, because He has taken one of His own children away from us? Does God make mistakes? Are we not sure of His love? Was it in anger that He came and caused us such grief? May we not be sure that the sorrow which came with such heavy fall was really God's best kindness for us, as well as for the beloved one He took to Himself? Is it not sin, then, for us to weep without any sweet submission and loving acquiescence?

> "Mother, I see you with your nursery light,
> Leading your babies, all in white,
> To their sweet rest;
> Christ, the Good Shepherd, carries mine to-night,
> And that is best.

> "But grief is selfish: I cannot see
> Always why I should so stricken be,
> More than the rest;
> But I know that, as well as for them, for me
> God did the best."

"Rabboni."

"Jesus saith unto her, Mary."—JOHN xx. 16

JESUS had not forgotten Mary's name in His experience of death. It was the ancient heathen belief that death washed from the soul all memory of the earthly life—its loves, its sorrows, all its recollections. But here we see Jesus on the other side of death, and the old affections are found unchanged in Him. He met Mary and His other friends, and took up the threads of the tender story of love just where they had been broken off three days before, when He died. This fact ought to be very comforting. Love is stronger than death. When our friends pass through death, whatever changes may be wrought in them or upon them, we know that there will be no change in their love for us. Death will not sever the ties that bind Christian hearts together on the earth. We shall meet again in the after life and remember each other and love each other as before, and take up the old threads of affection and go on weaving love's web for ever.

When Jesus had called Mary and she recognized Him by His voice, she at once answered Him in the one word "Rabboni!"—"My Master!" This name by which she called Him showed the loyalty of her heart, and the consecration of her life to Him. Many people are only a half-conception of Christian faith. They believe in Christ as a Saviour, but do not think of Him as Lord—their own personal Lord. They think of faith only as trusting for salvation, and do not understand it also as obedience and service. Mary had the true conception. Her answer to Christ's call implied the surrender of herself to Him. All true faith accepts Christ in two ways and under two names. First, it receives Him as Saviour, Jesus, trusting in Him alone for salvation. "Simply to Thy cross I cling." Next, it accepts Him as Lord, Rabboni, yielding the life to Him. The saved soul owes obedience, submission, loyalty, service.

True Christmas Joy.

" Mary Magdalene came and told the disciples that she had seen the Lord."—JOHN xx. 18.

ON this Christmas day we come to the hour of restored joy, which is even richer and deeper because fuller than the joy of the Saviour's birth. Christmas tells of the first coming of Christ to earth, with blessings for a lost world. But Jesus was lost to His disciples when He went down into the darkness of death. Mary's message is of a Saviour come again from the darkness, and come beyond death in immortal life. Only part of the joy came with the birth ; here we have the full joy, telling of accomplished redemption and glorious victory over death and the grave. Hope was lost on the Friday of Christ's death ; now the stars are shining again, never again to be eclipsed.

So this really is the full Christmas message. It tells not merely of a Saviour born, but also of a Saviour that has lived, obeyed, suffered, died, and risen again, and is able therefore to save unto the uttermost all who come unto God by Him. The shepherds and the Magi found but a little babe when they came to see the new-born King. We see a Saviour with the print of the nails in His hands and feet, who has wrought a full and glorious redemption for the world.

Jesus appeared to Mary after He had come again from death ; yet death had not extinguished one beam of His brightness. The resurrection was a type and prophecy of the future resurrection of all who believe in Him and sleep in Him. It shows us therefore that death does not mean destruction, is not the end of life. It is but an incident, an experience, and life goes on afterward without loss or marring. We ought to try to learn this blessed truth. Life is not worth living which is bounded by earth's little horizon and does not reach out into immortality. Indeed we do not really begin to live until we are living for immortality.

Dec. 26.

The Walk to Emmaus.

*" While they communed together and reasoned, Jesus Him-
self drew near."*—LUKE xxiv. 15.

THESE two friends, as they walked along with heavy
hearts, had only one theme : they were talking of
their sore loss and of Him whom they had lost. They were
so intensely absorbed in their sorrow as they talked of it
that they were not aware of the near approach of a stranger
until He had drawn up to them and joined them. Jesus
always draws near when His friends are talking of Him.
In an Old Testament book it was said that when the Lord's
people come together and speak of sacred things, the Lord
listens, and keeps a book of remembrance.

Here is something more. Two of Christ's friends talk
of Him, and He comes and joins them. How much those
Christian people miss who meet and pass hours together,
and have no theme of conversation but the silly gossip of
society, filled with backbitings and bits of malicious criticism and mischievous scandal, but without one single word
about Christ ! Does any one suppose that the Lord
hearkens to such conversation, or puts it down in His book
of remembrance ? Of course He hears every word of the
talk, and every word goes down in a book of remembrance,
and we must give account for every idle word. But He
does not listen and record the conversation in the sense
the prophet meant, with loving pleasure. Does any one
think Christ will draw near and become one of any such
party of Christians as often gather in parlours, deliciously
feeding on every bit of fresh gossip, but with never a word
about their Redeemer ?

What a blessing every hour of conversation would bring
if we would only talk together of Christ and His kingdom !
He would then draw near and join us, adding the joy of
His presence to our hearts. Shall we not talk together
more of our Lord ?

"Abide with Us"

"They constrained Him, saying, Abide with us."
LUKE xxiv. 29

IF the two disciples had not constrained Jesus to stay with them, He would have passed on, and they would have missed the blessed enjoyment of His company, and the disclosure of Himself which He made to them at the end. The lesson is for us. No doubt we miss many rich comforts and blessings because we do not earnestly constrain Jesus to tarry with us. He loves to be constrained. He does not go where He is not really and earnestly desired, where His presence is not eagerly sought after. Only love in us can receive and enjoy Christ's love.

The only reason we do not have more of the blessed fellowship with Christ is because we really do not want more. He is willing to be our abiding guest, entering into every experience with us in our work, in our pleasures, in our social life, in our temptations and trials ; but many of us do not want Him always with us. His presence would interfere with our methods of business, or with our way of living, or with our enjoyments and amusements. We do not then constrain Him to abide with us, and He passes on, and we miss the blessing He would bring.

If we were truly to desire Christ to abide always with us, He would never go away. What a life of benediction and joy we should live if He were indeed always with us ! Unbroken communion with Him would hold heaven close about us all the while, and thus these sordid earthly lives of ours would be permeated and struck through with the sweetness and fragrance of holiness, and transformed into the likeness of Christ Himself. Then all life's experiences would be transfigured. Joy would be purer, and even sorrow would be illumined. All through life this should be our continual prayer ; then in death our earthly communion shall brighten into heavenly glory.

Dec. 28

Prize Present Blessings

"Their eyes were opened, and they knew Him; and He
vanished out of their sight."—LUKE xxiv. 31

ALL along the way Jesus had walked with these disciples, pouring the warmth of His spirit upon them;
but they did not recognize Him until the moment of His
vanishing out of their sight. It is the same with us and
many of our best blessings. We do not recognize them till
they are taking their flight. We do not prize health till it
is broken. Our common privileges we do not value till
something deprives us of them. Our homes appear old-
fashioned till we are thrown upon the world homeless.

It is the same with our friends. We do not see the
beauties of their character, nor perceive their real worth,
until in some way we have lost them. This is specially
true of the friends who are nearest to us in our own households. They seem to us commonplace, because they are
always moving before us. Their help is so perpetual, and
their ministry is so unbroken, that we do not learn their
value to us. But some day one of these friends vanishes
out of our sight. The familiar form is seen no more. The
voice of tender love is heard no more. The quiet, gentle
ministry ceases. To-morrow we miss the friend; then in
the vanishing we learn what he was to us. Very sadly
one has sung,—

" And she is gone, sweet human love is gone!
  'Tis only when they spring to heaven that angels
  Reveal themselves to you; they sit all day
  Beside you, and lie down at night by you,
  Who care not for their presence: muse or sleep,
  And all at once they leave you. Then you know them!
  We are so fooled, so cheated."

Should we not get a lesson here in these closing days of
the year? Shall we not try to prize our blessings while
we have them? The vacant chair should not be the first
revealer of a loving friend.

"Rejoice in the Lord"

"Then were the disciples glad when they saw the Lord."
JOHN xx. 20

CHRIST'S death had caused them great sorrow; to have Him back again from death gave them unspeakable joy. Indeed there never would have been any Christian joy if Jesus had not risen from the dead. It was necessary that He should die for our sins; but if He had died and remained in the grave, no benefit could have come to us from His dying.

A dead mother cannot do anything for her children; nor could a dead Saviour have helped those who trusted in Him. We need a living Saviour, to whose feet we can creep with our penitence when we have sinned, and in whose hands we can be kept in safety until we reach glory. We need a living Friend, who will bless us by His rich love; whose strong arm will hold us up in weakness, and defend us in temptation; whose presence will restrain us from sin, and inspire in us all good thoughts and holy desires and aspirations. We want a living Comforter, who will stand for us in heaven and plead our cause there, and stand by us on the earth in all our imperilled life. We want a living personal Caretaker, who will look after all our interests, plan for our lives, order our steps, and provide for all our wants. We want a Prince who has won for us the battle over death and the grave, and is able therefore to bring us also from under the power of death.

No wonder, then, that the disciples were glad when they saw the Lord, when they had Him back again from the dead. We should be glad, too, and rejoice in the glorious truth of Christ's resurrection. We have a living Saviour. We have one in heaven who loves us. Our Redeemer holds the keys of death. No dark grave can hold us or any of ours who sleep in Jesus. We can enjoy as real communion with Jesus as did His first disciples, because He lives and is one with us.

Dec. 30

"Lovest Thou Me?"

"Simon, son of Jonas, lovest thou Me?......Feed My lambs ......Feed My sheep."—JOHN xxi. 15, 16

THERE are several great lessons which we should learn from Peter's restoration. One is that the first essential in a Christian worker is love for Christ Himself. Wisdom will not do. Eloquence will not do. We may delight in the work itself. People sometimes talk about a "passion for souls" as essential in one who would work for Christ; but this is not enough. Nothing less than a passion for Christ Himself will do to fit one for labour for souls. "I have but one passion, and that is *He*," said a great missionary. When we love Christ with all our heart, and not till then, are we ready to do His work. He will not entrust the care of His flock to any who are not loyal to Him and do not love Him. "Lovest Thou me?" comes before "Feed my lambs."

Another thought here for workers is, that they must *feed* the souls entrusted to their care. Entertainment is not the object, but feeding, spiritual feeding. But what is food for souls? Nothing but Christ Himself; and the way to feed others on Christ is to open up for them the holy Word, that they may see Christ and learn to love Him and trust Him and do His will. We must be sure that we give true soul-food, the pure Word of God, to those whom we undertake to feed.

Then more than feeding is here enjoined. The Master's words vary here: He bade Peter *feed* the lambs and *tend* the sheep; that is, give them all shepherd-care—love, protection, guidance, provision. The most important and responsible work in all this world is caring for souls. The responsibility rests, not on pastors alone, but upon all parents, all teachers, all Christians. We dare not do this work carelessly. It would be a terrible thing if through our negligence any soul should be marred or lost. They are Christ's lambs and Christ's sheep that we are set to shepherd; we must be faithful.

"Follow Me."

" When He had spoken this, He saith unto him, Follow Me."
JOHN xxi. 19

WE have come now to the last day of the year. For a whole year in these daily readings we have been walking with Christ. Is there any better word with which to close this book and close the year than this last invitation of Jesus—" Follow Me " ? This is the true outcome of all learning of Christ. Mere knowledge, though it be of spiritual things, avails nothing, save as it leads us to follow Christ.

We have seen Jesus in all the different phases of His life. We have heard many of His words. Now it remains only for us to follow Him. The outcome of seeing and knowing should be living and doing. The last day of the year suggests also the same duty. Who is satisfied with His life as it appears in retrospect from these evening shadows ? The past, however blotted, must go as it is ; we cannot change it, and we need not waste time in regretting. But the new year is before us, and if we would make that better than the stained past, it must be by following Christ more closely.

To follow Christ is to go where He leads, without questioning or demurring. It may be to a life of trial, suffering, or sacrifice—but no matter ; we have nothing whatever to do with the kind of life to which our Lord calls us. Our only simple duty is to obey and follow. We know that Jesus will lead us only in right paths, and that the way He takes slopes upward and ends at the feet of God.

The new year on which we are about to enter is unopened, and we know not what shall befall us ; but if we follow Christ we need have no fear. So let us leave the old year with gratitude to God for its mercies, with penitence for its failures and sins, and let us enter the new with earnest resolve in Christ's name to make it the best and most beautiful year we have ever lived.